To Mr Byers
I hope you
enjoy this book.

sincerely

Scott O'Grady

25 AUG '90

FIGHTER
MISSIONS

FIGHTER MISSIONS

BILL GUNSTON   LINDSAY PEACOCK
Derek Bunce   Patrick Bunce

ORION
BOOKS

New York

A Salamander Book

Published in the United States by Crown Publishers, Inc., 225 Park Avenue South, New York, 10003 and represented in Canada by the Canadian MANDA Group.

Published in Great Britain by Salamander Books Limited

ORION and colophon are trademarks of Crown Publishers, Inc.

Library of Congress Cataloging-in-Publication Data

Gunston, Bill
    Fighter missions/Bill Gunston and Lindsay Peacock
        p.   cm.
    Includes index.
    ISBN 0-517-57194-3
    1. Air warfare. 2. United States — Armed Forces — Tactical aviation. 3. Europe — Armed Forces — Tactical aviation.
I. Peacock, Lindsay. II. Title.
UG700.J33   1988
358.4'14 — dc 19   88-22529

10 9 8 7 6 5 4 3 2 1

First Edition

Credits

Project Manager: Ray Bonds

Editor: Eugene Kolesnik

Designers: Nigel Duffield, Philip Gorton, Paul Johnson

Color artwork: Derek Bunce

Special Photography: Patrick Bunce

Filmset by: The Old Mill

Color reproduction by: Kentscan Ltd., Magnum Graphics Ltd.

Printed in Belgium by Proost International Book Production, Turnhout.

Acknowledgements

Grateful thanks are due to the following who so generously gave of their valuable time to assist with the preparation of this volume. Lt Col Les Dyer and Capt. Bill Napolitano of the 510th Tactical Fighter Squadron; Capt. John Boyle of the 81st Tactical Fighter Wing Public Affairs Office; Wg Cdr Wright, Sqn Ldr James Kirkpatrick and Flt Lt Ray Goodall of No. IX Squadron; Flt Lt MacGregor of the Community Relations Office at RAF Bruggen; Sgt David Malakoff and Sgt Scott Graham of the 48th Tactical Fighter Wing; Wg Cdr Peter Hitchcock and Flt Lt Ian Dearie of No. 229 Operational Conversion Unit; Lt Col Roger Brooks of the 42nd Electronic Combat Squadron; Maj. A. J. N. Simkins of 656 Squadron, Army Air Corps; Sgt D. Aragon of the 20th Tactical Fighter Wing; Flt Lt Dancey at RAF Coningsby; Flt Lt G. C. Barr at RAF Wittering and Mark and Ray Hanna.

Contributors

The Authors
Bill Gunston is a former RAF pilot and flying instructor and has become one of the most internationally respected authors and broadcasters on aviation and scientific subjects. He is the author of numerous books, including several for Salamander, including "Modern Air Combat" (with Mike Spick), "The Illustrated Encyclopedia of Aircraft Armament", and "Modern Fighting Aircraft". Former technical editor of "Flight International" and technology editor of "Science Journal", Mr. Gunston is an assistant compiler of "Jane's All The World's Aircraft".

Lindsay Peacock is an aviation journalist and photographer who has written extensively on military aviation subjects for many international defence journals. He has travelled widely in pursuit of his subjects, including many visits to military airfields and aircraft carriers, observing activities and aircraft first-hand. He is also the author of books on specific aircraft topics, including some in the well-respected "Osprey Combat Aircraft Series".

The Artist
Derek Bunce was drawing aircraft as soon as he could sharpen a pencil. His enthusiasm for aviation spans the entire history of flight, and he has recorded all the significant events in superb colour brushwork, from Sopwith Camels to fighters of the future. An Associate of the Guild of Aviation Artists, he has worked as art director and illustrator with many international magazines and airlines, and produced display and other artwork for aircraft and systems manufacturers.

The Photographer
Patrick Bunce is a freelance photographer, following his father's enthusiasm for aviation, but wielding a camera instead of a brush. He has gained an enviable reputation for his imaginative work.

Contents

INTRODUCTION

THOUGH THE title of this book is "Fighter Missions", the coverage is rather broader than this implies and includes most of what might be termed air-combat missions. Those not included — because they are far removed from the basic subject — are such duties as strategic bombing, anti-submarine warfare, mine warfare and reconnaissance. To have attempted to include these, and supportive missions such as transport and air-refuelling tanking, would have been counter-productive, diluting the coverage of the true "combat" missions on which this book concentrates. We did, however, carefully consider including the AEW/AWACS mission, because this acts as a force-multiplier in magnifying the capability of every mission flown in the face of an enemy.

Each mission forms a self-contained section of the book. While the main part of the text is totally contemporary, describing a typical mission, minute-by-minute "as it happens", each section opens with an introduction which, among other things, fills in the historical background. In some cases one may be intrigued at the long history; for example, many aspects of the CAS (close air support) mission have hardly changed in 70 years. In others, one may wonder that some missions took so long to mature. For example, cannon firing AP (armour-piercing) shot could have been fitted to aircraft in 1917-18 (though as they would have had to be armoured they might have been large and ponderous aircraft), but there is no record of any attempt to use aircraft effectively against tanks until well into World War II. Even in the Soviet Union, where air-to-ground rocket projectiles were pioneered in the 1930s, the crucial importance of the specialised anti-armour aircraft does not seem to have been recognised until after the Nazi invasion on 22 June 1941.

Of course, the "fighter" has always been regarded primarily as a fighter of other aircraft. But ever since World War II the media have often found themselves hard-pressed to know how to describe many of the aircraft that equip modern air forces and other fighting services. In their simplistic view, everyone knows what a fighter is and everyone knows what a bomber is; and "anti-tank aircraft" is also generally admitted as being self-explanatory. So, in general, small fast jets tend to be called fighters even if their air-combat capability is essentially zero, and even if they are actually bombers. What makes it harder is that, while the word "fighter" conjures up images of dashing heroes in polka-dot scarves, the word "bomber" is pedestrian in the extreme. If you were to call a Jaguar, A-7 or F-111 pilot "a bomber driver" he would probably regard you as an F-15 jock indulging in insulting one-upmanship, yet in fact such an introduction would be entirely accurate.

The versatile warplane

Of course, some aircraft are versatile. Paraphrasing a common aphorism, "some are born versatile, while others have versatility thrust upon them". The two most versatile warplanes of World War II, the Mosquito and Ju 88, were each designed for a highly specialised mission. Only in the fullness of time was it appreciated that they could almost fight a war single-handed.

In today's world many important aircraft have had interesting histories. The F-104 was designed purely as an air-combat fighter but spent almost its entire combat life as a tactical bomber and reconnaissance aircraft. (In its twilight years the Italians built a stand-

off interceptor version armed with long-range AAMs.) The Jaguar
was designed mainly as an advanced trainer but matured as an
excellent attack and reconnaissance aircraft (which after
modification by BAe as an unstable research aircraft could be no
mean fighter!). The Harrier was reluctantly permitted to be
developed as a light close-support aircraft, by a government which
had decreed that there were to be no more manned combat aircraft
at all, yet later developed into one of the world's toughest air-
combat fighters which scored 20 plus to nil in the South Atlantic
and has consistently run up similar scores in mock combat against
the best fighters in Western air forces.

The F-111 was designed as a fighter but had to meet such a long
attack and ferry range requirement that it never became a fighter,
and one version serves with Strategic Air Command. In an exactly
opposite way, the F-15 was designed as a totally uncompromised
air-superiority fighter, making no concession whatever to any form
of attack capability, so that the battle-cry was "Not a pound for air-
to-ground!" Now — surprise, surprise — the F-15E is the USAF's
next dual-role all-weather attack aircraft. The F-16 was designed as a
simple LWF (lightweight fighter) yet matured as one of the world's
outstanding aircraft at such diverse missions as air combat, stand-off
interception, all-weather attack, reconnaissance and defence
suppression. Its original rival, the YF-17, was developed into today's
F/A-18, which as its designation indicates was boldly designed to be
equally good at both the fighter and the attack missions. One could
argue indefinitely about whether such versatility inevitably results in
a "Jack of all trades, master of none".

Some design teams have created basically versatile aircraft which
continued on page 12

Left: *The British-designed Harrier is arguably the most revolutionary warplane of the post-war era, being the first true V/STOL fighter to enter service. In its latest guise as the AV-8B Harrier II, it is an ideal vehicle for the close air support mission, for which purpose it serves with the US Marines.*

Above: *International collaboration is very much the name of the game nowadays and is perhaps best epitomised by the Panavia Tornado. Available in strike and air defence variants, this example of the latter derivative displays the markings of No. 5 Squadron, Royal Air Force.*

Below: *Another example of international co-operation is provided by the General Dynamics Fighting Falcon which is the subject of several co-production deals. This Belgian Air Force F-16A is typical, being partly manufactured and wholly assembled by SABCA in Belgium.*

Of all the aspects of modern aerial warfare, the fighter still retains the most glamour, perhaps largely by virtue of the fact that most people perceive the role of the fighter pilot as being in some ways akin to that of a gladiator of the skies, depending largely upon his own skill to outwit and vanquish an opponent. In reality, of course, the picture is very different as will soon become apparent from even the most cursory glance at the pages of this volume. For a start, many contemporary fighter aircraft need two crew members if they are to be used to optimum capacity in the execution of their missions, while there is still considerable debate as to just how broad the category of ''fighter'' really is. Certainly, some of the types discussed in this volume — the F-111 and Tornado are good examples — could more properly be described as ''bombers'' since their primary task is nothing more than that of putting ordnance accurately on target.

Similarly, in the anti-tank arena, use of the fighter nomenclature is perhaps being stretched a bit when one considers the TOW-armed Lynx

helicopter and yet it is truly a "fighter" for it most certainly fulfils a role that has traditionally been the preserve of fixed-wing aircraft.

In the following chapters, most of the tasks that are generally associated with the fighter aircraft are examined in some detail. Each separate chapter opens with a consideration of the historical evolution of the role under discussion before turning to describing a mission such as might be flown in the event of a "real war". Air superiority **(1)**, interception **(2)**, maritime **(3)**, anti-armour **(4)**, close air support **(5)**, defence suppression **(6)**, and interdiction **(7)** are the subjects examined and each mission profile looks closely at all aspects inherent in successfully accomplishing the objective, whether it be to kill an opponent in aerial combat or to destroy his capacity to wage war upon the ground. Planning, briefing, tactics and weapons employed are all described in detail while the part played by ground personnel is by no means overlooked for without them no modern air arm could hope to conduct effective combat operations for a prolonged period.

have then been quite substantially modified to tailor them specifically to particular missions. In the Soviet Union the outstanding example is the swing-wing MiG-23, which in its MiG-23BN and MiG-27 forms is tailored exclusively to the low-level attack mission. In the West the outstanding examples are the Tornado and Mirage 2000. The former is in service in quite considerably different IDS (interdiction/strike) and ADV (air defence variant) forms and is going into production in a third version for ECR (electronic combat and reconnaissance). The Mirage 2000 is basically an air-superiority fighter tailored entirely to high-altitude operations but, despite the complete unsuitability of its large delta wing, it is now also in service as the two-seat 2000N for low-level nuclear attack. Its wing limits its speed at sea level to 600 knots, compared with 800 knots for the Tornado, and it attempts to avoid having to penetrate close to its target by standing off and firing an ASMP cruise missile.

Defence suppression is a specialised form of attack mission. The USAF's family of Wild Weasel aircraft have all been versions of established tactical aircraft, such as the F-100, F-105 and F-4, probably to be followed by the F-16. A less-obvious form of defence suppression is performed by the dedicated tactical jammer and ECM aircraft, such as the US Navy's four-seat EA-6B and the USAF's two-seat EF-111A. These can accompany or precede attack aircraft, all the way to the target if necessary, or stand off in various ways. Further assistance, often crucial, is provided by such aircraft as AWACS and tankers.

The scenarios

It will be appreciated that, throughout the world, every air-combat pilot has to have some idea of who his enemies are, or who they might be. For nearly 40 years the Soviet Union and West European democracies (bolstered by the United States) have confronted each other in what has been called a state of armed peace. There cannot be a single reader of this book who does not earnestly hope that the policies of *glasnost* (openness) and *perestroika* (fundamental rebuilding or reorganisation) will make this confrontation part of history. At present, however, the NATO and WarPac air forces still regard each other as natural enemies.

Thus, for obvious reasons, the scenarios depicted and described in this book are those that both sides have discussed and trained for over the years, knowing that they would be acted out in the event of major conflict in Europe, and especially on the Central Front. It is

Top left: *The US Air Force's premier air superiority fighter is the F-15 Eagle, a type that also serves with the air arms of Israel, Japan and Saudi Arabia. This pair of F-15Cs are from the 36th Tactical Fighter Wing, a USAFE unit stationed at Bitburg AFB, in West Germany.*

Top right: *Yet another McDonnell Douglas product, based on an original Northrop design, is the F/A-18 Hornet. Serving with the US Navy and Marine Corps as well as some overseas air arms, it possesses genuine multi-mission potential as both an interceptor and strike aircraft.*

Left: *Seaborne air power has assumed awesome potential in the years that have elapsed since World War II. A carrier such as the USS America seen here is able to accommodate an Air Wing with more than 80 aircraft optimised for an impressive variety of missions.*

Right: *Genuine all-weather capability is possessed by the interdiction/strike version of the Tornado, which now serves with Great Britain, Italy, Saudi Arabia and West Germany in considerable numbers. An RAF example from No. 9 Squadron is seen leaving a shelter at Bruggen.*

fervently to be hoped that the appearance of this book will not be thought provocative or "warmongering". Our aim is naturally to tell it like it is. We could, of course, have invented a mythical far-away country for our scenarios, but this seemed pointless. Instead our objective has been to explain how the front-line crews of the NATO air forces train to fight in the European theatre. Had the publisher been based in Moscow we should have described the missions studied by the WarPac air forces. There would probably have been very few differences — though we in the West have long felt we have the edge in ability to get down really low "among the weeds".

A belief in "superiorities"

We are not really able to judge how far this belief is justified. Since about 1915 it has been a perhaps natural belief among combat pilots everywhere that they can do things a little better than their opponents. There have been many occasions when this costly belief has had to be abandoned, even if only temporarily. In World War II the Fw 190 and A6M "Zero" gave the Allies such a hard time, at least until 1943, that the only thing left was a belief in individual superiority of the Allied pilots. It is probably fair to suggest that every pilot in history, going in to engage an enemy, has had to be supported by a true belief in "superiorities" enjoyed by his own side. Preferably he can believe in superiority of his aircraft. If not, he has to feel he is better trained. Yet, at the same time, in the back of his mind he knows that the guys on the other side most certainly do not harbour any feelings of inferiority. Rather do they, in their turn, believe themselves to be superior. It helps enormously if such feelings can be backed up by some kind of evidence.

Those old enough to remember World War II will recall that

virtually every bit of printed paper published for public dissemination was studied by the "authorities" and, if necessary, tinkered with to boost the morale of the Allies (and especially the home public), downgrade or ignore the achievements or superiorities of the enemy and most certainly never suggest any cause for fear or apprehension about the future. People did not then produce books like "Fighter Missions". The nearest one got was the series of official APs (Air Publications) for training one's own aircrew, usually with simple black-line diagrams and often with typewritten text (after 1942 the quality improved). Even in these booklets it was almost automatic to let propaganda slip in wherever appropriate.

Today fashions have changed. To prepare this book the authors, artist and photographer visited many combat units and talked with

many front-line pilots, backseaters, right-seaters and front-seaters. The result ought to reflect current doctrines and opinions, at least those of the NATO air forces. The team have also had the benefit of long and close association with manufacturers, and so have been able to appreciate the problems and possibilities in meeting conflicting mission requirements. Thus, this assemblage of up-to-date information will probably be of value to both the aircraft engineer and the combat pilot, and certainly to the air-warfare enthusiast. In this book, as already noted, we tell it like it is, or at least like it seems to be.

Nowhere is the difference between "like it is" and "like it seems to be" more marked than in the vexed question of aircraft vulnerability. For over 30 years the men behind the SAMs and the triple-A have been absolutely confident that nothing can get past

A: The pilot of an 81st Tactical Fighter Wing Fairchild-Republic A-10A Thunderbolt II, engaged in making a gun attack on a Warsaw Pact armoured formation, spots an approaching Soviet MiG-23 ''Flogger'' fighter and elects to dive towards cover in order to reduce the risk of being shot down. **B:** Soviet MiG-23 ''Flogger'' makes a slashing attack on the A-10A, during which it launches a single example of the infra-red homing version of the AA-8 ''Aphid'' air-to-air missile. **C:** Faced with this threat, the A-10A pilot dips behind cover so as to employ terrain masking which succeeds in breaking missile lock. **D:** In the meantime, the pilot of the MiG-23 ''Flogger'' manoeuvres hard in order to try and gain a position from which a new attack can be initiated. **E.** A-10A pilot utilises the Thunderbolt II's superior turning ability to negate this new threat and move into a position from which either the GAU-8/A Avenger cannon or an AIM-9 Sidewinder heat-seeking missile attack could be made against the MiG-23 with a high probability of success.

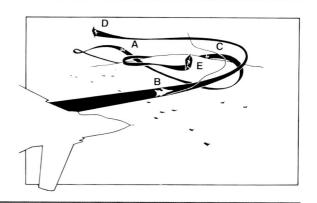

them, while the jocks in the cockpits have been equally confident that they can accomplish their missions. Today it is fashionable to skip the propaganda and try to present a completely objective appraisal, but the story one tells depends on who one talks to and who one believes. To some degree the reader must make up his own mind on how far the missions described in the following pages could really be flown against the most sophisticated modern threats.

The cost of progress

On the first day of World War II Ernest (later Lord) Hives, general manager of Rolls-Royce, said, "We must win this war; there's no point in coming a good second." The same philosophy applies to every aspect of modern airpower. In aircraft and aircrew performance, reliability, availability, tactics and training, there is no point in "coming a good second". So, since the start of air warfare 75 years ago, combat aircraft have never ceased to become more and more capable, which has meant more complicated and more expensive both to buy and to operate. This in turn has greatly increased the difficulty and cost of training the aircrew and the ground staff, and though a lot can be done with simulators and instructional rigs the combat pilot simply has to fly real missions (real to the extent that they are not simulated), and fly them quite frequently, if his skills are to be honed to the point where he will probably win, rather than come a good second.

This costs a lot of money. In World War II a ballpark figure for the cost of buying a fighter was about £5,000, and it cost about

Below: Multiple ejection bomb racks and fuel tanks are carried beneath the wings of this Grumman A-6E Intruder of the US Navy. Entering service in the all-weather strike role as long ago as 1963, the A-6 has been much improved since then and is still a key element of today's Navy.

Above: Despite its unprepossessing looks, the Fairchild-Republic A-10A Thunderbolt II is a potent performer in the anti-tank role. A major factor in its success in this task is the massive and powerful GAU-8/A Avenger 30mm gun, the magazine of which is shown here being loaded.

Right: Probably the finest interceptor in the world, Grumman's F-14 possesses one major advantage in that it is still the only fighter able to employ the Hughes AIM-54 Phoenix air-to-air missile which has the potential to destroy targets at ranges of around 90 miles.

£1,000 to train a pilot to the point where he was ready for operations. Today the corresponding figures are about £30 million and £3 million, which represents an increase many times greater than that due to inflation. As there is no sign of this trend changing one is reminded of the US Congressman who plaintively asked in 1922, "Why can't the Army have just one airplane and take turns flying it?"

The staggering increase in complexities and costs has various other effects, all presenting grave problems. Some are found in the process of deciding what aircraft to buy. In September 1944 the leaders of Nazi Germany decided that a programme should be launched for a new jet fighter. The entire process of drafting the requirement, conducting a competitive evaluation of the submitted proposals, designing the winning aircraft, building the prototype, getting it into the air and simultaneously laying down a vast scheme for manufacture of 1,000 aircraft per month took just 90 days. Today things take rather longer. For example, France and Germany launched the programme to build a new anti-tank helicopter in 1980. The formal agreement was signed on 29 May 1984. The first flight is expected in "1989-90". The first delivery is scheduled for 1997, and the French anti-tank version is to be ready in 1999. Thus, the pilots who will fly this helicopter in service may well not have been born when the project was launched. The mind boggles at the costs incurred in 19 years of industrial effort.

Development timescales

In the same way, Britain, the USA and Canada are collaborating on an ASTOVL (Advanced STOVL), which is unquestionably the most urgently needed item in the inventories of the respective air forces. This programme was launched in June 1983. Most of the aircraft and engine industries of the three nations are working on it. The date for demonstrating the available technology is 1995, the first flight might be in about 2000 and the planned in-service date is foreseen as 2005-2010! Of course, by 2010 the whole scenario of air

warfare is likely to have been changed completely, so the ASTOVL is likely to be out of date before it gets near a squadron. To put this all in perspective, if the Spitfire had been developed to a similar schedule it would have reached Fighter Command 17 years after World War II ended (though as Britain would have "come a good second" the RAF would have no longer existed).

New missions for old aircraft

Not only do modern aircraft take a long time to create but they also have to last a long time in service, with some aircraft nearing their 20th year in front line squadrons, which means that such factors as airframe fatigue, maintenance actions and what is called "total cost of ownership" over a long period become of the greatest importance. In the course of such long service lives the missions can change out of all recognition. Instead of flying in the stratosphere an attack aircraft may have to penetrate hostile airspace at tree-top height. Instead of carrying a single NW (nuclear weapon) it may have to carry ten tons of "iron bombs". Instead of attacking targets behind an army front line it may be tasked to hit powerful surface warships. Instead of operating over Arctic tundra it may find itself over scorching desert, or windswept islands in the South Atlantic! And who would have thought that an air force would be so short of fighters that it would hang missiles under trainers.

Of course, in the final analysis everything comes down to a question of what can be afforded. Many important programmes have proved vulnerable to budget cuts, which has meant that new aircraft capable of flying new kinds of mission have been cancelled.

Whatever the aircraft, however, it is more often than not the performance of the aircrew that counts most in combat. While the action described here may have been fictionalised, the missions are real; the authors have brought them to life so that readers can glimpse the complexities of the teamwork in the cockpit and on the ground "back at base". This book is a tribute to the immense skill and courage of all those who contribute to fighter missions.

THE INTERCEPTION MISSION

Evolution of the Mission

I F THE air-superiority mission vaguely resembles the mediaeval swordsman, who had to close with his opponent and then defeat him by superior agility — the battle perhaps enduring for several minutes while each adversary looks for the crucial opportunity — then the interception mission has more in common with the archer, crossbowman or modern sniper. The kill is effected from a distance, and the quarry frequently has no inkling of his deadly danger until a hail of cannon shells or a missile strike home, possibly from 60 miles (100km) away.

From the very start of interception missions the usual target was one or more enemy bombers, penetrating one's own airspace. In contrast, the air-superiority mission normally involves opposing fighters, engaging in furious manoeuvres in more or less neutral airspace, perhaps over a land battlefront. This kind of classic dogfight can be performed only in day visual conditions, but the interception mission can be, and usually has to be, flown in bad weather or at night. The interceptor thus has to be equipped with suitable long-range radar, and if possible also with an IR (infra-red) search/track set. It also must be armed with AAMs (air-to-air missiles), if possible with semi-active or active radar guidance in order to lock-on the target at a range of from 20 to 100 miles (32-160km).

The interceptor therefore has to be a relatively large fighter, with long range and endurance, and preferably with a crew of two. It is difficult to imagine a war scenario when interceptors would not need combat persistence, the ability to shoot down several enemy aircraft in a single mission. Comprehensive mission avionics, and, if possible, good stealth characteristics to avoid being detected, are clearly highly desirable. So, too, is high supersonic "dash" speed in order to reach the neighbourhood of fast targets quickly — but this burns excessive fuel.

On the other hand, there ought to be no need for dogfight agility rivalling that of the air-superiority aircraft. In other words, for a given total installed thrust and wing area the interceptor can be at least 50 per cent heavier. The fact that this would tend to demand a long paved runway is much less serious than it would be for the air-superiority aircraft, unless we believe our enemy would be so unsporting as to destroy our airbases with long-range precision missiles. Interceptors tend to be based in the homeland, well back from a front line, and to enjoy the facilities of a permanent airbase. (The startling exception is Sweden, where the air staff have sufficient imagination to see that no airbase could exist in a real war, and so even the big JA37 interceptor Viggens

Knights of the Sky

1918, typical of most countries

1944, RAF and Commonwealth air forces

1988, RAF but typical of most modern air forces

would in any time of crisis be dispersed safely into the countryside.)

In the earliest days of air warfare the word "interception" was sometimes used correctly to describe a mission flown by a defending fighter trying to bring down an invading heavy bomber or airship. Often these defensive missions were flown by large two-seaters, and the very last Zeppelin to be destroyed in combat was shot down off the English coast by a day bomber, an Airco DH.4!

But inevitably the mission was primitive by modern standards. The intercepting pilots had only the vaguest idea of where the enemy

Left: *The flying clothing worn by fighter pilots has paralleled fighter aircraft in becoming ever more complex and expensive. In 1918 the need was mainly warmth. In 1944 radio, oxygen and a Mae West were added. Today's suit and helmet serve many functions.*

Right: *To modern eyes the German airships which bombed Britain in World War 1 look impossibly vulnerable, but in fact they were difficult to intercept and quite hard to shoot down. The Zeppelin L.32, seen here, was one of the unlucky ones. Her crew of 22 were all killed.*

Below: *This Saab AJ37 single-seat all-weather attack Viggen — a truly outstanding aircraft — flies with the Swedish air force, one of the few air forces to recognise that in any European war any aircraft parked on an airfield will quickly be destroyed.*

In the early days of the interception mission pilots had to rely on a visual sighting of the target before effecting a kill. Today, complex avionics aid in the task of finding and destroying an opponent: radar "eyes" locate and isolate a target before computers calculate its relative position. And then, only when there is a probability of achieving a kill will the interceptor's powerful missile armament be unleashed on the unsuspecting foe.

bombers or airships might be, and relied entirely on searchlights and seeing bursting anti-aircraft shells. If they did manage to get near the enemy, they were likely to have to run the gauntlet of friendly AA fire, and until the end of World War I the margin of flight performance of the interceptors over their enemies was very small. If the enemy, even an airship, had a considerable advantage in height, the defending fighter might well be unable to reach it. For this reason, the first true interceptors were designed to loiter at typical airship height, lying in wait. In practice this was very hard to achieve.

Several of these pioneer interceptors were officially described as "gun carriers", the gun often being the powerful Davis, a recoilless weapon used in three sizes, firing shells weighing from 1.5lb (0.68kg) to 6lb (2.27kg). Some aircraft accommodated the guns and gunners in howdah-like nacelles attached to the upper wing, one example being the Robey-Peters. But the most extraordinary of all this early species of anti-airship interceptors was the Supermarine (Pemberton-Billing) P.B.31E, sometimes called the Night Hawk. This incredibly cumbersome quadruplane had its own electric generating plant to supply a

searchlight in the nose cockpit, while various gunners aimed a 1.5-pounder Davis and two Lewis guns. Nine tanks held fuel for an alleged 18 hours, by which time the gunners and single pilot might have been tired as well as cold — and probably feeling frustrated.

The radar revolution

By the 1930s the RAF and a very few other air forces had identified the interceptor as a small fighter endowed with the highest possible rate of climb. This was because the first warning of a raid by enemy bombers would be when they were seen and heard almost overhead, at perhaps 15,000ft (4,600m). The only alternative was to mount "standing patrols"; fighter squadrons would take-off and climb to the height at which enemy bombers might be expected, and patrol over a given region in the hope of finding "trade". Such a procedure was fine in theory, but in wartime would have imposed a severe drain on aircraft, pilots, maintenance man-hours, spares, fuel, oil and engine life.

From 1936 the whole of air warfare was increasingly revolutionised by the invention of radar, and the interception mission more than most. By the start of World War II the RAF and

Right: One of the best British fighters of World War 1 was the S.E.5a. It had a forward-firing belt-fed Vickers gun and a Lewis on a Foster mount above the upper wing which enabled it to be pulled back so that the pilot could change ammo drums.

Luftwaffe had no need to mount standing patols. Every time a fighter squadron was "scrambled" it could be sure of meeting the enemy, for with two-way radio it could be guided by a controller who, in turn, was in possession of accurate information on the enemy's position, height and strength long before a single bomber had come within visual or aural range. It was by such means that the Battle of Britain was won, but the Luftwaffe's answer was to give up precision attacks on such targets as fighter stations and instead bomb cities by night. A year earlier, and there would have been no answer at all. By October 1940, however, the first radar-equipped Beaufighters were in service with Fighter Command.

Such machines were the first of a totally new species of specialised interceptor which, for the first time in history, could hunt down enemy aircraft in darkness, or even in cloud, without any more than the most general guidance by ground controllers, as given to day squadrons, and without needing help from searchlights or seeing AA fire. Such aircraft relied entirely upon their own radar. Initially this was heavy and cumbersome, and needed a second crew-member to operate the radar controls and try to interpret the obscure and capricious indications.

Of course, this meant that the overall interception had to result from quite a long sequence: ground radar and observers, telephones, girl plotters, ground controller, voice radio, pilot, then aided by airborne radar, air observer's interpretation, intercom, and again an understanding of aural directions by the pilot. In order to shoot down the enemy it was generally regarded as essential to achieve

Right: *Soundly defeated over Britain in daylight in 1940, the Messerschmitt Bf 110 later proved an excellent basis for a night fighter. Equipped with ever greater loads of radar and other sensors, and heavier armament, the final Bf 110G versions stayed in action until the end.*

visual contact. In other words the pilot had to catch sight of the target and get it in his gun-sight first.

As World War II continued, so did AI (air-borne interception) radar improve. To a considerable degree this was effected by reducing wavelength, using the new technology of the magnetron to generate powerful radiation at wavelengths down to 3cm. As soon as the magnetron had been developed, in England, the invention was conveyed to the still-neutral United States, where it was described in an official history as "the most valuable cargo ever brought to our shores". As early as January 1941 the US Navy issued a requirement for something that a few months earlier would have been absolute science fiction: "A 3cm AI radar that is light, compact, simple, dif-

ficult to jam, operable by the pilot, and useful in night air interception with secondary capability in attack on surface vessels". The reader can readily understand the achievement in developing a radar that could fit into an ordinary single-seat fighter, and with its display in front of the pilot.

Though the most numerous of the new single-seat interceptors were Grumman F6F Hellcats, the very first were a dozen Vought F4U-1 Corsairs. The radar power unit and transmitter/receiver were installed in the fuse-lage, the antenna (aerial) was put inside a streamlined blister well out on the starboard wing, and the viewing scope was at the top of the instrument panel. The results were outstanding. Until 31 October 1943 Japanese bombers — dubbed "washing-machine Char-

lies" by the recipients — had roamed the areas round Bougainville and New Georgia (Solomon Islands) every night, largely to prevent anybody being able to sleep. From that day onwards every "Charlie" was destroyed. Indeed on one famous occasion an F4U pilot tested his guns and found a "Charlie" had got in the way! Suffice to say, from that time on, it was practical to put radar in virtually any fighter, even a single-seater.

Back in 1940-41 many seemingly crazy ideas had been proposed to beat the night raiders over Britain, and some were even tested. One was the Turbinlite: a big radar-equipped night fighter was supposed to fly in formation with two or more smaller fighters and, on finding a target, would illuminate it with a searchlight in the hope that the accompanying fighters would shoot it down. This idea must have been invented by someone with no experience of flying and little imagination, though the Turbinlite itself was the brainchild of a wing commander. Another short-lived idea was the LAM (long aerial mine), not unnaturally code-named "Mutton", in which a night fighter was supposed to bring down enemies by trailing an explosive device on a 2,000ft (610m) cable.

It took a long time for it to be appreciated that equipping a bomber with emitters — devices radiating electromagnetic waves — makes it thousands of times easier to intercept. RAF bombers of 1939-42 were difficult to intercept because over enemy territory they did not radiate anything except IR from the engine exhausts (which can never be eliminated, though the "visible" temperature can be reduced). From 1942 the "heavies" were fitted with a ground-mapping radar, called H_2S, and this broadcast the bomber's presence precisely like a lighthouse, sweeping a powerful beam to all points of the compass. From 1943 they were additionally fitted with a small aft-facing radar (Monica) to warn of the presence of enemy night fighters, and this gave the very same night fighters yet another unmistakable emission on which to home. Such interceptors as the Bf 110G and Ju 88G were equipped with Naxos-Z, which homed on H_2S, and Flensburg, which homed on Monica. Today, air forces have rather more understanding of the concept popularly called stealth, and try to avoid making the enemy interceptor's task so simple.

Above left: The Messerschmitt Bf 109E was the Luftwaffe's standard single-seat fighter during the Battle of Britain. Thanks to British radar the Luftwaffe was almost always brought to battle, and eventually gave up its attempt to conquer the RAF.

Below: Powered like the F6F by the R-2800 engine, the Chance Vought F4U Corsair was likewise the pioneer of single-seat night fighting, the pilot using his own radar scope to effect interceptions. The first British single-seat night fighter was the Lightning.

Left: Though it did not fly until July 1942 the Grumman F6F Hellcat powered by the R-2800 engine had such power and capability that it progressively swept the Japanese from the skies over the Pacific ocean. It later proved capable of night fighting using a 3cm radar.

Below: Here seen in the USA after World War 2, the Heinkel He 219 was one of the most formidable piston-engined night interceptors. It combined outstanding flight performance with a range of electronic aids and devastating armament. The latter included cannon firing upward at 65°.

The nuclear jet threat

The advent in 1945 of nuclear weapons suddenly changed the whole situation. It was realised that in a future war it would be unlikely for the sky to be filled with thousands of bombers. Instead there might be just one, but carrying a bomb that could destroy a city. Moreover, as it would probably be a jet, it would be flying at about twice the speed and twice the height of previous bombers. The interceptor would therefore not need so much combat persistence, but it would have to have almost total certainty of destruction against a single target, and to accomplish the interception in about half the elapsed time.

The first major change, devised and deployed originally by the US Air Force, was the collision-course technique. This was linked with a change in armament, to batteries of rockets of 2.75in (70mm) calibre, copied from the German wartime R4/M. Unguided, but stabilised in their flight by spinning rapidly, these packed such a warhead punch that even a single good hit could bring down a bomber, and two or three would practically guarantee destruction. Thus, if a sufficient number could be launched towards a bomber, spreading out because of their natural dispersion — the trajectories being far more random than those of gun-fired projectiles, despite their spin — then there would be a good chance of several hits even if the original direction of aim was much less precise than that necessary with fixed guns even of large (say 30mm) calibre.

In turn this led to the collision-course interception in which the fighter pilot is vectored by ground control to such a position that he can engage the target aircraft from abeam. Seen from the side, an aircraft presents a much bigger radar target than is the case when seen from astern, so the fighter can detect the target earlier and close on it with greater certainty, especially in the presence of countermeasures. The first and most important countermeasure is chaff, slivers of reflective foil or aluminised plastic film with a length similar to the wavelength of the fighter radar. To this day, chaff is by far the most common ECM (electronic countermeasure). It can be pumped out by a dispenser or ejected inside small cartridges which subsequently "bloom", but in either event the chaff ends up behind the aircraft that is using it. Chaff is clearly more effective in blinding a fighter's radar if the fighter is astern of the target. With the collision-course interception it has little effect.

How did the interceptor steer in order to engage the enemy accurately from the side? In its developed form, produced by Hughes Aircraft, the whole process was automatic. The fighter's radar detected and tracked the target, generating constantly changing sightlines and future positions. These were fed to a computer, which worked out how the fighter should steer in order to bring about the desired interception. The resulting output was then fed to the fighter's autopilot and thus to the flight-control system. With the North American F-86D Sabre of December 1949 the collision-course technique was achieved by a single-seater, armed with only 24 rockets. Most aircraft in this class were larger, and carried a greater number of FFARs (folding-fin aircraft rockets), the Avro CF-100 Mk 5 being able to blanket a vast area of sky with 152 in a single devastating salvo.

Self-homing guidance

By the mid-1950s Hughes Aircraft had moved on to a more advanced electronic fire-control system, the MA-1. This was a pioneer digital avionic system, and it was capable of guiding an interceptor, such as the Convair F-106 Delta Dart, through an entire engagement. It did not have to be a collision-course manoeuvre, and the weapon could be an FFAR, a guided missile (such as the Hughes AIM-4 Falcon, in various versions homing by radar or IR), a nuclear rocket (AIR-2 Genie) or a gun (the 20mm M61A-1).

This alone would have demanded a much more capable and flexible fire-control system, but in fact the MA-1 did far more than this. For

Interception Fighters

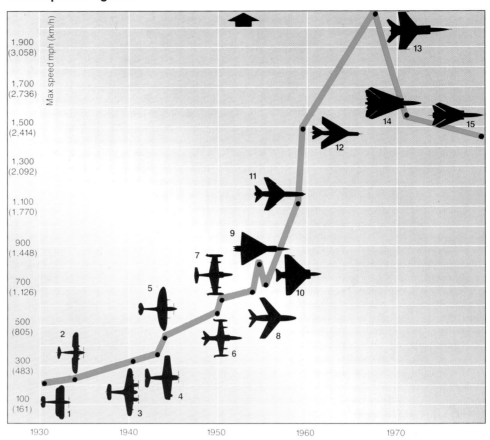

Above: Fundamental laws of mechanics limit the practical speed of a manoeuvring fighter. This shows how fighter speeds have gone up, then down, over a 50-year period. **1:** Hawker Fury. **2:** Dewoitine D.510. **3:** Bristol Beaufighter. **4:** F6F-3N Hellcat. **5:** Spitfire XIV. **6:** F-94C Starfire. **7:** F-89J Scorpion. **8:** F-86D Sabre. **9:** F-102A Delta Dagger. **10:** Javelin. **11:** F-8A Crusader. **12:** Lightning F.1. **13:** MiG-25. **14:** F-14A Tomcat. **15:** Tornado ADV. The arrow points to the never-completed Republic XF-103.

Above: Here flying in its twilight years with the New Jersey Air National Guard, the F-106A Delta Dart has served for 30 years as the principal all-weather interceptor defending the United States. Designed to carry missiles only, it was much later retrofitted with a gun.

Right: Cleverly dubbed by Lockheed "The Missile with a Man in it", the F-104 Starfighter was designed for speed — at the expense of weapons, turn radius and many other factors. The Japanese Air Self-Defence Force used these single- and two-seat versions in 1964-86.

one thing, the F-106 was one of the first all-weather interceptors to have complete supersonic capability. At heights in the neighbourhood of 35,000ft (10,670m) and above it was possible to work up to a peak Mach number of almost 2.3, though at the cost of tremendous fuel consumption. This dramatically reduced the time taken to fly from the fighter airbase to the location at which the engagement would take place, and at the same time it made it more difficult for the enemy aircraft to escape. At the same time, when travelling at such a speed any interceptor has virtually no manoeuvrability. Even quite small alterations in trajectory, in either the horizontal or vertical plane, call for considerable sustained g, in the horizontal plane accompanied by rolling to a large bank angle, and any idea of what might be called "manoeuvring" can be dismissed completely as wholly unattainable.

The relationship between speed, turn radius and acceleration (measured in units of g) is one of the fundamentals of mechanics, and is cons-

Above: AIM-4 training Falcon missiles swung out on their launchers from the huge internal weapon bay of an F-106. The F-102/F-106 series was planned in 1949. Such carriage of missiles may return in the 1990s when designers seek better stealth qualities, and reduced drag.

Wing Comparisons

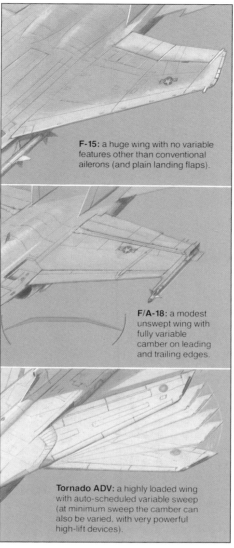

F-15: a huge wing with no variable features other than conventional ailerons (and plain landing flaps).

F/A-18: a modest unswept wing with fully variable camber on leading and trailing edges.

Tornado ADV: a highly loaded wing with auto-scheduled variable sweep (at minimum sweep the camber can also be varied, with very powerful high-lift devices).

tant for every type of aircraft. The turn radius is in fact exactly proportional to the square of the speed. If the radius of turn is 0.5 mile (0.8km) at 400mph (644km/h), it will be 8 miles (13km) at 1,600mph (2,575km/h), for a turn pulling the same g. There is nothing the aircraft designer can do about this. Thus, it often pays to slow down and regain the ability to change direction. Suppose we are flying in an old-time biplane fighter and discover we have an AAM on our tail, closing at Mach 4 but able to pull 30g! This sounds like imminent destruction, but in fact we can easily evade the missile just by waiting until it is about to hit us and then flying a maximum-rate turn (at perhaps 7g). This will take us well outside the lethal warhead radius, and the highly supersonic missile's 30g capability will not be able to prevent it from flying straight past us.

The too-fast fighter

The problem of having to fly in almost straight lines at high supersonic speeds reached its almost absurd climax with the Republic XF-103, planned in 1951 but finally cancelled in August 1957. Powered by a mighty turboramjet, with a variable inlet and also variable shut-off internal doors in the 82ft (25m) fuselage, the XF-103 was to streak towards its target at Mach 4, or about 2,645mph (4,255 km/h). It was to bring down the enemy with AAMs and FFARs, but simple arithmetic showed that there was no way the FFARs could be aimed against a manoeuvring target without

Left: Contrasts in basic wing design of three modern interceptors. The F-15 relies on the sheer size of its wing and tremendous engine power. The F/A-18 met a challenging requirement to fly fighter and attack missions from carriers. The Tornado wing is fully variable.

the required g acceleration getting into the range 15-25. Most fighters are stressed for about 7-8g, and today's F-16's ability to pull 9g is what many pilots would say is beyond the comfortable limit for the human body. There is no way a manned interceptor can manoeuvre at 15-25g, not ever!

Intercepting a very fast target does, however, tend to demand a very fast interceptor. When the US Air Force was developing the XB-70 Valkyrie, planned to cruise at about Mach 3 (say, 2,000mph, 3,220km/h), it suffered the high costs incurred mainly because of the problems such a bomber would pose for the defenders. Even cruising at a great height, in full view of Soviet radars, the B-70 was to travel so fast that intercepting missiles (SAMs fired from the ground or fighter-launched AAMs) would have had to start off heading almost exactly for the correct target future position. Major course corrections would not have been possible.

IR versus radar homing

The Soviet answer was the MiG-25. Work on this was continued even after the Mach-3 bomber itself had been cancelled, and it has ever since been the fastest combat aircraft in service in the world. No other aircraft so well emphasises the contrast between the air-combat fighter and the interceptor, because the MiG-25's dogfighting capability is non-existent. Not only is it not stressed for pulling harsh manoeuvres at low levels but its wing loading is 135lb/sq ft (659kg/m²) or almost double that of an F-15C, and with a wing whose supersonic profile is not optimised for high-g. The most telling comment on the MiG-25 is that this very specialised "straight-line" interceptor has since been redesigned into the MiG-31. This far more useful and flexible aircraft is designed for a maximum Mach number at high altitude of 2.2, and even this is considerably greater than that of most other modern interceptors. Indeed the evidence is that, so far, today low-level speeds are much more important.

There remains to be discussed the profound effect upon the interception mission exerted by the introduction of AAM armament. Indeed, one has only to imagine the problems confronting the would-be users of the first AAM to go into production to begin to appreciate the scale of these changes. This pioneer weapon, the German X-4, was rocket-propelled but it had to be steered all the way to the target by signals transmitted along a pair of fine wires unreeled behind the missile. The pilot of the fighter had to keep the target in his gunsight and then bring the tricky missile on to the same sightline, keeping it there until impact and warhead detonation. The command link used smooth variation of current for missile yaw and "bang/bang" (on/off) type control for pitch. The commands were sent out by manipulating a separate small joystick, so a crew of two was needed, one to fly the fighter and the other to fly the missile. And it was essential to keep flying directly towards the target all the time the AAM was in transit, which, with a heavily armed target, was courting disaster.

With the development of self-homing AAMs the interceptor's task became much easier, but

there were still major shortcomings. By far the most important kinds of AAM so far developed for service are the IR and SARH types. The IR (infra-red) homer senses the faint heat from high-temperature parts of the target and steers the missile towards these parts — actually towards the centroid, or best average location between a group of heat sources — until the missile hits.

Early IR missiles were not particularly clever. They tended to home on the sun, or the sun's reflection in a pool or greenhouse. The only part of a target aircraft at a sufficiently high temperature was the jetpipe and, if possible, the turbine seen from dead astern (unless

Above: The latest interceptor in RAF service, the ADV Tornado, has primary armament of four big Sky Flash (later AMRAAM) missiles recessed under the fuselage, backed up by Sidewinders and a gun. AMRAAM offers escape from the need to "illuminate" the target.

Below: Designed as a pure air-superiority fighter, the USAF's F-15 is now in production as a dual-role two-seat fighter/attack aircraft. Its huge wing is totally unsuited to maximum speed at treetop height, but, in particular, excellent for the fighter mission.

an afterburner was in use, in which case there was no problem). This meant that the attack had to be made from astern, as in the days of guns. In 99 per cent of the IR missiles made so far the pilot switches on the homing head, listens for a low growling in his headset and then manoeuvres his fighter astern of the target until nice juicy IR sources are "visible". The growling rises to an urgent singing note, confirming that the missile has locked-on and can be fired, secure in the knowledge that — in the absence of effective countermeasures, such as intensely hot flares — the missile will hit the selected target.

The semi-active drawback

By about 1963 much more sensitive IR homing heads had been perfected. These could detect the cold metal of a hostile aircraft, even from abeam or head-on, against the even slightly colder background. This made the interception almost simple. So long as the fighter could fly within a few miles of its target, heading towards it, the missile could be reliably locked-on and fired, no matter what the relative positions of the two aircraft might be. Using these new "all-aspect" AAMs, the enemy could even be engaged from head-on, but the IR missiles generally remained close-range weapons, unable except in the most perfect conditions of very clear air and very cold background to detect a target at great distances. Their one great advantage was, and remains, that they are "fire and forget" weapons. The moment the interceptor pilot has fired, he can forget that target and turn to a different one.

Look down, shoot down

This is not the case with SARH (semi-active radar homing) missiles. These require the target to be "illuminated" by radar from the fighter. The missile then detects the radiation scattered or reflected back the way it was sent out and homes on this necessarily much fainter radiation. It is coded to respond only to the radar from its own fighter, to avoid "own goals". Despite the low signal strength of the reflected radiation, the SARH missile can still home over ranges several times greater than the limit possible with IR. The latest Sparrows, for example, have a theoretical brochure range of 62 miles (100km), though practical range limits are somewhat shorter.

This is impressive, but SARH missiles suffer from a drawback which today is every bit as serious as the wire-guided X-4 would have been in 1944. To home on its target the AAM needs the target to be held in the beam from the fighter's own radar. This radar points ahead, so the fighter has to keep flying towards the target until the missile hits. This throws away the advantage of the missile's long range, and long before the SARH missile strikes home the fighter may well have been detected by the homing head of a short-range IR missile carried by the target. In the latter's final few seconds it may fire this IR missile which self-homes and quickly evens the score. Obviously, nothing could be more undesirable in an interception mission than having to continue to fly directly towards the target all the time our own missile is in the air.

In numerous exercises fighters armed with the AIM-7 Sparrow — which has a published range of up to 62 miles (100km) — have engaged simple targets such as F-5s at several times the effective range of the target's AIM-9 Sidewinders. Then, after firing (or simulating) a Sparrow shot, the big fighter would have to keep heading towards the target for so long that, just as its own Sparrow hit home, it would come into firing range of the "enemy".

747-style combat aircraft

Nobody has fitted fighters with missiles and radars facing backwards, and a better answer is

Above: Launch of an AIM-54C, the current production version of the US Navy's Phoenix. This missile has its own homing radar and can destroy targets from ranges in excess of 124 miles (200km). Though the F-14 will carry the active-radar AMRAAM, this missile does not meet the Navy's range requirement. Two companies are battling to replace Phoenix.

Left: Peel-off by F-15C Eagle fighters of the 18th TFW, Pacific Air Forces. From the outset the F-15 could fly the air-superiority close combat mission as well as night and in-weather interception (though the USAF's idea of "in-weather" is much less severe than the RAF's). The later F-15E is a multirole two-seater.

FIGHTER MISSIONS

to give the AAM active guidance; in other words, to fit it with its own small radar. The first AAM in service with this capability was the US Navy's AIM-54 Phoenix, carried only by the F-14A and D Tomcat. From the outset this was not only the world's longest-ranged AAM, with the ability to kill from a distance of over 124 miles (200km), but also one of the first with "look-down, shoot-down" capability.

Today, virtually all penetration of hostile airspace is carried out at the lowest possible height, to minimise the chance of being detected and tracked by enemy radars. It follows that the interceptor has to shoot down from above, and it was very difficult to make radars able unfailingly to lock-on to enemy aircraft yet ignore the gigantic echo from the ground immediately beneath. Today's missiles, and interceptor radars, can kill low-flying aircraft no matter how close they are to the ground.

Should it ever be needed, they can also shoot down aircraft perhaps 40,000ft (12,200m) higher than the fighter.

A slow fighter

When truly long-range AAMs were first developed it was thought that the interceptor could be used merely to carry a load of missiles

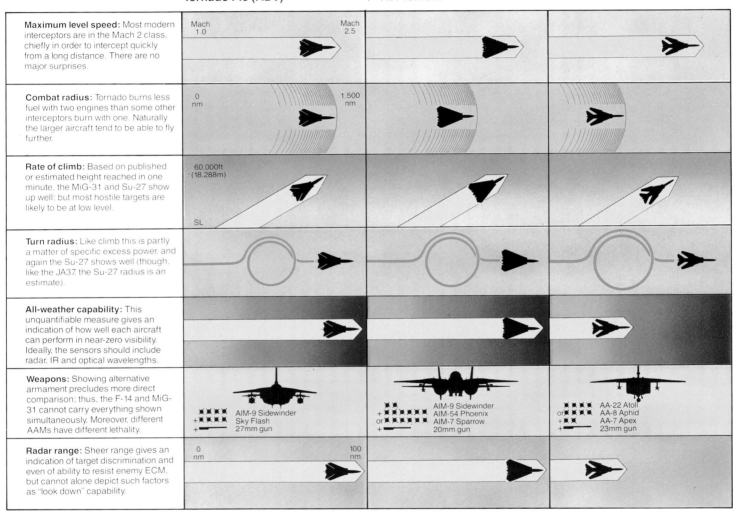

These diagrams are intended to afford a broad basis for comparison; they are essentially qualitative, not quantitative. Obviously, the objective is to compare like with like, and to portray each parameter at its limiting value under what might be termed typical mission conditions. Thus, most performance values assume a weapon load less than the maximum. The top row (level speed) is for a flight level around 35,000ft (10,670m), while turn radius (one of the more difficult quantities to pin down) assumes medium height at about 400kt (750km/h). Possible weapon loads are shown with "and/or" qualification.

◀ F-14A Tomcat

Power plant: Two P&W TF30-414A (20,900lb/93kN)
Span: (min sweep) 38ft 2.5in (11.65m)
Length: 62ft 8in (19.1m)
Max TO weight: 74,349lb (33,724kg)
Crew: 2

◀ Tornado F.3

Power plant: Two RB.199 Mk 104 (17,000lb/75kN)
Span: (max sweep) 28ft 2in (8.6m)
Length: 59ft 4in (18m)
Max TO weight: 61,700lb (27,986kg)
Crew: 2

◀ MiG-23MF

Power plant: One Tumanskii R-29B (27,500lb/122kN)
Span: (min sweep) 25ft 6in (7.77m)
Length: 52ft 1in (15.88m)
Max TO weight: 41,670lb (18,900kg)
Crew: 1

aloft, thereafter acting as a kind of airborne launch station. This was attempted by the US Navy in the late 1950s, when the Douglas F6D Missileer, carrying six big Eagle AAMs, was ordered to protect the battle fleets against distant enemy aircraft. The F6D faintly resembled today's A-6 and S-3 in being a relatively slow, long-span machine, with good lifting capability and endurance. It was cancelled in 1960, partly — it was said — because the outgoing Navy Secretary could not comprehend the concept of "a slow fighter".

Stealth and detection

In fact, the relatively slow, un-agile platform orbiting aloft while armed with very long-range AAMs, and with an accompanying large surveillance radar, is as valid as that of the offensive counterpart, the large transport-style aircraft carrying perhaps 50 long-range cruise missiles. Today the stealth cruise missile poses by far the greatest threat to a nation's major surface installations, and few if any modern interceptors could shoot one down. Quantum advances are needed in the detection and tracking ability of fighter radars and IR sets, and in the homing systems of long-range air-to-air missiles.

| MiG-31 | Su-27 | F-4E Phantom II | JA37 Viggen |

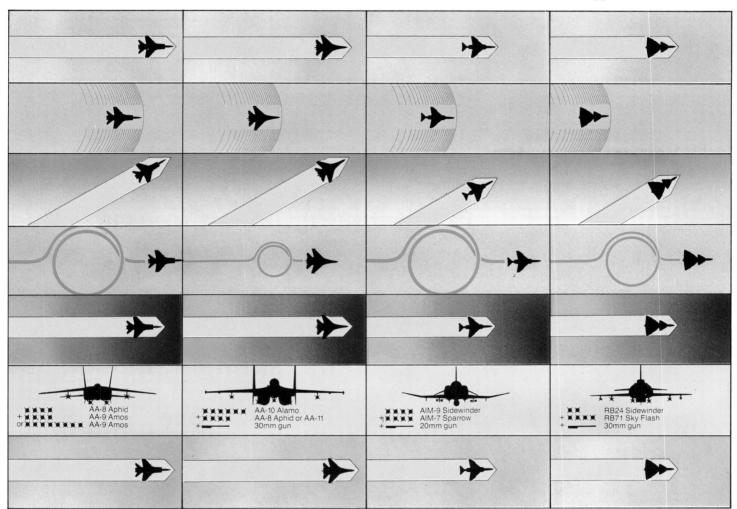

◀ MiG-31

Power plant: Two Tumanskii R-31F (30,865lb/137.3kN)
Span: 45ft 11in (14.0m)
Length: 70ft 7in (21.5m)
Max TO weight: 90,725lb (41,150kg)
Crew: 2

◀ F-4E Phantom II

Power plant: Two GE J79-17 (17,900lb/79kN)
Span: 38ft 5in (11.7m)
Length: 63ft 0in (19.2m)
Max TO weight: 60,360lb (27,379kg)
Crew: 2

◀ Su-27

Power plant: Two Tumanskii R-32 (29,955lb/133.25kN)
Span: 48ft 3in (14.7m)
Length: 70ft 11in (21.6m)
Max TO weight: (est) 65,000lb (29,500kg)
Crew: 1

◀ JA37 Viggen

Power plant: One RM8B (28,108lb/125kN)
Span: 34ft 9in (10.6m)
Length: 51ft 1.5in/(15.58m)
TO weight: ("normal armament") 37,478lb (17,000kg)
Crew: 1

The Tornado Mission

AT the forward operating location at Benbecula, an island in the Outer Hebrides off the west coast of Scotland, a handful of RAF Tornado F.3 interceptors from No. 5 Squadron stand on alert, ready and waiting to deal with any enemy aircraft attempting to attack sea or land targets after passing through the strategically important Greenland-Iceland-UK gap (GIUK). The GIUK gap is also strategically significant to the Soviet navy in that any Soviet ship requiring to leave the northern Russian ports must transit this choke point in order to build up naval strength in the open ocean. Meanwhile, far to the north, on an air base in the Kola peninsula, half-a-dozen Soviet Tupolev Tu-16 "Badgers" take-off on the start of a long-range anti-shipping strike mission, their target consisting of a convoy far out to sea in the north-east Atlantic Ocean. Elsewhere in Scotland, fighter controllers are alerted to the coming threat and initiate the first of a series of actions that will culminate in the destruction of the Soviet strike package long before it reaches its target.

0815 hours

They have been at Benbecula for the best part of four days now and are beginning to feel that they are missing out badly, the little amount of information that has filtered through to the makeshift dispersal facility indicating that their air defence dedicated colleagues on the mainland are seeing rather more action.

Indeed, since the half-a-dozen No. 5 Squadron Tornado F.3s flew in from Coningsby, they have been called upon to scramble only once and even that was a false alarm — a USAF Military Airlift Command C-141B Starlifter en route to Europe having for some unaccountable reason strayed far off course.

They are there, in the Outer Hebrides, to cover the north-west approaches and, specifically, to counter the threat posed by Soviet warplanes attempting to move through the Greenland/Iceland/UK (GIUK) gap. Interdictor/strike aircraft using this corridor can either attack targets situated on the British mainland or, as is much more probable, hit sea convoys engaged in transferring much needed men and equipment to the European theatre.

Apart from the brief flurry of excitement caused by the MAC transport, the No. 5 Squadron pilots have flown only rarely and the few sorties which have been completed have done little to relieve the tedium, use of in-flight refuelling — from either a VC-10 or a Tristar tanker — enabling them to remain airborne for prolonged periods. After four or five hours in the cockpit, there is growing discomfort — helmets weigh ever more heavily, oxygen masks pinch uncomfortably and cramped muscles begin to show signs of seizing up through lack of exercise.

Such discomforts are, however, accepted as being nothing more than part of the job and even though they have encountered little in the way of "trade", there is still a very keen sense of anticipation of battle. Inevitably, this is mixed in with a modest amount of envy, for they are all too well aware that other fighter

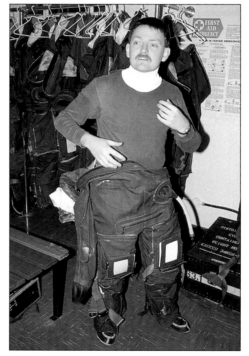

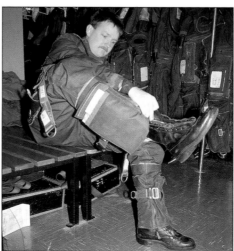

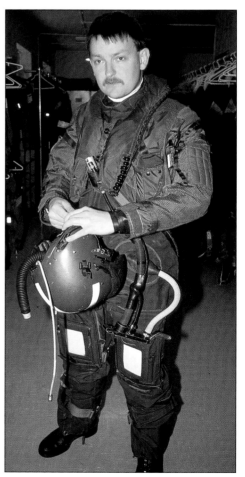

Left, below left and below: Survival in the hostile environment in which modern interceptors will be expected to fly and fight requires much specialised flight kit. In this sequence of illustrations, a Tornado pilot dons gear which includes an immersion or "poopy" suit, leg restraint devices, a pair of rather cumbersome boots and the inevitable "bone dome".

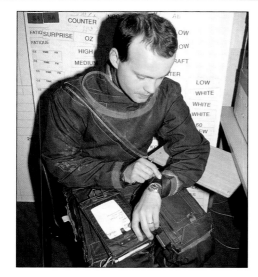

Above: In peacetime, pre-mission briefing is usually accomplished on the ground before walking out to the aircraft but it is possible for Tornado crews to receive instructions while on cockpit alert duty. Here, a pilot synchronises his watch during a briefing.

Above: Preparation for a mission is a quite complex process which invariably includes a detailed briefing covering a number of points. These always include the objectives of the sortie to be flown as well as the examination of weather, tactics, weapons and communications.

Below: Outside the squadron's hardened accommodation, personnel assigned to ground defence duties occupy bunkers located in and around the complex of aircraft shelters which provide protection for the Tornado F.3 interceptors between sorties.

units stationed at RAF airfields on the east coast have been kept far more busy. All they can do is wait and hope . . .

The Soviet Tu-26 "Backfire" is, of course, perceived, with its sophisticated array of weapons and electronic equipment, as being perhaps the most serious threat but this potent warplane is, in reality, only one of several Soviet combat types with the ability to attack via the so-called "back door", moving through the GIUK gap to outflank the heavy concentration of defences along the east coast in order to approach from the west. To date, though, "Ivan" has shown no inclination to employ this tactic, all of the raids which have so far occurred having been mass frontal attacks from the traditional axis of approach to the east.

On the crew-room wall, the hastily applied legends "Frontal Aviation means just what it says", and "Who is A. Lert and why is he doing these dreadful things to me???" just about sum up their frustration, for, in addition to the occasional fruitless patrols, four days of cockpit readiness also lie behind them . . . four days of tedium as, kitted up and ready to launch at a moment's notice, they while away the hours.

On the first day, things hadn't been too bad, the anticipation of combat helping to keep them keyed up, waiting for the scramble call. Day two started off reasonably well, the detachment commander and his wingman launching within minutes of beginning their spell of cockpit readiness, but they were doomed to disappointment for it was this sortie which encountered the errant C-141B. Since then, it has all been downhill.

At first, pilot and navigator crews managed to keep themselves reasonably well occupied, checking out systems and generally reassuring themselves that the aircraft was in good shape for the mission demanded of it. Frequent checks of the Tornado F.3's key systems help them to maintain a fairly high level of concentration, although, quite understandably, their thoughts stray to the probability of combat. Nobody says much about that but all wonder how they will fare when the time comes. They needed action, but were no longer optimistic that they would get it.

Yesterday, to help time pass, one or two crew members took books out to the cockpit, spending long sessions of the alert period quietly reading while they awaited the call that never seemed to come. Somewhat ironically, one of them — who had best remain nameless — was making solid progress with Tolstoy's *War and Peace* and was even beginning to entertain visions of completing this classic novel without ever once seeing action. He was soon to be proved wrong . . .

0820 hours

At the sector operations centre (SOC) at RAF Buchan in north-east Scotland, fighter controllers study the air picture which is built up using data received from a variety of sources. On the Continent, elements of NATO's Air Defence Ground Environment (NADGE) relay information to Buchan, as do the station's own radars and those at various satellite stations in the Northern Isles, Saxa Vord's contribution being particularly valuable since this facility is ideally placed to observe air traffic attempting to pass through undetected.

Today, at least, there is evidence of aerial activity way up to the north, facilities in Norway having detected several radar returns before they were reduced to little more than idle speculation in the face of sustained barrage jamming. It is possible that it is a bluff on the

Right: Having reached the hardened shelter in which his Tornado is housed, a pilot performs a quick external pre-flight inspection. Weapons, flight control surfaces and panels are normally examined closely during the pre-departure walkaround.

part of "Ivan", but with a convoy now embarking on the final and most hazardous stage of its trans-Atlantic crossing into Greenock on the Clyde it is equally possible that Soviet forces are preparing to attack.

 0822 hours

A controller at Buchan reaches for a telephone which connects him directly by landline to the temporary operations facility at Benbecula.

"I suspect we might have some trade heading your way before too long. Bring another two Tornados to five minutes readiness and the last two to 15 minutes readiness."

 0823 hours

At Benbecula, the officer manning the operations desk returns the handset to its rest, rises and pokes his head through an adjacent hatch. Three faces look up at him enquiringly, while other aircrew are more intent on a game of cards, although the shouts of "cheat . . ." seem to indicate that they are not taking the game too seriously.

 0824 hours

"OK, Mac, George," says the officer, "that was Buchan — they want two more aircraft on five minute standby. You'd better get out there now. As for you Dick, you're on 15-minute standby as of now . . . same goes for you too, Mike."

"Does this mean we might actually get to fly today at last . . . ?" says one pilot, as he quickly gathers up his kit, before disappearing out the door at a brisk trot. Within moments, his navigator and another crew follow, clambering aboard a Land Rover that is waiting to take them to their aircraft, which are dispersed in a number of hides situated close to the end of the runway.

 0825 hours

As they move out, two other crews are already on alert, waiting in their respective cockpits with power on and radios alive so as to receive any call to scramble that might come. Recent construction has resulted in some hardened shelters appearing on the airfield skyline and one or two of these are now in use but facilities at Benbecula are generally still somewhat primitive, with all of the ongoing construction work having been suspended for the time being. In view of that, any scramble order will be relayed from air traffic control via conventional radio. Navigation systems are also aligned, ready for a hasty departure and all that can be done to speed the launch procedure has been done. Soon the order to scramble will come from Buchan.

Above: While the pilot continues his careful pre-flight inspection, the Tornado navigator climbs the steps and settles into the rear cockpit where he quickly gets down to checking out the aircraft's complex array of avionics systems with the aid of built-in test equipment.

Left: Only when he is satisfied that all is in order will the pilot occupy the forward cockpit. Once securely strapped in, he will devote his attention to a long and complex sequence of pre-start checks, before using the auxiliary power unit to bring the Tornado's engines to life.

Right: With the canopy closed and both engines running smoothly, the crew are kept busy with still more checks before they leave the protection of the shelter. These include verifying that control surfaces are working satisfactorily and aligning the inertial navigation system.

Left: *Satisfied at last that the Tornado is in good shape, the pilot advises the ground crew that he is ready to leave the shelter. Outside, armed guards patrol in NBC kit, ready to deal with any intruders who might try to interfere with the smooth flow of operations.*

while others monitor the movement of key flight control surfaces and pull the chocks clear in a sequence of highly co-ordinated actions polished by frequent peacetime practice.

0838 hours

The pilot of the leading Tornado activates his radio again, uttering the brief message, "01 scramble taxi." A click from the tower operator is the only response but is sufficient to let him know his message has been heard and understood. The engine note deepens momentarily as the pilot adds just enough power to get the aircraft moving clear of the shelter, turning right on to the taxiway a few seconds later. Opposite, from another shelter, another Tornado emerges, its nose suddenly dipping as the pilot brakes to a halt and waits until lead has rolled past before also moving out on to the taxiway.

0833 hours

Even as the two new alert crews are hastily pre-flighting their aircraft and settling in to their cockpits, so is the word to scramble fighters being passed from Buchan to Benbecula. Information received by the SOC reveals that at least half-a-dozen potentially hostile aircraft are heading south-westerly on a course that will bring them within reach of the Tornados at Benbecula, and the order to launch is quickly passed by landline.

0834 hours

Satisfied that the launch order is authentic, the tower controller activates the radio and begins to speak, "Ranger 01, 02. This is Mayfly."

"Roger, Mayfly."

"Er, 01, 02 to intercept unidentified tracks, vector 290. Climb flight level 250 for transit. Call TAD075, back-up TAD125. Scramble, scramble, scramble, acknowledge."

"01, scramble. Vector 290, 250, TAD075, back-up 125."

0835 hours

Within moments of the order to launch being received, the pilots begin start-up procedures, employing the rapid take-off panel to bring the aircraft to life, fuel flowing into the combustion chambers, as the auxiliary power units are engaged. Outside, ground crew perform their few remaining tasks, armament specialists removing the final safing devices from the clutch of missiles that each Tornado carries

0840 hours

As they take the active runway, lead again speaks to air traffic control. "01, take-off . . ." Again, the only acknowledgement comes in the form of a click as the controller flicks the switch on and off. A brief glance to the right reveals that his wingman is in place and the two pilots quickly exchange hand signals before pushing the throttle levers hard forward and releasing the brakes. The high-pitched whine of the engines at idle is quickly replaced by a deepening, crackling roar as power increases and the afterburners ignite, propelling the pair of aircraft down the runway at ever-increasing speed. Heavily laden with fuel and missiles, they still use little more than 4,000 feet (1,200m) to get airborne, personnel on the ground listening to the noise fade and then reappear as, reversing track, the two Tornados head out over the sea.

0845 hours

Once airborne, they separate, the gap between the two aircraft opening out to about 7,000 feet (2,100m) laterally and some 2,000 feet (600m) vertically as they head north-west at high subsonic speed. They pursue a course which, if all goes well, will permit them to head-off the approaching bomber formation and choose the optimum moment to initiate their attack. Data on the opposition force is still filtering into Buchan from a variety of sources, and it appears that it consists of no more than half-a-dozen aircraft — probably cruise-missile-armed "Backfires", although this has still to be confirmed.

They will, however, be working with an E-3 Sentry operating out of the US air base at Keflavik, Iceland, on "TAD075", this being a cryptic reference to a secure communications channel. Already they have been identified on

the Sentry's radar, their "squawk" (transponder code) standing out clearly on the tactical displays inside the cabin of the E-3 as they move further out over the sea.

Despite some evidence of electronic interference, the enemy aircraft are being tracked on radar, the US Air Force Sentry monitoring them as they move down the GIUK gap in a south-westerly direction at low level. It is highly unlikely that the Soviet crews will be unaware that their aircraft are being "painted" by radar, for their own warning receivers are almost certainly picking up the Sentry's radar signals and providing a visual reference to the approximate location of this "threat" by means of a display scope.

Indeed, it is hoped that their almost certain knowledge of this fact will persuade them to modify their tactics, experience having already revealed that, wherever a Sentry patrols, there are usually also some Eagles in attendance not too far away. Since Keflavik is also home for the F-15Cs of the 57th Fighter Interceptor Squadron, the consensus of opinion among those controlling the interception is that the approaching bombers will follow a slightly different track so as to position themselves beyond the range of the US fighters.

 0853 hours

The bluff works, and the enemy formation changes course, coming around on to a new track which will take them further to the east of Iceland. Aboard the orbiting Sentry, a controller smiles to himself as he notes the slight change of course, bringing this to the attention of another member of the battle staff within a matter of moments. Shortly afterwards, a coded message is transmitted over a secure data link channel, staff at Buchan being among the few agencies that are privy to its contents.

Now, the enemy aircraft will pass much closer to the Tornados which continue to maintain strict radio silence as they move further out over the grey and uninviting waters of the Atlantic. This is not to say that the Tornados are not in contact with controlling agencies but rather that such contact is purely one-way, the Tornado crews keeping a listening watch and reacting to orders but not acknowledging them. Barely a minute after the enemy formation take's up its new heading, crews aboard the Tornados learn of the change.

 0855 hours

They also observe electronic "silence", holding their Marconi AI24 Foxhunter radars in stand-by mode so as not to alert the enemy force of their presence. Only when they are advised to activate their radars will they electronically "unmask" and go about the task of intercepting and, if all goes well, destroying the opposition.

Right: *The four belly-mounted Sky Flash missiles and the muzzle of the Mauser cannon that form part of the Tornado's impressive armament are visible on the lead aircraft as it heads for the runway. Moving fast, little time will pass before it is airborne and hunting its targets.*

Above: *Tip vortices swirl from the lead aircraft as the pair of Tornados begin their take-off roll. Just visible in the heat haze laid down by four RB199 engines working at full augmented thrust is the lead element of a second pair which will soon follow them.*

Above left: *Moving clear of the confines of the hardened shelter, the nose of the Tornado dips momentarily as the pilot checks the brakes, before moving on to the adjacent taxiway. In the rear, the navigator is busy, checking the equipment he will use.*

Right: *As the approaching Tu-16 Badgers move nearer, the Tornado crew are hard at work. In the front cockpit, the pilot is setting up a missile attack while his navigator monitors the developing action by means of radar data and the tactical evaluation display console.*

Below: *With the afterburner flame glowing brightly in the gloom and with the main gear almost retracted, the lead Tornado gets airborne in typically noisy fashion. In a few minutes, it will be well out to sea, moving fast to cut off the formation of enemy bomber aircraft.*

Tornado F.3 (ADV) Cockpit

In essence, it is little more than a cat and mouse game played for the very highest stakes, with the odds now tilted heavily in favour of the interceptors. Certainly, on paper, they possess most of the advantages. They have the assistance of ground and airborne controllers to help them find their targets; they have their own radar with which to perform the interception; they have an impressive selection of weapons; they have superior manoeuvrability and speed; and, to some extent, they have surprise in their favour.

For the opposition, the advantages are few. They had originally hoped to penetrate to the target area without being detected. Now, having analysed the characteristics of the radar that is observing them and correctly identified it as that of an E-3 Sentry, they are aware that they have failed in that objective. In view of that, they are naturally expecting to run into some opposition and are alert to that eventuality. They have a varied assortment of deception equipment, including chaff, flares and jammers with which to decoy enemy missiles and disrupt enemy radars but that is just about the extent of the defensive measures they are able to employ. They are, to put it bluntly, in big trouble unless a miracle saves them . . .

 0908 hours

"Ranger 01, Candy 31 (E-3 call sign). Targets in your one o'clock, crossing right to left, range 30 miles, speed 500 knots and are identified as hostile. Clear engage . . ."

 0909 hours

It is only now that they "unmask", the navigator bringing the AI24 radar into play. Initially, it operates in pulse-Doppler mode employing a high pulse repetition frequency (PRF) as it searches for the targets while they pull round in a left-hand turn which should put the Soviet aircraft ahead of and below them. Within a matter of seconds, utilising one of the two cathode ray tube (CRT) displays situated high up on the right-hand side of his cockpit, the navigator locates the targets on the radar.

They are ahead, the leading element consisting of a pair of Tu-16 "Badgers" flying adjacent tracks with about two miles (3km) lateral separation. Four miles (6km) behind is the second pair and four miles further back is the third pair, the formation showing up on the Tornado cockpit displays as two columns of three aircraft, with the rearmost aircraft still some way beyond visual range at about 20 miles (32km) in front of the two interceptors.

Pilot and navigator of the lead Tornado confer briefly to establish the form that the interception will take, the pilot then activating his radio and advising his wingman of the game plan. "Lead to two. We'll walk up the line starting from the rear. You move wide and take the right-hand column. Confirm."

"Er, two to lead. Move wide to engage right column."

Even though they are flying at little more than 250 feet (76m) above the sea, the hostile aircraft show up clearly on radar. It is shaping up to be a classic interception and the navigator quickly switches to the track-while-scan mode.

0910 hours

Each target is assigned an individual letter, commencing at "A" and the navigator begins to set up for automatic target sequencing, it being possible for the Tornado F.3 to engage up to four hostile aircraft in rapid succession with a high probability of success. On this occasion, since the lead crew will only be engaging the three aircraft on the left-hand side of the enemy formation, the attack profile is quite straightforward, and the navigator quickly inserts the relevant data into the computer.

In the meantime, the pilot stays "head-up" as they stalk the six bombers, alert to the possibility of enemy "Fulcrum" fighters even though the Sentry has given no indication of the presence of any such threat. At the moment, they have stabilised about 20 miles (32km) behind the rear pair of "Badgers", matching speed and holding the targets at about the one o'clock position while the navigator manipulates the radar controls so as to ensure that Sky Flash missile launch constraints are satisfied and that the optimum position is achieved when the time comes to fire.

Almost simultaneously, the navigator utilises the weapon control panel that is located adjacent to his left knee to select the armament that they will employ, in this case one of the four Sky Flash semi-active radar homing missiles housed beneath the aircraft's belly. Earlier, soon after take-off, he had taken a few moments to verify that the missiles were tuned to search in the correct frequency band for "energy" emanating from the Foxhunter's J-band radar illuminator, signals originating from this source being received via a rear reference aerial once the weapon is on its way to the target.

0912 hours

As he works, he advises his pilot of developments and requests small course corrections from time to time, similar actions taking place in the second Tornado which has now manoeuvred into a near ideal position to begin its attack sequence.

0913 hours

"Locking-on . . . wait . . . wait . . . come starboard five degrees . . . wait . . . wait . . . locked-on . . . fox one . . ."

0913:20 hours

On hearing the words "fox one", the pilot, who has also been observing the developing tactical situation via the head-up display

Right: With the wing almost entirely enveloped in vapour, the leader's Tornado reefs around into a hard right turn as it manoeuvres to engage one of the Tu-16 Badgers high above the Atlantic Ocean. Within a few seconds, a Sky Flash missile will be on its way.

Left: *Seconds after getting airborne, the pair of Tornados will take up a new heading as they move to intercept the Tu-16s. They will also adopt battle formation, separated laterally and vertically by several thousand feet so as to achieve valuable mutual support in case of any threat.*

Right: *Launch of Sky Flash missile uses a unique ejection system whereby twin rams drive the weapon through disturbed airflow into smooth air before the rocket motor ignites. In this way, the risk of the missile failing to separate from the aircraft cleanly is entirely eliminated.*

Below left: *As the moment of missile release nears, the pilot devotes virtually all of his attention to the head-up display, on which appears data pertaining to the ever evolving tactical situation. Once missile parameters are met, he will hit the launch trigger on the control column.*

ADV Missile Ejection System

screen, depresses the trigger on the control column, an action which instigates launch of the first Sky Flash. A fraction of a second later, the Frazer-Nash cartridge-powered twin-ram ejector system activates, two long-stroke arms extending to thrust the Sky Flash through the disturbed airflow that surrounds the Tornado and which can, in certain adverse circumstances, prevent separation. As the missile moves, so too do its thermal batteries energise, furnishing the modest amount of power that is required by Sky Flash sub-systems such as the movable control surfaces.

Within two or three seconds of the firing button being depressed, the batteries are fully up to speed and it is only then that the missile actually leaves the rail, driven by an Aerojet Mk.52 Mod.2 single-stage solid-propellant rocket motor which boosts it to a speed of Mach 4 in less than three seconds. Following burn-out, Sky Flash continues to coast towards its target, its velocity diminishing as it travels further away from the launch platform. Fuse inhibiting devices also trip out after it has travelled a certain distance.

 0913:25 hours

As it goes, the inverse-monopulse seeker head tracks the designated target by observing reflected radar energy from the AI24's J-band continuous wave illuminator while the aft-facing antenna monitors "raw" CW energy put out by the AI24. The latter effectively acts

Left: *It is impossible to over-emphasise the value of supporting aircraft such as the E-3 Sentry (AWACS) for control and direction. A dedicated AEW platform it features a most capable radar and will play an important part in any future air war scenario.*

Below: *Long range tanks, Sidewinder and Sky Flash missiles are normally carried by the Tornado F.3 which also possesses a single Mauser cannon for use in the event of "head-to-head" combat. Most crews will, however, prefer to engage enemy aircraft from long range.*

as a reference signal, enabling the seeker head to measure Doppler shift and, in turn, establish target velocity. In this way, Sky Flash is able to overcome problems posed by land or sea "clutter".

Steering commands originating from the seeker head are fed via a miniaturised autopilot to the control surfaces, one pair of cruciform wings controlling movement in pitch while the other is responsible for roll.

ray of countermeasures kit to life and readying themselves for the impending electronic "battle" on which will depend their survival.

Now, alert to the danger, the Soviet formation begins to effect countermeasures, releas-

ing clouds of chaff (small strips of conducting material whose length is designed to make them good reflectors of radar energy) and activating jammers in a desperate attempt to throw their pursuers off track. At this point, however, the Tornados' AI24's ECM "hardening" comes into play, since it possesses a quite remarkable degree of resistance to these tactics, being able to "reject" spurious returns.

0913:56 hours

Travelling at close to five times the speed of the rearmost Soviet aircraft, it takes barely 30 seconds for the missile to overhaul the "Badger" at which it has been fired, the tail gunner of that aircraft catching no more than a brief glimpse of the onrushing weapon. Even as he depresses the switch that will activate his microphone, the warhead detonates directly below the "Badger's" port wing, blast effect and shrapnel conspiring to cause a catastrophic structural failure which results in the entire wing assembly separating from the fuselage. A second later, a huge cloud of spray marks the end of the Tu-16 which breaks into literally thousands of pieces on impact with the sea.

0914 hours

Apart from some floating debris, the only indication of the Badger's abrupt demise can be seen on the cockpit displays of the two pursuing Tornados. These now show only five targets and one of those has just seconds of flight remaining, for another missile is already on its way from the wingman's aircraft . . .

This second "Badger" also disappears from view in a welter of spray but this time an alert observer on another Tu-16 witnesses its destruction and quickly notifies his pilot, prompting him to break radio silence and warn the remaining elements of the formation of the danger that lurks behind. Thus far, the Soviet crews have been proceeding more or less as normal, maintaining radio and electronic silence so as to minimise the risk of betraying their presence.

For the moment, they choose to maintain formation integrity, recognising that their best chance of survival lies in the protection that is offered by use of mutual support. Aboard each of the four remaining aircraft, those crew members who are responsible for managing defensive systems snap into action, bringing the ar-

0914:40 hours

Within moments, both Tornados have engaged afterburner and accelerated to close on the next pair of "Badgers", the navigators in each running through the same preparatory ritual as they set up to fire two more missiles at the still-unseen targets which continue to head south-west, even though they now stand little chance of executing their own attack on the still-distant convoy. The missile launched by Ranger 02 guides extremely accurately, confirmation that it has found its target coming very

A: Leading Tornado F.3 fires Sky Flash missile which accounts for first Soviet Badger. **B:** Tornado wingman claims second Badger. **C:** Lead fires again and inflicts damage on third Badger. **D:** Wingman claims fourth Badger. **E:** Lead destroys fifth Badger. **F:** Sixth Badger misjudges avoiding manoeuvre and strikes sea, the aircraft breaking up on impact. **G:** Lead re-engages damaged Badger and finishes this off with AIM-9L Sidewinder from close range. **H:** Tornados move off to make rendezvous with Tristar tanker prior to returning to base.

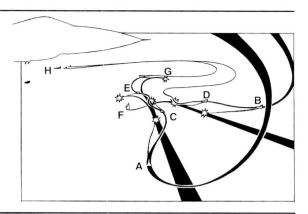

quickly, when yet another radar return abruptly disappears from the screen in the pursuing fighter.

0916 hours

The second missile — fired by the lead Tornado — performs marginally less well, a combination of evasive action and electronic "spoofing" deceiving it sufficiently to cause its warhead to detonate just outside the lethal zone, and it succeeds only in inflicting moderate damage on the "Badger". Blast effect causes the Soviet bomber to stagger slightly; the control column jerks savagely but the pilot manages to hold on and quickly stabilises the bomber before calling for a damage report.

The news is not good, shrapnel fragments from the Sky Flash warhead having penetrated the starboard wing in a number of places and a thin plume of fuel can clearly be seen issuing from the punctured fuel cells. Worse still, though, is the information that the starboard aileron has been fairly hard hit and is showing signs of disintegration. Already, the pilot is aware that he is having to work quite hard to retain control at this low level. There is a tendency to roll to the right, becoming ever more pronounced and requiring increasing amounts of muscle-power to counteract.

He decides to reduce power and climb, reasoning that a combination of lower speed and the more rarified atmosphere to be found at altitude will be doubly beneficial. For a start, it should partly alleviate the worst effects of the fuel leak, the rate of consumption being significantly less at altitude than that at low level. In addition, it would also reduce stress on the damaged control surface, making the job of actually flying the damaged aircraft somewhat less fatiguing.

On the negative side, they will, of course, stand out like the proverbial sore thumb and for a few brief moments he contemplates turning back but quickly dismisses that idea, acknowledging that his chances of reaching a safe haven are virtually non-existent. At the same time, he ruefully recognises that the possibility of surviving long enough to carry out an attack is now also exceedingly slim.

0916:45 hours

Twenty miles (32km) behind, the crews of the two Tornados are momentarily perplexed by his manoeuvre but continue in pursuit of the leading pair of Soviet bombers, the pilot of Ranger 01 giving a fairly wide berth to the damaged machine so as to avoid coming under fire from its tail gun armament.

Breaking radio silence for a few seconds, the pilot of the lead Tornado speaks, "Lead to two. Not sure what's going on here. Let's take out the lead elements and then hold back a few moments and see what gives, 'kay?"

"02, check . . ." comes the reply.

0917:30 hours

Within a minute, it has become clear that the trailing Badger has decelerated, the gap between the fighters and the damaged aircraft

having closed quite considerably. Lead speaks again, "Er, two. I reckon he's damaged. What d'you think?"

"Could be right there, skip."

"'kay, here's what we'll do. Let's stay on the leading pair and mop up tail-end charlie with a nine-lima afterwards. You got that, two?"

"Roger lead, see you later . . ."

0918 hours

The Tornados have closed the gap on the leading pair of "Badgers", the lead fighter again letting fly with a Sky Flash which rapidly overhauls and destroys the left-hand bomber. Even as Ranger 02 prepares to fire, however, the blip that represents his target suddenly disappears, its pilot having been unnerved by the sudden and fiery end of the adjacent Tu-16. Initiating violent evasive action in an attempt to disrupt the aim of the fighter pursuing him, he misjudges his altitude and flies into the sea. The luckless "Badger" disintegrates almost instantaneously.

0920 hours

Ranger 02 reaches the scene to witness a few

Above: With the interception of the Soviet "Badgers" having been successfully accomplished, the pair of Tornados alter course in order to rendezvous with a Tristar tanker of No. 216 Squadron which will furnish additional fuel to both aircraft for the return flight.

Below: Having provided fuel to one of the brace of Tornados, the Tristar continues to orbit while the Wingman receives his allotment. A hose and drogue system is employed to transfer fuel. Soon after topping off their tanks, the pair of aircraft are ordered home.

Above: Having joined up with other returning fighters, the Tornados pull heavy vortices as they break for landing back at Benbecula on completion of a highly successful mission. Within minutes of landing, ground crews will be hard at work rearming them for another trip.

Right: With gear down, wings fully spread and flaps and slats deployed, the leader brings his Tornado back over the boundary fence. Once on the ground, he will employ reverse thrust to decelerate before moving swiftly to the relative security of the hardened shelter complex.

pieces of wreckage still floating on the grey waters below. Circling for a minute or two to verify its demise, the Tornado eventually turns to reverse track, rolling out on a near easterly heading back towards home base.

In the meantime, Ranger 01 — having accounted for two Tu-16s already — has turned to deal with the straggler, again giving it a wide berth as he sets up for a Sidewinder shot.

In the rear cockpit of the leader's aircraft, the navigator can hear a faint humming, the distinctly unmusical sound that comes back to him over the intercom system indicating that his pilot is actually enjoying himself. It is a sound that has been most noticeable by its absence during the previous few days. He is about to remark on the fact when the noise abruptly stops, giving way to the sound of the pilot's voice, "OK, Mike . . . let's set up for a nine-lima attack."

"Right, Dave," he responds, hitting the necessary switches on the weapons control panel before adding, "It's all yours."

 0921 hours

They have closed to within five miles (8km) of the crippled "Badger", the small dot that is the Soviet aircraft being visible through the combiner glass of the head-up display unit. It is only now that they have positively identified the

type of enemy warplane, although suspicions that they were engaging a force of "Badgers" had been steadily growing strongly during the last few minutes.

 0921:30 hours

Now, they stabilise four miles (6km) directly aft of the Tu-16 and prepare to let fly with a single AIM-9L Sidewinder infra-red homing air-to-air missile. In the HUD, the pilot can see his target almost dead ahead, a minor correction being all that is necessary to position the "pipper" directly over the enemy aircraft. Through his earphones, he can hear a healthy growl which confirms that the missile's seeker head has searched for, located and locked-on to its objective. He flips aside a cover on the stick top and thumbs the revealed red button which enables the missile head to lock on to the target. The slight change and quickening of growl tone encouragingly indicates a good missile lock on to the crippled "Badger". He pauses for a moment and then pulls the trigger. Moments later, through the HUD, he sees the smoke trail left by the missile as it closes on its target.

Ahead, the "Badger's" tail gunner observes the flash of missile ignition and alerts his colleagues in the cockpit that they are under attack. Unable to manoeuvre fully and freely, the Badger pilot commands ejection of a number of infra-red flares and turns to the right as hard as he dares.The fairly gentle evasive manoeuvre fails to outwit the Sidewinder's seeker head which remains firmly locked-on to the harassed bomber, a last minute course reversal and a sudden descent being only marginally effective in throwing the weapon off.

 0921:45 hours

Detonating directly above the Badger, shrapnel from the warhead causes still more

damage to the starboard wing, the aileron fluttering momentarily before peeling away and spiralling downwards to fall in the sea. Now leaking fuel from a score of points and only barely controllable, the Tu-16 somehow manages to continue but it is fast becoming evident to the Russian crew that they are unlikely to escape as the Tornado is still prowling behind, preparing to administer the *coup de grâce.*

 0923 hours

For the crew of the leading Tornado, what looked like being another bad day has been entirely transformed, their second Sidewinder homing unerringly to its mark from a range of no more than three miles (5km). In the front cockpit, the pilot looks on in near disbelief as the "Badger" erupts in flame, the detonation from the missile's warhead being followed by a truly massive explosion as fuel and armament ignite and virtually tear it apart in mid-air.

 0925 hours

"Er, lead to two. What news?"

"Hallo lead. Splash three Badgers and I've got you visual for a rejoin to starboard."

"Roger, two. Rejoin to starboard . . ."

 0926 hours

Switching channels, the pilot of the leading Tornado makes a brief in-flight after-action report, "Candy 31. Ranger flight's splashed six "Badgers". Lead has one Sky Flash 'n two nine-limas remaining. Two's got two Sky Flash and four nine-limas. Fuel state's getting marginal. Any orders for us?"

"Affirmative, Ranger 01. Nice work. Vector 085 for rendezvous with tango (tanker aircraft) then proceed to CAP at Papa five. Expect early relief on station. Candy 31 out."

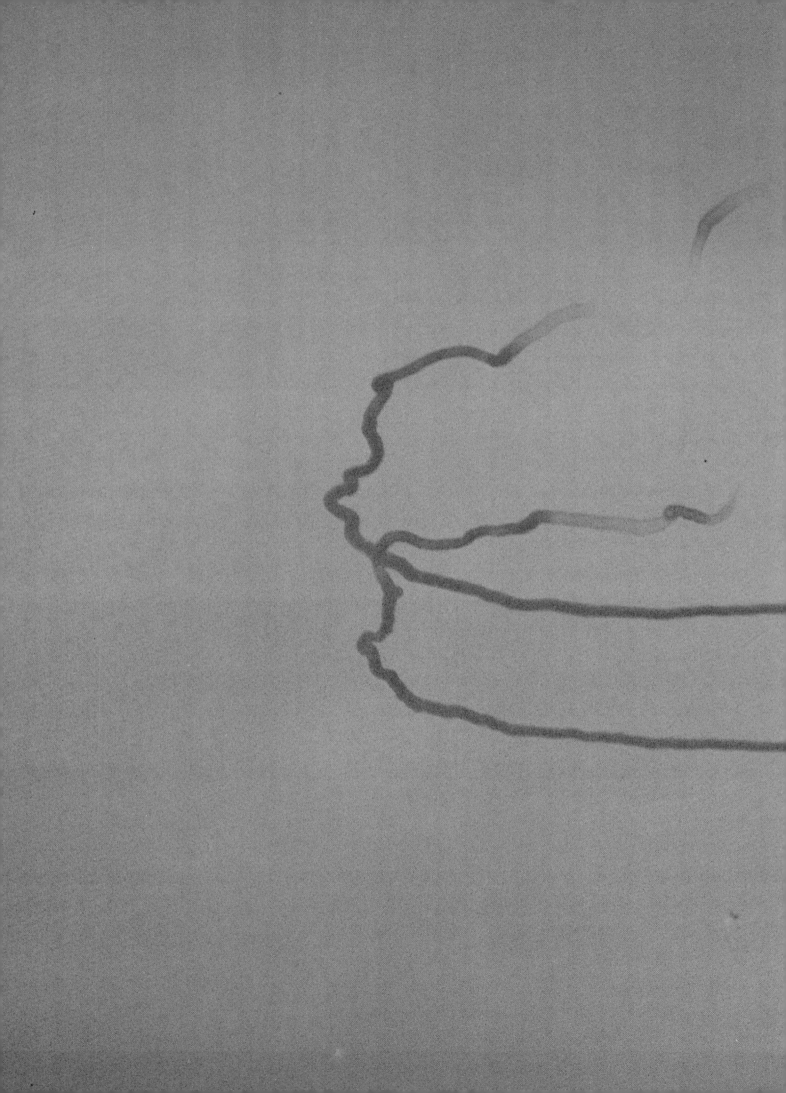

THE AIR SUPERIORITY MISSION

Evolution of the Mission

FUNDAMENTALLY, the air-superiority mission is similar to the interception mission. It is flown by a fighter bent on the destruction of enemy aircraft in the air. The fighter may be vectored (guided) by friendly ground, airborne or shipborne controllers, and may use its own radar or other sensors, and it may use AAMs (air-to-air missiles) to kill one or more "hostiles" from a distance. Where this mission differs from the interception mission is that the air-superiority fighter can take on agile enemy fighters, and is prepared to engage them at close quarters.

Once it has done so, the fight has much in common with ancient swordplay. It is usually a one-versus-one combat. Both adversaries watch each other constantly, use their own agility to the utmost, can indulge in feints and other ruses, and look always for the vital — possibly split-second — opening in which they can effect the kill. No matter whether the fighter uses a gun or an AAM it has to point towards its target, or rather, more precisely, to where the target will be in perhaps one second's time.

Modern air-superiority fighters may have a multimode radar, IR (infra-red) sensor and various other devices, but the close engagement between fighters has, so far as the author is aware, not yet reached the point at which it can safely or usefully be sustained at night, in cloud, in a snow blizzard or in any other blind conditions. It calls for a fighter aircraft with the best possible pilot view, the lowest wing loading (weight divided by wing area), the greatest possible SEP (Specific Excess Power — a measure of surplus engine thrust available for manoeuvre) and the greatest possible power of manoeuvre. This power of manoeuvre must be in attitudes, rotation about axes, slip/skid, dive/climb and in all other variations, the objective always being to hit the enemy with gunfire aimed straight ahead or with a self-homing AAM. Of course, it goes without saying, the fighter needs a suitable weapon-aiming system. Yet almost 80 years ago it is doubtful if even the most sci-fi aviation enthusiast had ever considered the problems, beyond the thought that an unsporting pilot might take a gun aloft in his cockpit. But criticism is easy with hindsight!

Imagining aerial war

Before the start of World War I in August 1914 the very idea of fighting in the sky was no more than a vague idea. Indeed, when in 1909 Fred T. Jane prepared the first of his famous annuals describing all known aircraft, he included a contribution on "Aerial Warfare"

Above: A Bristol F.2B Fighter of 22 Sqn at Vert Galand on the Western Front. The photo was taken on 1 April 1918, the day 22 Sqn imperceptibly changed from being "RFC" to being "RAF". Its equipment was unquestionably the best two-seat fighter of World War 1.

Below: A captured Fokker D.VII on an RAF airfield at about the time of the Armistice (November 1918). So good was this fighter that defeated Germany was explicitly required to hand every one over to the Allies as part of the war reparations. They were thwarted by wily Anthony Fokker!

written by an admiral in the Royal Navy — the greatest available expert on the subject — whose only conception of what might happen in future was that friendly *airships* might be seen towing targets for their partner to practice quickfire shooting!

In 1910 rather undisciplined young officers in the US Army, who had been taught to fly by the Wright brothers, started firing rifles from the air (and hitting targets on the ground, despite sitting on the lower-wing leading edge with nothing to hold on to). A little later Col Isaac N. Lewis visited them and fired his brilliant new machine gun in the air. This gun, though not specifically designed for air fighting, had the advantages of air cooling, compact design and feed by 47- or 97-round drums which fed reliably no matter what the attitude or accelerative forces on the gun. The French Hotchkiss had some similar features, but it was fed by a long strip of cartridges which stuck out to one side, which was often very inconvenient. Hotchkiss, and Vickers in Britain, also made massive guns of calibres up to 47mm. Though ponderous, slow-firing and with low muzzle velocity, these fired shells which could bring down an enemy aircraft with a single well-aimed shot.

The "stick and string" era

At the same time, it must be remembered that aircraft — aeroplanes and airships — of 75 years ago were basically a spidery structure covered with fabric. Bullets and even shells could pass straight through without doing

Obviously, the basic mission of a "fighter" is to destroy hostile aircraft. Fighters have been called scouts, pursuits, Zerstörers (destroyers) and interceptors, but today we also sometimes add the prefix "air superiority" to show that we are concerned mainly or totally with the primary air-combat mission. In particular, we have an aircraft designed for "eyeball confrontation" in close, rapidly manoeuvring combat.

more than making two holes in the fabric. There are many combat reports of pilots firing long bursts, even using incendiary ammunition, at large bombers and at airships without any visible effect.

Today the notion of air superiority means the ability to win in close combat, using guns and "dogfight" missiles. It conjures up a picture quite different from "interception" which can be achieved at supersonic speed, relies totally upon radar and other sensors (some on the ground or in AWACS aircraft) and aims to kill at a great distance. But in 1914 few people had any idea about air fighting at all.

When the first units of the British Royal Flying Corps flew across to France — itself a major accomplishment — one pilot asked, "What do we do if we meet a Zeppelin?" Encountering a hostile airship was constantly in the minds of the young RFC pilots, some of whom had more or less unofficial ideas about using shotguns, pistols and various other weapons. The only official answer to the pilot's question was to point out that Zeppelins usually flew far above the ceiling of the B.E.2a biplane, but that a bold pilot might try to effect a mid-air collision. Meanwhile, RFC No 4 Sqn, staying at home with explicit orders to defend against the German airships, issued their observers with a Lee-Enfield rifle and 50 rounds withdrawn one by one from a canvas bandolier.

Back in 1912 the far-sighted British Admiralty had asked Vickers to build an aeroplane carrying a machine gun. The result was a series of EFBs (Experimental Fighting Biplanes), carrying an observer to fire the gun in the nose of a tandem-seat nacelle with the pusher engine

Above: *The excellent British S.E.5 and 5a fighting scouts had a synchronised Vickers gun (not visible here) firing past the propeller blades and a Lewis mounted so high it missed the propeller entirely. In front of the pilot (here holding a Very signal pistol) can be seen the Aldis optical sight which was used for aiming.*

Below: *Designer Geoffrey de Havilland can be seen in the cockpit of the first B.E.2, which could be called Britain's first military aircraft. It was designed to be inherently stable, and nobody thought about fitting armament on the aircraft.*

at the rear. Numerous other aircraft adopted a similar layout, but most had such poor speed and climb that they could not reach enemy aircraft seen overhead. Later it became common practice to patrol at the greatest practical height in order to wait for the enemy to appear. But until the end of 1915 weapons remained primitive. On 25 July 1915 Capt Lanoe G. Hawker succeeded in shooting down three German two-seaters, all armed with machine guns, from a Bristol (tractor-engined) Scout whose sole armament was a single-shot Martini carbine fastened on the right side of the fuselage at a diagonal angle so that it cleared the propeller!

This feat remained very much the exception. Other pilots improvised with various forms of armament, some believing in towing a kind of grappling hook on a cable. A refinement, the British "Fiery Grapnel", combined a multi-hook device with an incendiary charge intended to set fire to airships. An alternative was the Ranken dart, which when dropped on to an airship from above was supposed to pierce the fabric and gasbag and then explode.

The forward-firing gun

Such ideas gradually faded, while the forward-firing machine gun or cannon became all-important. For at least three years prior to the war inventors had proposed various ways of enabling a machine gun to fire safely between the blades of a tractor propeller, but nobody showed interest. One of the inventors was Raymond Saulnier, of the famed Morane-Saulnier company. Because he could not guarantee reliable operation of the gun, he fit-

ted steel deflectors to the back of his propeller blades. In the spring of 1915 Morane-Saulnier display pilot Roland Garros, by now in uniform, took this aircraft to the front. Ignoring any proper interrupter or synchronizing gear, he merely dived at the first "Hun" and opened fire. In a few days he scored five victories, before being brought down in German hands by engine trouble. Quickly, Anthony Fokker did better than merely copy this crude idea: his designers perfected a proper synchronizing gear.

The result was the Fokker E-series, E meaning *eindecker* (monoplane). Though otherwise unimpressive, their ability to fire straight ahead with one, two or even three machine guns proved deadly to the un-agile Allied machines. So grievous were the Allied losses that in January 1916 the RFC decreed that each aircraft on a reconnaissance mission "must be escorted by at least three other fighting machines". The fighter had arrived. Within six months the almost standard armament was two machine guns, either both on top of the fuselage or one on the fuselage and the other mounted on the upper wing. Almost the only variation to this was to fit one or more guns at an oblique angle to fire upwards, but these remained exceptions.

Aiming the aircraft

Having established the dominance of the forward-firing gun, aimed by aiming the whole aircraft, further improvement naturally enhancing the fighter's speed, rate and angle of climb, and manoeuvrability. Despite the increasing weight of aircraft, it became essential to rely on absolute structural integrity, even in steep dives at full throttle and in all the unnatural attitudes that might be encountered in the course of a combat.

One of the most trusted machines, with no flight limitations, was the Bristol F.2B. This two-seater was at first flown straight and level, like a bomber, the backseat observer firing at the enemy. Results were disastrous. Once it was realised that the Bristol should be flung

round the sky like a single-seater it did well, and despite the dogfight manoeuvres the observers of Bristols scored roughly as many kills as did the pilots with their forward-firing guns. But the vast majority of fighters remained single-seaters.

In late 1916 the Royal Naval Air Service achieved local air superiority over the Western Front with the Sopwith Triplane. This brought a quick over-reaction by the enemy who built at least 14 types of triplane as an "answer". In fact the undoubted agility of the short-span triplane did not really make for a superior dogfighter, and at the end of the war the best fighters on both sides were all biplanes.

By this time few pilots went out alone, as had many of the famous aces. Complete squadrons of nine to 12 aircraft were the norm, and the Germans made a deliberate policy of forming their "Jastas" into large "circuses", typically comprising four Jastas of 14 fighters each. The pilots in these crack formations won their place by their combat record. Each painted his aircraft in an individual scheme using the brightest colours and designs to strike fear into the enemy. Previously, individual pilots had attempted to attack from above, if possible diving from the direction of the sun to avoid being seen until too late. By 1917 the big formations resulted in a massed opening engagement — not often taking the opposition by surprise — which within seconds disintegrated into dozens of separate engagements which were often one-against-one or two-against-one but seldom involved a larger number.

Above: *This Fokker E.III was fitted with no fewer than three guns, but offsetting the advantage in firepower was the sluggish flight performance caused by the extra weight. After all, an engine of 100 horsepower only just sufficed to take off and climb.*

Below: *Three generations of fighter cockpits are exemplified by the Sopwith Camel of 1917, the Supermarine Spitfire of 1940 and the McDonnell Douglas F/A-18 Hornet. The difference between the first two were mainly ones of degree only, but today's technology is different.*

The Cockpit Environment — Distance of Engagements 1917 to the Present

By 1918 hundreds of painful lessons had been learned, but in the 20 years between the World Wars not much happened beyond a dramatic increase in fighter engine power and a progressive change from the fabric-covered biplane to the all-metal cantilever monoplane, with retractable landing gear, flaps, enclosed cockpit and constant-speed propeller. Many pilots resisted this change. To them, survival in a dogfight depended on having unfettered all-round vision and the greatest possible manoeuvrability. The new fighters were often inferior in both respects to their predecessors. On the other hand, they were much tougher, faster and more heavily armed. Hispano-Suiza's installation of a shell-firing cannon between the cylinder blocks of a geared V-12 engine to fire through the propeller hub — an

Above: *The Gloster Gladiator was identical in technology to fighters of World War 1, merely having a much more powerful engine, oxygen, radio and four guns instead of two. Despite its agility it could not survive against the Messerschmitt 109.*

idea actually tested (with a different kind of engine) by Blériot in 1911 — was instrumental in getting air forces used to the advantages of larger guns, able to kill from a range of half a kilometre. In contrast, Britain stayed with rifle-calibre, but for the first time worked from basic principles in calculating the number of strikes needed to bring down an enemy and the likely available firing time. The answer came out at eight guns, each of which possessed the ability to fire at a rate of 1,200 rds/min, or 20 per second.

Above: *Messerschmitt Bf 109D-1 fighters used in the advanced training role in late 1939. In many ways the Bf 109 was surprisingly deficient, yet in the hands of the most experienced fighter pilots in history it shot down many thousands of enemy aircraft.*

Below: *The Focke-Wulf Fw 190 was designed four years later than the Bf 109, and it was one of the best piston-engined fighters of all time. Extremely small, it nevertheless could carry a torpedo or a 4,000lb bombload, besides having heavy armament and armour.*

The need for cannon

In the crucial Battle of Britain in 1940 the RAF used the resulting eight-gun fighters against Bf 109Es with two machine guns and two 20mm cannon. As in the case of the aircraft themselves, the balance was pretty even, and victory went to the better pilot. But the writing was on the wall: machine guns simply lacked killing power against modern aircraft. Soon the RAF adopted a battery of four 20mm cannon as standard armament, though a few pilots harmonised these to converge at ranges no greater than those they were used to with rifle-calibre.

Such changes in aircraft and guns had almost no effect on the basic principles of air fighting. Pilots still strove to engage with the advantage of height, if possible "out of the sun", and to get on the tail of an enemy, all the while continuing to look in every direction possible. Prior to an engagement, however, most air forces had thought in terms of units of nine to 12 aircraft, often called squadrons, which trained in tidy formations that looked good in peacetime. During 1936-39 the infant Luftwaffe was tried out in the Spanish Civil War, and experience here quickly showed the need for smaller and more flexible groups. The result was the *Rotte* (loose pair) and *Schwärm* (two *Rottes*). These were eventually adopted by the Allies, the Schwärm becoming the finger-4 with aircraft arranged like the tips of the fingers of one hand. Whenever a whole squadron held formation, two aircraft would

Above: *Thanks to brilliant design (helped by being later than, say, the Spitfire or 109) the P-51 Mustang could outpace both those earlier fighters despite having greater fuel capacity. From January 1944 the Merlin-engined versions ranged far over Germany.*

Below: *Japan's Mitsubishi A6M Zero was likewise renowed for its long range, which in 1941 was also combined with deadly manoeuvrability and firepower. But it had to soldier on in only slightly improved versions which by 1943 were outclassed by Allied fighter aircraft.*

Bottom: *One of the "more powerful Allied fighters" was the F4U Corsair, flown by the US Marines, Navy, Royal Navy and RNZAF. Its 2,000/2,400hp engine overcame its bulk and weight and enabled it to slaughter the lighter yet flimsier Japanese fighters.*

act as "weavers" at the rear, with higher throttle settings to enable them to weave in the horizontal plane searching the sky to the rear.

In the Battle of Britain fighters operated for the first time under close direction from the ground by Controllers who, thanks to the invention of radar, were continually told the enemy's positions, altitudes and strengths. This led to an attempt to deploy defending forces in formations at Wing (typically three squadrons) strength, but the benefits were the subject of acrimonious argument.

By this time it was clear that large twin-engined fighters could not safely engage in close combat with good smaller fighters. Indeed, there was much argument about the ideal smaller fighter. Yakovlev in the Soviet Union had no doubt it should be small and agile, and criticised such machines as America's ten-ton P-47. In Japan the almost total success of the A6M Zero in 1940-42, against indifferent opposition, suggested that with two cannon and excellent agility an engine of 1,100hp was sufficient. Too late, new Japanese fighters were developed with engines of double this power, able to meet such 2,000hp fighters as the F6F and F4U.

Jet propulsion

The latter seemed big, but with the coming of jet propulsion fighters tended to become considerably larger still. Early jets were typically 100mph (160km/h) faster at all heights than their predecessors, but they were less agile, much more expensive and had considerably shorter mission endurance. In the new problem of compressibility, which caused progressive loss of control and very undesirable flight characteristics above Mach 0.8 (or thereabouts), most early jets were if anything worse than the Spitfire, which could dive to 0.92. Just one new fighter, the USAF's F-86, flown in

Above: *One of countless strange weapons of World War 2, the Mistel (Mistletoe) comprised a Ju 88 with its nose packed with high explosives guided near its target by a fighter (Fw 190A) mounted on top. The idea was unwieldy and warhead delivery uncertain.*

Below: *As in the case of all-weather interceptors, the story of the air-superiority fighter is one of rapidly increasing flight performance up to 1960, followed by a decline. The latest fighters can in theory reach Mach 2 at high altitude, at the expense of a lot of fuel and travelling in a straight line. 1: Fokker E-type. 2: Sopwith Camel. 3: Boeing P-26. 4: Grumman F3F-1. 5: Supermarine Spitfire I. 6: Me 262A. 7: NAA F-86A. 8: NAA F-100A. 9: Lockheed F-104A. 10: Dassault Mirage III. 11: MiG-21F. 12: McDonnell Douglas F-4B Phantom II. 13: General Dynamics F-16.*

Air Superiority Fighters

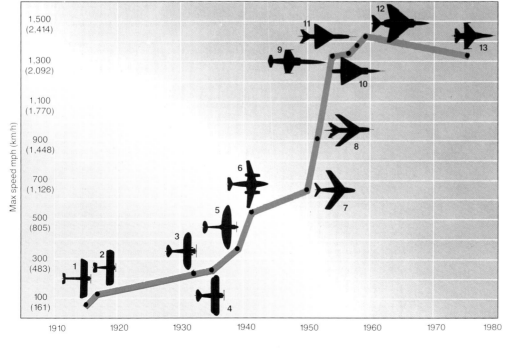

1947, demonstrated superb handling at all times and the ability to dive to beyond Mach 1.

The problem of compressibility affected not only speed but also the effective ceiling at which high-speed aircraft could manoeuvre. It was not unknown for a fighter to reach, say, 48,000ft (14,630m) in a ceiling climb and yet be totally unable to engage in combat above about 30,000ft (9,144m). This powerful phenomenon was the first time pilots had been faced with external influences, over which they had no control, which prevented them commanding the trajectory of their aircraft, and thus of fighting in the air.

The importance of the pilot

Of course, not all earlier fighters had been equally agile, and some had suffered from tricky or even dangerous handling, but pilots could learn to master this. As in air combat, if a pilot could get through the dangerous initial period and survive, he was then likely to become really expert and, if it happened to be wartime, run up a big score. But a pilot needed more than the ability to fly his aircraft to the limits; he also needed to be able to shoot.

The exploit of Capt Hawker, flying crabwise while loading and firing a single-shot gun, is something very few pilots could do even to-day. Of course, the fighter pilot's job was made immeasurably easier once guns fired straight ahead and kept firing as long as the trigger was depressed, but there were still problems. Countless pilots have been so excited upon meeting the enemy for the first time that they have forgotten, until it was rudely made apparent, to reset their armament from SAFE to FIRE. Even then, they are faced with the problem of aiming.

The history of fighter gunsights is fascinating. It began with ring-and-bead sights and various collimated optical-tube sights, some of which were low-power telescopes. More than about x3 was useless, as vibration would make it difficult to hold the sight on target. Today, the problem of aiming fixed guns at an enemy aircraft ahead is the same as it was in 1916, with the proviso that in 1916 an aircraft flying at 80mph (129km/h) at low level would be far more influenced by bumpy air than one flying at 600kt (1,110km/h). Indeed, anyone used to flying Tiger Moths or micro-lights will wonder that any World War I pilot could indulge in accurate shooting at all. Of course, the objective is to send out a stream of bullets or shells in such a direction that the target and the projectiles reach the same place at the same time. In other words, you aim at where the target will be in perhaps one second's time.

Sighting on target

The aim-off clearly depends on target speed, target relative attitude (maximum for a beam shot) and one's own gun's muzzle velocity. A low-velocity gun, such as the World War I cannon or the MG FF of World War II, needs far more deflection than a gun such as today's Oerlikon KCA or Aden 25 with m.v. of over 3,400ft (1,050m/s). Aim-off does not depend on target range, but at long ranges the gravity drop of the projectiles becomes important.

Very few pilots are able to shoot accurately at long ranges, and to have much hope of success most need to get in as close as possible. For over 40 years 600ft (183m) has been considered a good firing range, because apart from easing aiming problems the brief projectile flight time almost eliminates the effect of target evasive action after pulling the trigger.

The gyro gunsight

The problem of deflection shooting was greatly eased by the introduction of the gyro sight, developed at Farnborough in the 1930s (and subsequently by Ferranti) and introduced in 1941. Oddly, this valuable sight was first used in Stirling bomber turrets, but it swiftly became standard in fighters and, in conjunction with a manually inserted range on the throttle and a target wingspan on the sight, enabled the pilot to shoot quite accurately by lining up the target in a ring of bright dots. Subsequently, radar was introduced to give target range automatically, and in the 1970s American research led to the IF/FCS, the integrated fire/flight control system. With this a pilot can open fire at near the limits of gun range, with horrendous deflection and,

Top right: The first Spitfires, delivered to the RAF in 1938-41, had rifle-calibre machine guns only. By 1942 Spitfires were fitted with two 20mm Hispano cannon. This restored example shows the locations where, in some versions, two extra 20mm could be fitted.

Right: The Lockheed F-104 Starfighter was the supreme example of the fighter designed for speed, climb and height. It carried the brilliant new Vulcan 20mm gun, fitted to almost every US fighter since the 104, and two Sidewinder heat-seeking air-to-air missiles.

Below: The Saunders-Roe SR.53 was an attempt to combine the range and endurance of a turbojet with the tremendous speed, climb and height of a rocket. It was a delight to fly, but the production SR.177 version was cancelled in April 1957.

Left: *The strange withdrawal of Britain from the world fighter market in 1957 made it almost easy for Dassault of France to sell the Mirage III. As early as 1961 traditional British customers such as South Africa and Australia went to the French; these Mirages are Swiss.*

Below left: *McDonnell at St Louis were never asked by any customer to build the Phantom II, yet they eventually completed nearly 5,200! These two are F-4Fs of the West German Luftwaffe which, like many Phantoms, will eventually be subjected to a major and comprehensive upgrade programme which will extend their service life to the year 2000.*

without special skill, make almost every round strike home. So far this extremely valuable coupling of the sight and an automatic flight control system has not yet reached the squadrons. Neither has the ability of the F-16AFTI (Advanced Fighter Technology Integration) to fly one way while pointing in another, or to keep pointing straight ahead while slipping or skidding sideways, or moving diagonally up or down, been put to practical use. Certainly, such capabilities, together with enhanced manoeuvring gained from some measure of thrust vector control, are likely to be introduced in the Lockheed F-22A or Northrop F-23A (the candidate Advanced Tactical Fighters).

The quest for range

Going back to 1950, this was a time when new ideas proliferated. The notion of extending fighter range by towing, or "parasiting" by latching on to a bomber's wingtips, was not only resurrected but taken a step further with the amazing McDonnell XF-85 Goblin, designed to drop from inside a large bomber, unfold and enter combat over enemy heartlands to protect its "mother ship". After shooting down enemy fighters, it was to hook back on to its parent and be folded back inside. A similar idea had been tried with US Navy airships in the 1930s. Later such aircraft as the British SR.53 rocket/jet fighter were proposed as parasites carried into enemy airspace pick-a-back on Vulcan bombers.

The only range-extension idea that proved its worth in practice was the much simpler one of flight refuelling, first practised by the Meteor F.8s of RAF No. Sqn in 1951. These very successful trials suggested that four hours was about the limit for a fighter pilot. Beyond that, his various discomforts seriously reduced fighting efficiency. Today the Tornado F.3 can fly four hours without using its flight-refuelling probe, and the practical fighter mission can cover quite large areas of the globe.

By the early 1950s fighters were being developed that were capable of supersonic speed in level flight, and this automatically made it possible to open up the flight envelope in height as well as in Mach and indicated airspeed. The spectre of compressibility became past history, but arguments remained. Having talked to fighter pilots in Korea, Lockheed's Kelly Johnson found a strong wish to have more speed and height, even if it meant "throwing out the ejection seat, half the

fuel and replacing the radar gunsight by a piece of gum stuck on the windshield". He thereupon designed the F-104, the "missile with a man in it", but this brilliantly fast and seemingly almost wingless fighter proved to have many shortcomings.

Combat persistence

The even faster Republic F-103 was never completed. On the other hand the McDonnell F-4 Phantom II, flown in May 1958, proved to have such a range of capabilities that, despite its great size, it became the yardstick against which other 1960s fighters were judged. Though in Vietnam it was almost never able to use this capability, it marked the emergence of the true fighter able to hack it in close combat and also (as described in the section on Interception) kill from beyond visual range.

Of course, the latter capability rests upon use of the AAM (air-to-air missile). Some early supersonic fighters were designed to carry only one or two AAMs. The Mirage IIIC, with

Right: *The Bracket, or Offensive Split, forces the Bad Guy to pick one from a pair of defending fighters. The supporting fighter (**No 2**) is able to reverse his turn and get in behind the enemy. The F-15 (and indeed the MiG-29) has excess power to do this.*

Below: *Flown nine-years after the MiG-29, France's Dassault-Breguet Rafale prototype is hoped to lead to both land-based and carrier versions by the mid/late 1990s. But the Mikoyan design bureau have already completed much of the flight-test programme of the MiG-29 successor.*

The Bracket

The Modern "Office"

The Growing Threat

MiG-21MF

MiG-23MF

MiG-29A

Su-27A

MiG-31

booster rocket pack, carried just a single AAM as its only armament. The RAF's Lightning and Soviet MiG-21F carried just two AAMs each, and no guns (later versions did incorporate guns). Not only was it reluctantly forced on the experts that the gun remained vital for close combat, but the notion of "combat persistence" gradually gained recognition. A costly supersonic jet carrying a single missile is obviously limited in value, especially if (as very often happened 25 years ago) the missile malfunctioned. In contrast the F-4E carried an internal gun (of 20mm calibre and firing 6,000 rds/min), four Sparrow medium-range radar-guided AAMs and four Sidewinder infra-red homing short-range dogfight AAMs. This gave combat persistence in excellent measure. Obviously, there are limits to how much adrenalin an average pilot possesses, and to how much fuel the fighter carries to feed thirsty afterburners. In theory an F-4E could down ten or a dozen bad guys in one mission. In practice things are not that simple.

Combat manoeuvres

Poor US air-combat results in the Vietnam War were partly due to political constraints, but partly to lack of pilot training. The result was the setting up by the USAF and Navy of specialised fighter schools where already fully combat-ready fighter pilots were given an intensive and really demanding course which, by every means possible (and they are constantly being refined), their skills in close combat were honed to a razor sharpness. There are today dozens of kinds of close air combat with numerous standardised manoeuvres. In general, the objective is to use one's own aircraft to the limits while keeping aware of the overall situation at all times. There are very few rules that have no exceptions, and the rules are often modified by a particular fighter's capabilities.

One good general rule is continuously to maximise one's own energy. Energy can be speed or height, so the rule can be interpreted as "never get low and slow", though even this has exceptions and a well-flown helicopter can be hard to shoot down. There are a few situations known as "telephone boxes" because there is no place to go; the hapless pilot has got himself into a tight combination of relative position, speed, height and other factors from which, in theory at least, extrication is impossible.

Since 1960 there have been several hundred air combats under many contrasting circumstances. The only factors common to almost

FIGHTER MISSIONS

all have been that altitude has seldom exceeded 20,000ft (6,100m) and speed has seldom exceeded 400kt (740km/h), though there has been an extremely small number of cases where speed was much higher. The locations have included large areas of Israel, Egypt and Jordan; South-East Asia; Algeria; Indonesia; Nigeria, Angola, Chad and other parts of sub-Saharan Africa; Aden, Oman and other Arabian borders; the western and eastern frontiers of India and Pakistan (the latter now being Bangladesh); Libya's Gulf of Sirte and frontier with Egypt; most of Lebanon, especially including the Bekaa Valley; Central America, the border between Honduras and Nicaragua; the Falklands; the Iran/Iraq border; and, briefly, India's frontier with China. Despite its duration and bitterness, fighting over Afghanistan does not appear to have involved air combat, for the simple reason that only one of the combatants possessed combat aircraft.

Predicting the future

In an atmosphre of *Glasnost* nobody anywhere wishes to consider the prospect of armed conflict between East and West, and virtually everyone in the world takes comfort in the belief that a major war is rapidly

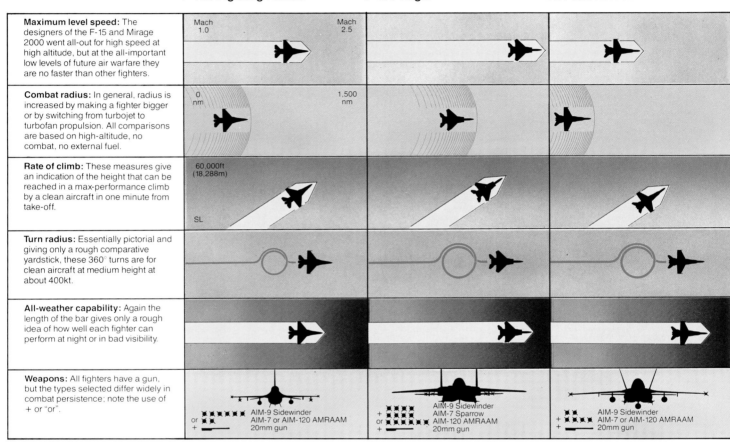

	F-16C Fighting Falcon	**F-15C Eagle**	**F/A-18A Hornet**
Maximum level speed: The designers of the F-15 and Mirage 2000 went all-out for high speed at high altitude, but at the all-important low levels of future air warfare they are no faster than other fighters.	Mach 1.0 / Mach 2.5		
Combat radius: In general, radius is increased by making a fighter bigger or by switching from turbojet to turbofan propulsion. All comparisons are based on high-altitude, no combat, no external fuel.	0 nm / 1,500 nm		
Rate of climb: These measures give an indication of the height that can be reached in a max-performance climb by a clean aircraft in one minute from take-off.	60,000ft (18,288m) / SL		
Turn radius: Essentially pictorial and giving only a rough comparative yardstick, these 360° turns are for clean aircraft at medium height at about 400kt.			
All-weather capability: Again the length of the bar gives only a rough idea of how well each fighter can perform at night or in bad visibility.			
Weapons: All fighters have a gun, but the types selected differ widely in combat persistence; note the use of + or "or".	or / + AIM-9 Sidewinder, AIM-7 or AIM-120 AMRAAM, 20mm gun	+ / or / + AIM-9 Sidewinder, AIM-7 Sparrow, AIM-120 AMRAAM, 20mm gun	+ / + / + AIM-9 Sidewinder, AIM-7 or AIM-120 AMRAAM, 20mm gun

These diagrams are essentially pictorial, providing a rough comparitive basis for measuring the performance and capability of seven of the world's more important air superiority fighters at present in service. The point should be made that not all are similar in timing; the F-15 and MiG-21MF were both in service in the mid-1970s, and while the JA37 only entered production after 1980 its basic design stems from 1965-67. It is also important to remember that Soviet aircraft which have only recently become well-known in the West may in fact have been flying for a long time (MiG-29, 1977, for example). Also, the appearance of the MiG-29 in the West has radically changed assessments of its capabilities and it is now perceived as being a very fine fighter indeed.

◀ F-15C

Power plant: two P&W F100-220 (23,450lb/ 104.3kN)
Span: 42ft 9.75in (13.05m)
Length: 63ft 9in (19.43m)
Max TO weight: 68,000lb (30,845kg)

◀ F-16C

Power plant: one P&W F100-220 (23,450lb/104.3kN) or GE F110-100 (27,600lb/ 122.8kN)
Span: (over missiles) 32ft 10in (10.01m)
Length: 49ft 3in (15.01m)
Max TO weight: 37,500lb (17,010kg)

◀ F/A-18

Power plant: two GE F404-400 (16,000lb/ 71.2kN)
Span: (over missiles) 40ft 4.75in (12.31m)
Length: 56ft 0in (17.07m)
Max TO weight: 49,224lb (22,328kg)

receding from all likely futures. Yet work is at present continuing unabated in most countries in the development of weapons, nowhere more so than in the Soviet Union and major Western nations..

Throughout all recent history the NATO air forces, which sincerely believe they have to be ready to stop Soviet aggression Westwards, have cosily believed that their aircraft are superior to their opposite numbers. Quality,

they say, always wins over quantity. Many front-line fighter pilots say it is like "Ladas versus Porsches".

Such attitudes have ben dealt a rude blow by the appearance of one of the more recent (but by no means the *most* recent) Soviet fighters at the Farnborough airshow in 1988. Everyone knew the aircraft concerned, the MiG-29A, could put on an impressive show of flying. With unrivalled specific excess power

— for example, giving a take-off run of 290m (950ft) and initial climb of 65,000ft/min — it was expected to give everything in the West a real run for its money. But its crucial avionics were naturally thought to be backward. Its "look down, shoot down" radar was asserted by Washington to have been made possible "only by stealing the secrets of the Hornet radar", the APG-65.

Unfortunately for Western defence analysts

MiG-21MF	MiG-29A	Mirage 2000	JA37 Viggen

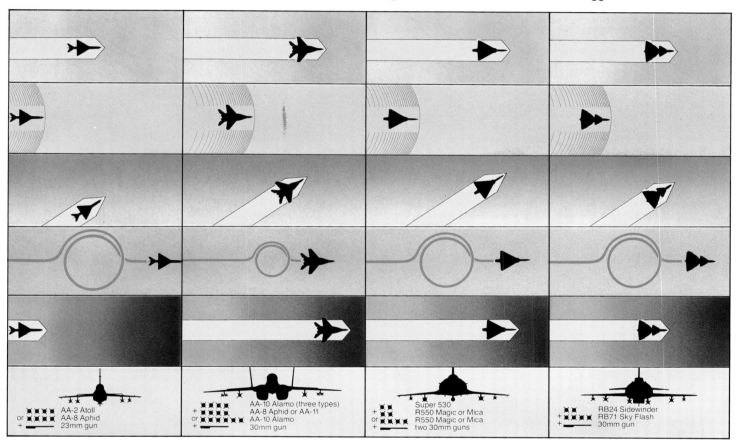

◀ MiG-21MF

Power plant: one Tumanskii R-13-300 (14,550lb/64.73kN)
Span: 23ft 5.5in (7.15m)
Length: (inc boom) 51ft 8.5in (15.76m)
Max TO weight: 20,725lb (9,400kg)

◀ Mirage 2000C

Power plant: one SNECMA M53-P2 (21,385lb/95.1kN)
Span: 29ft 11.5in (9.13m)
Length: 47ft 1.3in (14.36m)
Max TO weight: 37,478lb (17,000kg)

◀ MiG-29A

Power plant: two Tumanskii R-33 (18,300lb/81.4kN)
Span: 37ft 2.7in
Length: 56ft 8.2in (17.32m)
Max TO weight: about 39,000lb (18,000kg)

◀ JA37

Power plant: one Volvo RM8B (28,108lb/125kN)
Span: 34ft 9.25in (10.6m)
Length: (excl probe) 51ft 1.5in (15.58m)
TO weight: "Normal armament" 37,478lb (17,000kg)

55

the boot proved to be on the other foot. The Mikoyan designers were only too happy to talk about the MiG-29 fire-control system, which they rightly believe to be far in advance of anything even asked for by a Western air force — and the MiG-29 was in large-scale service in 1983.

Can't help bullseyes!

This enhanced accuracy was manifest in 1978 during the air gunnery tests of early MiG-29s. Computer software faults kept shutting off the 30mm gun after it had fired either four or six shots — but every single target was still destroyed. According to the designers, if they had known how super-accurate the gun aiming sub-system was they would have halved the capacity of the ammunition tank.

Normally a main computer interlinks the radar, IRST, laser and weapons, but all can operate autonomously. Another plus, nowhere near service in Western air forces, is a helmet-mounted sight. The MiG-29 pilot can look all over the sky and still keep all vital ''instrument'' and weapon-aiming numbers and symbols in front of his eyes. The helmet sight was in the MiG-29 regiments in 1983. Something similar may be hustled into NATO air forces in the early 1990s, because of the MiG-29 shock.

Western fighters have nothing but a radar, and so cannot make a ''stealthy'' approach on a hostile target. Not so the MiG-29 pilot, who can elect to override any computer-commanded switch-on of the radar — as

Left: *Among Western fighters there is little that can safely tangle with an F-16, which was the first modern fighter designed for sustained manoeuvring at 9g. Here a two-seat F-16B leaves visible wing-root vortices as it pulls up in full afterburner with the wing in high-camber.*

Below: *Most air combat photography is taken from astern the target, but this MiG-21MF got in the way of an Israeli F-4E Phantom. The picture was taken during the 1973 Yom Kippur war, when most Phantoms could carry guns only in external pods. A lucky shot?*

Top: *Another cavorting F-16, this time an F-16C with the General Electric F110 engine performing in 1988. Designed in 1972-75, the F-16 still provides the ultimate target for air combat performance at which designers of non-STOVL aircraft continue to aim.*

Above: *Photographed in England in September 1988, the MiG-29A is bigger than the F-16, very much more powerful, can pull a little more than 9g and has a much more comprehensive avionic fire-control system, as well as the ability to choose three AAM guidance systems.*

would normally happen on entering cloud — and can choose to trackdown his quarry using just the EO (electro-optical) sensors.

Winning war

Except for fighting around Israel, India, the Gulf of Sirte and the Falklands, most of these encounters have been more or less sporadic and, not to put too fine a point on it, unprofessional. Even the prolonged Iran/Iraq conflict has been punctuated by only sporadic engagements between opposing aircraft, in daytime ''eyeball'' engagements that, so far as one can

tell, have added little to the technology or the technique of air warfare.

Even in the remaining theatres, numerous conflicts have done little to update or rewrite the textbooks of air combat. This is perhaps remarkable. In the Six-Day War waged by Israel in July 1967 supersonic aircraft joined battle on both sides, and AAMs were used in anger. Such aircraft and weapons have been used many times since, but there have been few surprises. The overwhelming lesson of the Six-Day War is that, if you want to win a war — not a mere air battle but a war — then destroy your enemy's air power before it takes off. Today this lesson is a thousand times more important. Once the enemy aircraft is in the air, the best we can hope for is a successful outcome to an air combat. To achieve this, the enemy must be engaged and brought to battle, which in itself involves correct operation of ground and airborne radars and defence systems, communications networks and IFF transponders, and correct split-second decisions by many people. Once having been brought to battle, the enemy must be prevented from escaping and prevented from winning. He must be destroyed.

We always fondly imagine we are better than the bad guys, but unfortunately they have exactly the same ideas and attitudes, whoever ''we'' or ''they'' might be. Whatever the disparity in pilot proficiency or aircraft capabilities, there remains a very large measure of pure luck in the outcome of air combat, though many pilots will try to deny this. Right up to the present day, a significant proportion of aircraft lost in conflict have been ''own

goals'', usually to ground fire but occasionally even to misguided shooting by friendly fighters. And the folklore of air combat has never ceased to be periodically enhanced by fresh stories of pilots falling for such old tricks as giving them urgent instructions in their own language. Unquestionably, with 100 per cent stealth-designed fighters the outcome of air combat will be even more uncertain. In contrast, targeting large warheads against the precisely located and immovable airbases would give results that can be predicted with total confidence. But perhaps that would be considered unsporting.

Vertical rolling scissors. Unquestionably the top dogfighters of East and West are (in 1988) the MiG-29A ''Fulcrum'' and the General Dynamics F-16 Fighting Falcon (preferably with F110 engine). In this illustration we imagine an inept MiG-29 pilot overshooting an F-16, caught out by the sharp break **A.** At **B** the F-16 turns and barrel-rolls, to come into firing position at **C.** By this time the MiG pilot has woken up, rolls into the break and spoils the F-16's aiming solution. The eventual outcome of this air would be even.

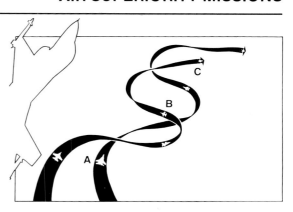

The Eagle Mission

F-16 Fighting Falcon strike aircraft of the Hahn-based 50th Tactical Fighter Wing are being "bombed-up" in anticipation of a mission against a WarPac build-up of troops and armoured fighting vehicles close to the forward edge of the battle area. At nearby Bitburg, in West Germany, meanwhile, elements of the 36th Tactical Fighter Wing are readied to perform the fighter escort mission, flying combat air patrol cover for the marauding strike force, with F-15C Eagles armed with AIM-7 Sparrow and AIM-9 Sidewinder air-to-air missiles. Across the border at a WarPac air base in East Germany, Soviet MiG-23 "Floggers" regularly launch and recover as they try to disrupt Allied air and ground operations. In the forthcoming strike, the "Floggers" will again be active but will fail to prevent the F-16s from achieving their objective, their attempts to intervene being forestalled by the Eagles operating from Bitburg. However, an inconclusive engagement between an F-15 and a "Flogger" highlights the problem of defective armament.

 1015 hours

At Bitburg, personnel of the resident 36th Tactical Fighter Wing are beginning to show signs of wilting under the pressure of sustained combat operations. For the aircrews assigned to USAFE's premier air superiority outfit, fatigue is becoming a matter for very real concern. Tempers are starting to fray in the face of the need to fly at least three missions a day.

They are, of course, not unique in this, for the sortie generation rate is being matched (and sometimes exceeded) by fellow pilots of the NATO alliance but the kind of flying undertaken by many of them is of a rather different nature. While air-to-ground is not an activity to be tackled lightly, it is perhaps less stressful in that survival is based upon evasion, with discretion invariably being perceived as the better part of valour. For the Eagle-drivers of the 36th, however, the need to achieve air superiority almost inevitably demands that they "tangle" with enemy fighters. At the bottom line, one cannot kill an enemy without first engaging him. It is this requirement which is at the root of the problem. Regular high-g aerial battles conspire with the ever-present threat of death at the hands of a numerically superior opposing force to cause the fatigue which has already claimed at least two victims.

For the ground crews, the constant need to turn round aircraft in minimal time so that they might re-enter the battle creates pressure of a different but, potentially, no less deadly nature. Once again, fatigue is evident, and here the situation is perhaps worsening for continuous combat is inevitably accompanied by a steady deterioration in aircraft serviceability. Thus far, ground crews have managed to maintain a high percentage of the Wing's assets in a combat-ready state but degraded-system operation is becoming increasingly commonplace and it will soon be necessary to withdraw some of the 70-odd Eagles from the fight so as to perform essential maintenance.

Already, the availability and status boards of

Above: At the 36th Tactical Fighter Wing's home base at Bitburg, West Germany, maintenance personnel work constantly to restore the F-15C Eagle fighters to a state of fully mission capable, a task that is not made easier by the fact that each Eagle occupies its own hardened shelter.

Bitburg's three F-15 squadrons are showing that many aircraft require more than routine servicing and the maintenance officers of each are hoping that the coming night will bring a respite so that some of this work can be done by day-break tomorrow. None of them is overly optimistic, however, for the initiative still lies very much with the Warsaw Pact forces, which continue to press hard in the hope of achieving a major breakthrough.

 1017 hours

At the moment, the scheduling officer of the 525th Tactical Fighter Squadron has more immediate concerns to resolve. It is shaping up to be another hectic day. Already, half-a-dozen aircraft are airborne, escorting a strike package while four recently returned Eagles are being turned-round, ready to fly again when needed. Missions scheduled for later in the day are certain to require at least ten aircraft, and since it is usual to prepare at least one spare per cell of four, he is well aware that he and his colleagues are in for a hard time.

Now, Wing headquarters has tasked him with furnishing four aircraft for a CAP (Combat Air Patrol) mission just across the line which marks the forward edge of the battle area (FEBA). Idly scratching his head, he studies the boards as he attempts to solve the increasingly difficult equation of current aircraft availability versus anticipated requirements. If all goes well, he reckons he should be able to keep everyone reasonably "sweet" by "pulling" four aircraft from missions planned for later in the day but the gamble he is about to take makes no allowance for unplanned unserviceability and it will take only a minor problem to throw a king-sized spanner in the works.

 1018 hours

Turning to an NCO, he explains, "Jack, I'm thinking of diverting four of the aircraft on this afternoon's mission to satisfy an immediate. Tell me, what's the status on the four birds that just got back? How long before we can regenerate them?"

"Ah, stand by one," comes the response, the NCO picking up a phone, dialling and speaking briefly. Returning the handset to its receiver, the NCO says, "bout an hour, sir. They've all got minor problems that the tech guys are tweaking right now. Mostly a case of switching line replaceable units, I guess."

 1020 hours

"Hmmm. OK, let's slot those four in on the afternoon mission. Right now, we'll take 012, 020, 025 and 047 for the immediate. Gimme' 028 as the spare. Better give the line chief a call to let him know. Who's on duty down there, by the way?"

"Flanagan, sir...he's a good man...."

"That's one thing we need right now. Oh, and Jack...."

"Yessir?"

"Keep your fingers crossed that we don't foul up."

"Sure thing, boss...."

Above and above right: Clad in NBC protective clothing, weapons specialists of the 36th TFW prepare a load of AIM-7 Sparrow and AIM-9 Sidewinder air-to-air missiles for fitment on the Eagle. A full load of weapons will comprise four examples of each missile.

Below: In addition to guided missiles, the McDonnell Douglas F-15 Eagle also packs a powerful close-in punch in the shape of a single Vulcan M61 20mm cannon. Ammunition for the associated magazine is seen here being loaded by two more busy munitions technicians.

Left: *Relatively secure inside its TAB-V hardened aircraft shelter, a 36th TFW F-15 Eagle undergoes routine servicing by ground support personnel wearing protective NBC kit. Weapons specialists will shortly move in to re-arm this Eagle which has just returned from a successful combat sortie.*

Below: *Elsewhere on the airfield, Eagles begin to leave their hardened shelters at the start of a CAP mission in which they will provide protection for a strike force of F-16 Fighting Falcons operating from nearby Hahn. On this occasion, five Eagles will taxi although only four will actually launch and fly the Mission.*

1022 hours

Not many feet away, in another part of the squadron's hardened operations centre, five pilots congregate around the Intelligence Officer (IO) for a quick briefing on the area in which they will be working. Only four of them will actually perform the mission but it is usual to crank-up a spare which will accompany the formation to the runway end and take the place of any aircraft that is forced to abort for technical reasons. Therefore, five pilots go about the process of preparation.

Thus far, though, the Bitburg Wing has suffered only two runway aborts and the job of "spare" is universally viewed with loathing by pilots. While they accept the necessity of being fully prepared to fly a mission, they find the almost inevitable return to the HAS anticlimactic and an additional strain on nerves that are already taut. However, since nobody has yet conceived a better alternative, it is something that they must learn to live with....

1023 hours

"OK, guys," begins the IO. "You'll be flying top cover for a bunch of F-16s from the 50th at Hahn. They're putting up a 12-aircraft package — eight air-to-mud and four low CAP."

He pauses for a moment and looks around for a pointer, eventually settling on a large ruler which lies nearby on a map table.

"Right, their target is a river crossing right in here. Ivan's got a whole mess of troops and armour stalled just across the other side and he's been working real hard to break out. Only trouble is, every time he puts up a temp'ry bridge, our guys come along and knock it down again. Latest intelligence indicates he's working on two crossings right now — here and here — and it'll be up to the guys from Hahn to try and take them out.

"Threats.... There's quite a bunch right now but Ivan's had three days to build up. Shilkas, of course, but they shouldn't bother you too much. Hand-held IR-homers as well — once again, they shouldn't be a problem unless you get sucked down. S'far as we know, there's no radar-guided missiles but fighters will almost certainly be a headache, which is where you come in.

"As you can see," he continues, moving the pointer quickly around the map to pick out two locations, "there's a couple of fighter bases not far away and they've been pretty

busy, tryin' to mess up our guys, so far without too much luck. Your job'll be to position yourselves right around here and forestall any approach. Problem is, we've got a whole bunch of stuff working over the real estate 'round here — us, the Brits and the Krauts — so you'll have to go visual since we don't want you nailing any of our guys to the wall. You'll be carrying Sparrows but it's unlikely you'll get a 'missiles free' situation developing so don't count on getting to use them. Nine-Limas and guns, no problem.

"Time on station is 1230. That's a few minutes before the Hahn guys are due to roll in, so basically you'll be trolling for bear. TOT's 1234 so you'll prob'ly have to proceed direct to the CAP station if you're gonna' get there on time. Guess that just about takes care of ev'rything for now so you better go to it. I'll give you the latest intelligence just before you walk out..."

1026 hours

Moving to the nearby plotting table, the five pilots set about planning the routing they will take to their designated CAP station, using a "safe" departure corridor from Bitburg that, by a happy coincidence, will enable them to head more or less directly to the working area.

On this occasion, navigation is a fairly straightforward matter, the job of planning being slightly compounded by the desire to arrive on station on time. An early arrival is clearly to be avoided for none of the pilots is anxious to remain in the area exposed to enemy threats for any longer than is strictly necessary. Late arrival is equally unwelcome since it could compromise the chances of success by exposing the strike package and low CAP elements to enemy interference. By adjusting their cruising speed slightly, the five pilots are able to develop a flight profile that will bring them to the correct point in space at the correct time.

1048 hours

With flight planning complete, the element leaders then devote a few minutes to discussing tactics with their respective wingmen. Since they routinely flew together during pre-war training and have since successfully completed several combat missions as a team, they have now developed an almost instinctive feel for the tactics and techniques that the other will employ. As a result, this phase of preparation takes very little time to complete, for most procedures are second-nature, honed to near-perfection in countless training sorties against other elements of the 36th TFW, in "Red Flag" exercises over the vast ranges near Nellis AFB, Nevada and in mock combat against the F-16Cs of the Brentwaters-based "Aggressor" outfit. Nevertheless, both lead pilots do devote a few moments to an informal briefing of the "spare" pilot who is less familiar with their unique idiosyncracies even though he is well-versed in the doctrine of aerial combat as practised by the 36th TFW and other USAF fighter units. Instinctive reaction is imperative for the successful outcome of combat and, therefore, the necessity to take time to brief the "spare" pilots.

Top: *Seen from the vantage point of Bitburg's control tower, the first pair of F-15s rotate for take-off after a reasonably short ground roll. Within minutes, they will be heading east at medium altitude to take up their designated patrol station.*

Above: *The pilot of this Eagle wastes no time in "cleaning-up" his aircraft once airborne at the start of yet another combat sortie. In the wing root, adjacent to the engine air intake, can be seen the muzzle of the fearsomely effective Vulcan M61A1.*

Right: *While one wave of fighters departs at the start of yet another mission, ground support personnel busy themselves preparing a recently returned group to return to the fray in the shortest possible time. Here, a refuelling hose replenishes an Eagle.*

1050 hours

While they go through the planning stages, other personnel are equally busy elsewhere. In five shelters, ground crew sweat a little as they ready their charges for action, a task which involves manhandling missiles on to stores stations, topping up depleted fuel tanks, replenishing gun magazines, "tweaking" sophisticated avionics systems and generally ensuring that the Eagle for which they are responsible is in good shape to perform the coming mission. Each aircraft will depart with a "full bag" of missile armament — four AIM-7M Sparrows and four AIM-9L Sidewinders — but it looks as though the situation around the probable battle area will predicate against the use of the semi-active radar-homing Sparrow.

1055 hours

As the process of preparing the aircraft nears completion, so do the other strands of pre-departure activity begin to reach a climax. Back in the hardened aircrew facility, with planning now finished, the five pilots gather for the mission briefing, a detailed process addressing a multitude of aspects. Radio frequencies — for chat between the disparate elements of "Buckshot" flight and for the relay of data to and from the primary control agencies, of which the NATO E-3A Sentry is arguably the most important — are discussed and noted. Aircraft call-signs — pertaining to the Eagles themselves and to the Sentry, which today is using "Boresight" — are scribbled down. Weather information is also covered quickly (today, it is good, with only a thin layer of cloud at around 15,000ft (4,570m)), but most of the time is spent on attempting to preview the various eventualities that "Buckshot" flight might encounter. Most are SOP (standard operating procedure) but the list is continually being added to as combat experience rises. Some of the items discussed relate to actions that should be taken in the event of contact being lost between leader and wingman or of combat damage being sustained but weapons parameters are also reviewed. The latter is an action which might seem superfluous but it is one that has already begun to pay real dividends for it has enabled 36th

Above left: With afterburners glowing brightly, the last aircraft in the four-ship formation heads away from Bitburg, pulling around into a fairly tight turn as it departs in order to waste no time in taking up its slot before setting off towards the East German border and an encounter with the enemy.

Above: The quartet of Eagles maintain tight formation as they move through the safe corridor to the east of Bitburg. Once clear, they will spread out into battle formation, with several thousand feet of lateral and vertical separation between each pair.

TFW pilots to achieve a particularly high kill probability per engagement, in the process cutting down on needless expenditure of valuable and expensive missiles.

Navigation is also referred to but the brief invariably terminates with a few words from the squadron's intelligence officer, reviewing "threats" in the immediate vicinity of Bitburg itself, reminding pilots of what they may take with them (precious little), of what information they are permitted to divulge should they fall prisoner (name, rank, service number and date of birth), and of the "rules" relating to escape and evasion.

1100 hours

With briefing now complete, pilots gather up charts and other impedimenta and move to the nearby survival gear room, where personal kit — including g-suits, helmets, oxygen masks, life vests and gloves — is stored, to suit-up for the coming sortie, removing the velcro-backed low-viz unit patches which adorn their flight suits in the process. One or two take time out to visit the toilet, having learnt from bitter experience that there are few discomforts that can compare with a full bladder in a high-g situation — but all are ready within five minutes. The section leader returns to the

operations room for a last look at the detailed "war map" that extends from floor to ceiling on one wall.

1120 hours

"Hey, shotgun," calls a voice, "Your carriage awaits...."

Picking up his helmet bag, the leader of "Buckshot" flight heads for the door, pausing only long enough to shout, "OK, guys...time to get movin'."

Outside, a van stands ready, engine idling and doors open, a huge helmeted gum-chewing negro at the wheel. An armed guard watches from a nearby fox-hole as the five pilots clamber on board, the last man in reaching around to pull the door shut. Even as the door latches closed, the driver lets in the clutch with a bang and the vehicle sets off at an electric pace, snaking and weaving as it whizzes across the concrete towards the shelters. In the back, still sprawling on the floor where he has been thrown by the sudden acceleration, the last man bellows, "Goddammit, Jackson. ..d'you have to do that ev'ry time I ride with you."

"Just using spoiling tactics, sir," is the reply. "Don't want no Commie bastards drawing a bead on us, now do we...."

Above: Flying at medium altitude and toting a full load of four Sidewinder and four Sparrow missiles, the pilot of this Eagle is most definitely "head-up", continuously scanning the sky so as to detect enemy "threats" before they present too much of a hazard.

Below: Well to the rear of the main battle area and reasonably secure from interception by WarPac fighters, a solitary Boeing E-3 Sentry orbits as it electronically monitors the evolving scene of battle. Here, two of its crew monitor the various communications networks.

 1130 hours

Inside five different TAB-V shelters, five pilots go through the routine business associated with every departure. Even the urgent demands of war do not eliminate the need for paperwork but inspection of airframe manuals takes little more than moments since the five F-15Cs allocated to this mission are all fully combat-capable. Confident that their prospective mounts are in good shape, each pilot very quickly signs the acceptance forms, before turning his attention to the pre-flight inspection, the normal quick peacetime walkaround being taken at a rather more leisurely pace. Control surfaces are examined, weapons are scrutinised, panels are inspected...then, satisfied, each pilot quickly climbs the ladder to the cockpit. Crew chiefs invariably follow them up to assist with the strapping-in procedure.

Below, other members of the ground crew plug long intercom leads into jack sockets in the sides of the aircraft, for once the Eagle's twin Pratt & Whitney F100 turbofan engines are running, normal methods of communication are impractical in the confined quarters of a HAS and it is not always possible for a pilot to observe hand signals during the series of pre-departure checks.

 1137 hours

In the shelter which houses the flight leader's aircraft, its pilot secures maps and charts before pulling on the handle which activates the so-called jet fuel starter (JFS). This device is essentially an auxiliary power unit which sits between the pair of F100s. Once it is running, it provides sufficient electrical power to permit use of the intercom and cockpit instrument displays.

 1140 hours

A few quick checks and he is into the main engine start procedure as the shelter's massive doors slide sideways. Daylight floods in, and prompts him to adjust the brightness of the head-up display unit.

Once again, the services of the JFS are employed, the starboard engine being started first. With both F100s idling and with the various engine-related instruments furnishing satisfactory readings, the JFS is quickly shut down and the pilot then turns his attention to pre-flight checks of control surfaces. Flaps and the massive dorsal airbrake slide out and in or move up and down, before a few moments are spent confirming that the vital ailerons and all-moving tailplanes operate freely. Outside the aircraft, ground crew members move smartly about, occasionally bending low to watch as they verify that all is apparently in order via the intercom system, the long leads snaking out behind them as they go about their duties.

Pre-departure checks are not confined to these all-important surfaces for the pilot also activates a BITE (Built-In Test Equipment) program, by which on-board computers automatically examine key items of the avionics package and hydraulics systems installed in the F-15C.

 1145 hours

Again, all the indications are good and the pilot then switches to the task of setting up his navigation equipment, first aligning the inertial navigation system by punching in the shelter co-ordinates which are painted on the wall. En route waypoint co-ordinates are also entered so as to provide "insurance" should the primary TACAN system become inoperative. An IFF (identification friend or foe) code is also dialled in to the transponder, this frequently changed "squawk" permitting other air and ground-based elements of the NATO alliance to "interrogate" the F-15 and verify that it is indeed "friendly".

 1150 hours

With those tasks out of the way and with time to roll fast approaching, Buckshot lead activates the radio and speaks briefly.

"Buckshot flight. Check in."

"Two...Five...Three... Four."

Unless anything unforeseen occurs — such as a surprise enemy attack on the airfield itself — that is the only communication that will occur before departure, the four primary pilots and the spare having been briefed to taxi to the runway at a pre-determined time.

Before that moment arrives, however, weapons specialists have one last duty to perform — removing "safing" devices which inhibit accidental firing of missile armament. As they

undertake this task, Buckshot lead and his colleagues rest their hands on the instrument panel shroud where they can be clearly seen by a member of the ground team and where, incidentally, it is impossible for them inadvertently to activate any switch.

 1154 hours

Ground crew quickly remove their intercom leads from the sockets in the side of each Eagle before "buttoning up" the access panel. From now on, communication is solely by hand signal but there is little that remains to be done, beyond the formality of a departing salute. In reality this is nothing more than a traditional gesture but one which is invariably observed by pilot and crew chief.

 1155 hours

Gently manipulating the throttle levers, Buckshot lead provides just sufficient additional power to propel his aircraft clear of the shelter, halting just outside for a few moments for the dual purpose of checking the brakes

Below: This extremely good view of the Eagle's "front office" reveals it to be fairly typical of 1970s technology. Controls for the head-up display unit are visible in the upper right corner while the throttle levers, control column and communications equipment are also quite evident.

and arming his ejection seat. Behind, the doors of the shelter are already closing...they will remain firmly shut until such time as the Eagle returns to its eyrie.

1157 hours

Ahead of him as he taxis towards the runway, Buckshot lead sees four other Eagles holding at the taxiway access points, these sliding into the correct position once he has moved past, the pilot of number two moving to take up station behind and to the left. Three and four adopt similar spacing while number five brings up the rear, ready to roll forward in the event of his being needed. In peacetime, it is usual to hold at a point just short of the runway for "last chance" checks. In war, however, time spent on the ground is cut to the absolute minimum so as to reduce vulnerability to enemy attack. Lead and his wingman therefore move straight on to the runway, halting only momentarily in order to exchange hand signals indicating that all is well.

1200 hours

Brakes are released, throttles are pushed hard up against the stops, afterburners ignite and, with each engine gulping fuel at the prodigious rate of 860lb (390kg) per minute, the first two Eagles quickly accelerate away down Bitburg's runway under the impetus of close to 50,000lbs (22,680kg) of thrust. Behind, the next two aircraft take the runway and follow identical procedures, beginning their departure roll just 20 seconds later.

As they pass the 100-kt mark, the noses lift more or less as one. Seconds later, they are airborne, wallowing slightly as they encounter jet wash left by lead and his wingman who are visible ahead as they pull around into a right-hand turn on to an easterly heading. Back on the ground at Bitburg, the pilot of the spare Eagle curses briefly as he returns to the shelter he had left just a few minutes earlier, consoling himself with the knowledge that he will get the chance to fly later in the day.

1202 hours

As the Bitburg-based Eagles manoeuvre on to their new heading, activity at nearby Hahn is beginning to peak, with bomb and missile-laden F-16s emerging from their shelters. They move towards a runway which bears visible evidence of hasty repairs, Hahn having been hard-hit by a dozen or so Soviet fighter-bombers just a couple of days earlier. Matters could have been worse, however, for despite achieving almost total surprise, the Soviet pilots failed fully to press home their attack and many of the bombs that were dropped ended up detonating more or less harmlessly in the heavily wooded surrounds to the base.

Right: *As with virtually all modern Western fighters, the Eagle incorporates the HOTAS (Hands on Throttle and Stick) philosophy whereby all of the key controls that a pilot is likely to require during the course of an aerial engagement are, most sensibly, at his fingertips.*

Above: *Buckshot lead breaks hard left to take up battle formation as the Eagles move towards the combat zone. At the moment, the aircraft is still in dry power but afterburner will soon be selected to provide a welcome power boost during the ensuing combat.*

Below: *In the meantime, the second element of Eagles hold close formation for a few seconds longer. They, too, will soon move into a new formation so as to enhance their chances of spotting an enemy first, before he is able to gain a dangerous position of advantage.*

HOTAS (Hands on Throttle and Stick)

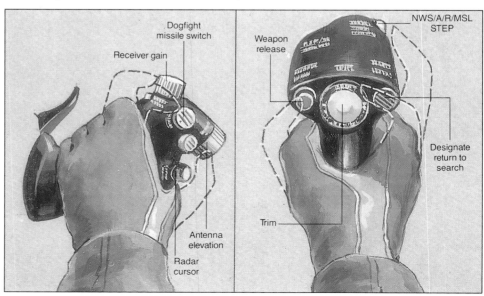

Even then, Hahn was put out of action for a matter of hours while the runway was patched up and cleared of unexploded ordnance.

 1220 hours

At 40,000ft (12,200m), the Eagle drivers are well aware that their movements are being observed by both friend and foe alike, their own radar warning receiver equipment providing confirmation that they are being ''painted'' by radar as they move east towards the FEBA. Many miles to their rear, a NATO Sentry orbits serenely as it electronically monitors the aerial battlefield, each sweep of the saucer-shaped rotodome updating the developing picture that is presented to the battle staff via cathode ray tubes and relayed to the ground by means of digital data link equipment. The four Eagles are clearly visible on the displays and have been identified as friendly. To their north, a group of RAF Tornados also heads east and the fact that they are at very low level does not prevent their being ''seen'' and recognised as friendly by the E-3A, as is a group of A-10A Thunderbolt IIs working over the main ground battle area. Also visible in the ''big picture'' are the F-16s from Hahn and these too are at low level, hoping to use terrain to mask their approach until the last minute.

Across the FEBA/FSCL, above enemy-held territory, there is also evidence of aerial activity but the nature of the threat is by no means easy to determine although some clues are provided by the pattern of that activity. To the south, a clutch of aircraft heading west at low level are clearly visible. These are almost certainly WarPac interdictors, and a group of accompanying fighters may be discerned weaving to and fro above them as they enter Allied airspace. Attempts at jamming the Sentry's radar have caused some inconvenience but thus far have failed to achieve the objective of ''blinding'' the E-3A.

Controllers on board the Sentry monitor the progress of the enemy aircraft as well as that of a group of Luftwaffe F-4F Phantoms

that have been tasked with countering this threat. If all goes well, interception should take place before the WarPac machines have penetrated too far.

 1229 hours

The Eagles have reached their designated CAP station and have descended slightly, the lead element of Buckshot flight maintaining an altitude of around 30,000ft (9,144m) with the second element about two miles (3km) away, in loose trail some 5,000ft (1,500m) higher.

Use of continuous fluid manoeuvring with co-ordinated cross-overs enables battle formation to be held, the two aircraft in each element never coming closer than 5,000ft (1,500m) apart and only occasionally allowing lateral separation to exceed 8,000ft (2,440m). In this way, they are able to maintain visual contact and, more importantly, clear each other's ''six'', that most vulnerable quadrant of sky directly to the rear of each fighter.

Previous opportunities to fly and train together means that each section leader and their associated wingmen are well versed in such tactics and there is accordingly no need

for any verbal communication as they manoeuvre and observe the rear quadrant.

It is here that the greatest danger lies, an approach from the rear offering a couple of important tactical advantages to any attacking fighter. Firstly, it provides him with the greatest opportunity of approaching unseen and no self-respecting fighter pilot wishes to fall victim to an unseen opponent. Secondly, despite the great improvements that have been made to infra-red missile seeker heads, it is still the optimum spot from which to employ IR-homing missiles, heat generated by the powerplant — whether in afterburner or

A: Pilot of Buckshot Three launches a Sidewinder heat-seeking missile which is successfully decoyed by an infra-red flare, permitting the MiG-23 ''Flogger'' to escape undamaged. **B:** Pilot of Buckshot Two launches Sidewinder in diving attack on another ''Flogger''. **C:** Buckshot Leader engages a MiG-23 with yet another Sidewinder which unaccountably fails to detonate. **D:** Buckshot Three lets fly with his second Sidewinder and succeeds in destroying a MiG-23. **E:** Boeing E-3 Sentry monitoring the battle.

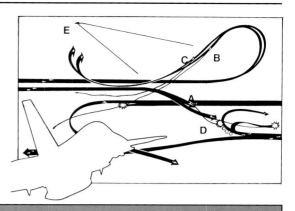

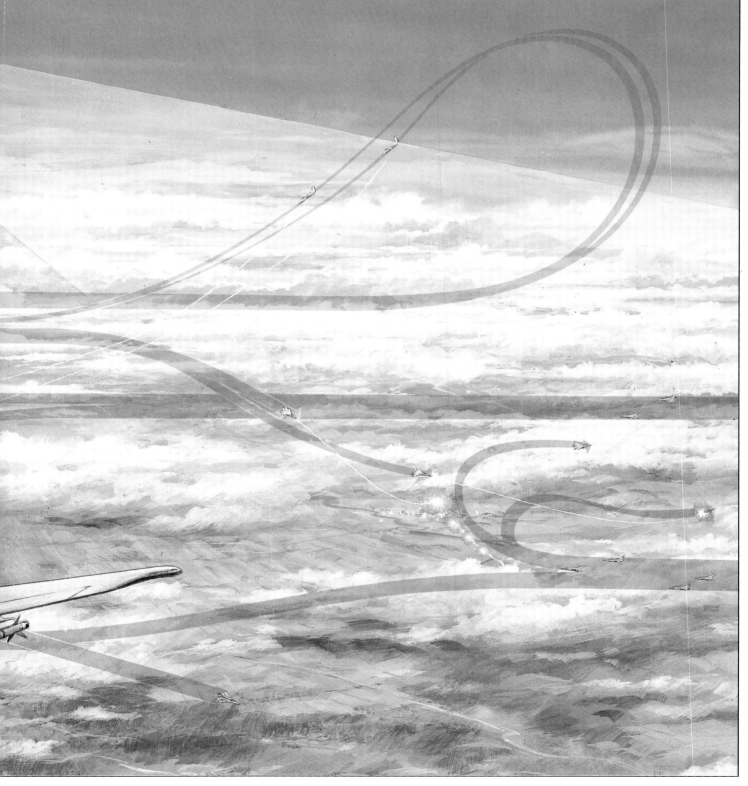

dry — offering the best "tracking signature" and, in consequence, the greatest probability of achieving a kill.

 1229:30 hours

Thus far, they have avoided using their own Hughes AN/APG-63 radar, not so much from a desire to remain undetected, since, in the radar-rich environment through which they have passed and in which they now fly, that is virtually impossible. They know that the enemy knows where they are — what the enemy does not know, however, is what they are. He certainly has clues as to the fact that they are Eagles, their operating altitude being one, but in the absence of being able to analyse the characteristics of their radar he cannot know for certain.

They could, for instance, be EF-111A Ravens preparing to employ jamming signals so as to mask the approach of Allied fighter-bombers....they could be F-16s or F-4s attempting to accomplish an elaborate bluff and draw valuable fighter assets away from the real objective....or, as in this instance, they could be Eagles performing a CAP cover mission. The only way to find out is to go and look....

 1230 hours

On board the F-15s, radios have been pre-tuned to Boresight's frequency and it is from this source that the first intimation of the impending action comes.

"Buckshot flight, Boresight. Fighter-type plots launching from airfield in your two o'clock, 'bout 40 miles (64km) east of your present position. Sure looks like they're gunning for you."

"Rog, Boresight..." he responds, adding for the benefit of his colleagues, "Buckshot, go button seven."

On the new frequency, Buckshot lead speaks again, "'kay, let's go see...."

Rolling out on to a new heading which should take them directly towards the oncoming fighters, he activates the radar momentarily, permitting it to make a few quick sweeps before ceasing its scan. On the

F-15 Single Man Philosophy

Above: *No fewer than 13 personnel occupy the main cabin aboard the Boeing E-3 Sentry, monitoring the display consoles, operating the integral computer, servicing the radar and dealing with the multiplicity of communications links.*

Left: *Subscribing to the single pilot philosophy, skilful placement of key controls where they are easily accessed by the pilot, as in the case of HUD, permits him to handle an intense multi-threat situation without too much risk of being overloaded by the developing tactical scenario.*

Below: *Cruising at an altitude of 30,000 feet, a single Boeing E-3 Sentry can observe the action over an impressively large area. This illustration looks at the Pulse Doppler Elevation Scan (PDES) mode whereby the height of various targets may be established by vertical scan.*

E-3A Pulse Doppler Elevation Scan Mode

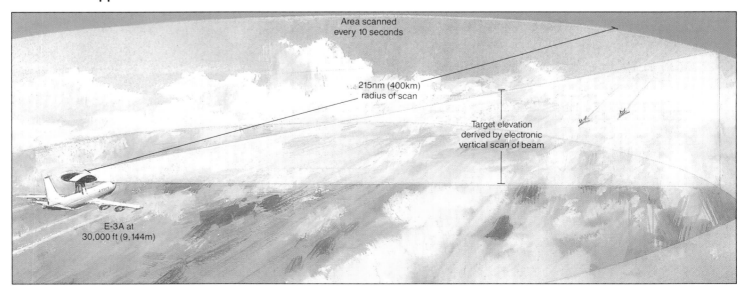

Area scanned every 10 seconds

215nm (400km) radius of scan

Target elevation derived by electronic vertical scan of beam

E-3A at 30,000 ft (9,144m)

CRT display adjacent to the HUD control panel, the image is temporarily "frozen" — several blips stand out clearly, each indicating a potential target for Buckshot flight.

1230:30 hours

As the Eagles move east to engage the onrushing enemy fighters, the first of the Hahn F-16s is just minutes from the river crossing, its pilot concentrating his attention on setting up his ordnance for the impending attack. Above, two pairs of Sidewinder-armed Fighting Falcons ride "shotgun" at medium altitude. Operating beyond the reach of small arms fire and outside the lethal envelope of the much-respected ZSU-23-4 mobile AAA, their job is to engage any fighters that succeed in evading the Eagles. They will remain on station for barely three minutes, furnishing low-CAP cover while the fighter-bombers strike before withdrawing to safety just 30 seconds after the last bomb-laden F-16 deposits its load of deadly ordnance.

1231:30 hours

At a combined closure rate in excess of 1,000 mph (1,610km/h), it takes very little time for the opposing forces to come together. Buckshot lead again activates his radar which provides a visual clue in the form of a target indicator box on the HUD. This notifies him that they are slightly below at about his one o'clock position some 15 miles (24km) away and closing at 980 knots (1,130mph/1,820km/h).

At present, the enemy fighters are still BVR (beyond visual range) but, since he knows roughly where to look, Buckshot lead manoeuvres his Eagle in order to put the potential opponents at his 12 o'clock position, thereafter using a telescopic sighting device that is secured to the cockpit shroud to scan the sky ahead. Within moments, he sees two aircraft some six miles (10km) away, almost instantaneously identifying them as MiG-23s.

1232 hours

Depressing the microphone button on the throttle lever, he speaks, first informing other members of Buckshot flight of the enemy's location and then issuing commands relating to the conduct of the ensuing battle.

"Tally ho. Two bandits 12 o'clock, six miles. Three, four look for the rest. Two...Immelmann, go....."

This is perhaps a risky manoeuvre, since it involves pulling up into a half-loop before rolling out on to a reciprocal track, an action which fleetingly exposes two sets of Eagle tailpipes to a tempting "Atoll" or "Aphid" IR-homing missile shot. It is a calculated risk, though, for Buckshot lead is convinced that the Soviet "Floggers" are after the Fighting Falcons. If his surmise is correct, lead and his wingman should end up in the opposition's six o'clock, handily positioned to launch their own attack with Sidewinder missiles. If it is not, he and his wingman could well be in serious trouble....

1232:05 hours

As he releases the microphone button, he hauls back on the control column, feeling his arms go heavy under the loads imposed by a force that equates to seven times that of gravity and sensing the pressure generated by his g-suit which instantly inflates to prevent his blood from draining southwards to pool in his legs. He grunts slightly to alleviate the worst effects of the g-force but is well aware that his peripheral vision is slightly impaired during this manoeuvre, delaying the roll-out for a

Left: In aerial combat, the head-up display unit is a key piece of kit, providing visual clues to the pilot as to his own speed, altitude and heading as well as information pertaining to enemy aircraft. The HUD's combiner glass, placed above the controls, dominates the cockpit coaming.

fraction of a second while he scans the scene below. On this occasion, his gamble pays off and he clearly sees two "Floggers" flash past beneath him in a westerly direction.

1232:10 hours

In the meantime, Buckshot three and four have detected the other four Soviet fighters on their own radar. Flying some ten miles (16km) behind the leading element and operating under strict GCI (ground controlled intercept) procedures, they are clearly gunning for the F-16s, having stayed low in the hope of being able to sneak past in the ground "clutter" and disrupt the strike elements which are now no more than a minute from opening their attack on the temporary bridges.

Although outnumbered, Buckshot three and four succeed in partially fouling up this ploy, altering course slightly and diving to try and head the four "Floggers" off. As they descend, Buckshot three acknowledges that he and his wingman will almost certainly be unable to prevent some of the fighters from getting through.

1232:14 hours

He decides to try a speculative Sidewinder shot, more in hope that the sight of a missile heading their way might prompt the Soviet pilots to forget about the attack echelons and instead take evasive action. He quickly selects a missile, the seeker head located in its nose beginning its scan pattern and very quickly detecting heat generated by skin friction on the fast-moving lead "Flogger".

In his earphones, Buckshot three discerns a faintly audible buzz, which grows in intensity as the range between the opposing fighters diminishes. At seven miles (11km), it is developing into the familiar growl which indicates a satisfactory "lock-on". He thumbs the red firing button, the weapon's motor igniting a fraction of a second later and driving the missile clear from its pylon beneath the wing of the swooping Eagle.

1232:32 hours

Through the HUD, Buckshot three's pilot sees the AIM-9L accelerate away from him, a trail of smoke marking its swift passage through the sky as it heads towards the low-flying MiGs, a pronounced right-hand curve indicating that it has thus far succeeded in retaining lock-on and is still tracking the lead aircraft. Then, in quick succession, decoy flares blossom brightly behind the lead MiG which pulls up into a steep climb in an attempt to break lock of the onrushing Sidewinder. His wingman, taken by surprise by this sudden (and unannounced) manoeuvre, holds his course for a couple of seconds before pulling around into a hard

Right: Once committed to action and with enemy fighters in sight, Buckshot Three manoeuvres hard in order to obtain a good firing position. Within moments, he will let fly with a speculative AIM-9 Sidewinder heat-seeking missile.

right-hand turn that exposes the belly of his aircraft to Buckshot three and four, who immediately follow.

1232:40 hours

Meanwhile, for an instant or two, it looks as if the pilot of the lead MiG has left his evasive action too late. The Sidewinder evidently begins to follow before wobbling as if uncertain, its sensitive seeker head momentarily confused by the sudden appearance of a multiplicity of attractive "targets". Then it locks on again, homing unerringly to detonate harmlessly in close proximity to one of the decoys, an explosion that is witnessed only by the other two MiGs which continue westwards, still intent on engaging the F-16s.

1232:45 hours

Aware that the last two MiGs have succeeded in evading the quartet of Eagles, the pilot of Buckshot three switches radio channels and gets off a quick call, warning the leader of the strike force that they can expect interference. "Buckshot three to Vixen lead. Two Floggers heading your way."

A momentary click in his earphones confirms that his message has been heard, but he has other more pressing concerns on which to focus his attentions, for he and his wingman are now in hot pursuit of the MiG wingman.

1232:20 hours

Meanwhile, Buckshot lead and his wingman have converted their height advantage into speed and are now diving in pursuit of the leading pair of "Floggers" which continue to head westwards. Whether they are unaware of their danger or whether they foolishly choose to ignore it is impossible to say — either way, the end result is the same. Within a matter of moments, the two Eagle pilots have selected

Sidewinders, the healthy growling tone in their respective headphones confirming that the missiles are locked-on and tracking their separate targets.

1232:30 hours

Launch occurs almost simultaneously, the two missiles accelerating away from the F-15s and beginning to overhaul the speeding "Floggers". As the Sidewinders leave the rails, lead calls, "Left turn, go..." and the two aircraft turn as one. This sudden change of direction incorporates a cross-over manoeuvre which puts the wingman out on the left and which enables each pilot to check for the danger on the other's six o'clock.

1232:35 hours

Below him, as he turns, Buckshot two catches a brief glimpse of a "Flogger" heading more or less east and is about to inform lead of this when he sees that it has an Eagle in hot pursuit. Behind this pair of aircraft, another Eagle weaves from side to side, the pilot of Buckshot four covering Buckshot three's tail as it manoeuvres for the kill.

1232:40 hours

From his grandstand seat high above, Buckshot two forgets all about the missile he has just launched, being more intent on watching the combat that is taking place below. He clearly observes a sudden bloom of flame and smoke as the predatory Eagle lets fly with a Sidewinder before he is jerked back to reality by the voice of Buckshot lead.

"Looks like you just nailed a MiG, two."

Unaware of events below and to his left, Buckshot lead has been devoting some of his attention to following the track of the two MiGs they had engaged and clearly sees an explosion as one of the Sidewinders detonates.

Seconds later, the mortally damaged "Flogger" — its control surfaces rendered useless by a mixture of blast and shrapnel damage — hits the ground and breaks apart, a momentary burst of flame caused by igniting fuel marking its final resting place.

The other "Flogger" is more fortunate. Although the weapon launched by Buckshot lead homes accurately, for some unaccountable reason it fails to detonate. In his cockpit, the leading Soviet pilot — still unaware that his wingman has been shot down — looks on in astonishment as the Sidewinder overhauls his aircraft and continues harmlessly on into the distance. He activates the radio and calls to his colleague but there is no response. Aware now that he is on his own, he opts for discretion, staying low and fast as he turns to the left to fly parallel to the border for a few moments before swinging around on to an easterly track for home.

 1232:45 hours

Above, Buckshot lead — still furious at the missile malfunction — contemplates pursuing but quickly realises that they are unlikely to catch him. He is tempted by the possibility of a Sparrow shot but acknowledges that the chances of the missile retaining radar lock on a low-level manoeuvring target are exceedingly slim and unlikely to achieve anything more than frightening an already alarmed Soviet pilot. On this occasion, it is clearly sensible to save the valuable weapon for a better target.

 1232:49 hours

His headphones crackle briefly, heralding a shouted message, the voice of Buckshot three rising in excitement.

"Three to lead. Just got one of the mothers...."

"There's no need to shout..." lead responds.

"Sorry skip, You should see it.... he's splattered all over the ground...."

"'kay, three, button it, will ya."

 1232:32 hours

Buckshot three's brief and totally conclusive combat also involves trading height for speed, the pair of F-15s accelerating to around Mach 1.3 as they pounce on the "Flogger" whose hapless pilot is clearly heading for home base as fast as he can go. Narrowing the range to little more than two miles, Buckshot three selects a missile and grins to himself as the tone in his earphones reveals that the MiG's afterburner offers an attractive target, infra-red flares ejected by the enemy fighter failing to distract the Sidewinder's seeker head.

 1232:38 hours

Intent on securing his first victory in aerial combat, Buckshot three feels the slight jolt that accompanies missile launch and watches gleefully as the weapon quickly overhauls the MiG. Only minor adjustments are necessary as it homes on the bright red plume of flame

Above: Below him, a heavily armed MiG-23 "Flogger" begins to take fairly violent evasive action in an attempt to shake-off the on-rushing Sidewinder. Simultaneously ejecting infra-red decoy flares, his ploy is successful, the Eagle's weapon misses and detonates harmlessly.

Below: Meanwhile, high above, Buckshot Leader pushes over into a dive in pursuit of the first pair of "Floggers" which press on, evidently unaware of the danger they now face. Seconds later, Buckshot Lead and his wingman each launch a single AIM-9L Sidewinder.

emanating from the opponent's tailpipe.

Afterwards, the victorious Eagle pilot was to claim that the missile disappeared into the exhaust nozzle of the MiG and literally blew it apart in mid-air. But that was not the case, a sudden deviation in the MiG's flight path resulting in the missile actually detonating alongside the starboard aft fuselage section.

Above: Seen through the combiner glass of the head-up display unit, an AIM-9L Sidewinder heat-seeking missile rapidly accelerates away from its launch platform and begins to track the enemy aircraft. Within moments, it explodes close to one of the MiGs inflicting mortal damage to the fighter.

1232:45 hours

Blast effect peels the all-moving tailplane away, causing a more or less immediate loss of control, the aircraft beginning to roll and pitch nose-downwards.

Almost instantaneously, fragments of the warhead penetrate the fuselage with disastrous consequences for the engine. Thrown turbine blades shred adjacent fuel and hydraulic lines and the entire aft fuselage is almost immediately engulfed in flames, the uncontrollable fire quickly spreading forward to the main fuel tanks. In the cockpit, the Soviet pilot instantly registers the missile hit but that is his last conscious thought.

 1232:47 hours

A split-second before the MiG strikes the ground, the main tanks blow apart, causing the fuselage to disintegrate into three distinct sections, wreckage being spread over a narrow swathe of ground almost three-quarters of a mile long. Secondary explosions follow as the missile and gun armament — comprising four AA-8 "Aphids" and a GSh-23L gun pack complete with some 200 rounds of 23mm ammunition — cooks-off in the intense heat.

 1235 hours

"OK Buckshot formation. Vixen's done its stuff. Let's go on home."

 1315 hours

Back at Bitburg, ground personnel busy themselves readying the freshly returned

Below: A few miles behind, the pilots of Buckshot Three and Four hold formation at medium altitude just before letting down for recovery. Within minutes of landing, they will return to the operations facility.

Above: *With the brief but quite conclusive combat now over and with Vixen formation having done its work well, the F-15 Eagles rejoin formation briefly before setting a course that will take them back to home base at Bitburg which is less than 30 minutes away.*

Below: *Buckshot Leader and his wingman maintain loose formation as they near the field and set up for landing. With main and nose gear down and locked, Buckshot Two employs the dorsal airbrake to kill off speed shortly before touch-down.*

Above: *The pilot of Buckshot Three holds his aircraft in a nose-high attitude so as to maximise the aerodynamic braking effect as he rolls down the runway shortly after touching down. The huge dorsal airbrake is also fully deployed behind the cockpit.*

Below: *With speed rapidly diminishing under the influence of aerodynamic braking, Buckshot Three's pilot allows the nose of his Eagle to settle slowly to the ground, before turning off the active runway and heading for the shelter complex he had left one hour earlier.*

Eagles for another mission, replacing expended Sidewinder missiles, replenishing fuel tanks and fixing the occasional defective item of avionics kit.

In the squadron's operations facility, debriefing is almost over, this having involved a detailed analysis of the tactics employed as well as subjective assessment of the quality of the Soviet pilots. It is generally agreed by the four Eagle drivers that this was poor. Inevitably, a considerable amount of time is spent in replaying the combat, gun camera film and corroboration from his wingman confirming Buckshot three's claim, while Buckshot lead verifies that his wingman's missile had also found its mark, confirmation coming from an F-16 pilot who had observed the explosion while moving to intercept the two Floggers which evaded the Eagles. They, incidentally, failed to disrupt the strike but did survive to fly and fight another day, a brief engagement between one F-16 and a "Flogger" proving inconclusive.

Still angry about the defective Sidewinder which he, understandably, feels deprived him of a certain victory, Buckshot lead complains to almost anyone who is prepared to listen and is only slightly mollified by the assurance that stocks of this weapon will be thoroughly checked out. In less than 90 minutes, though, he will be airborne again on another mission, and this time the missiles he carries into action will not let him down....

THE
CLOSE AIR SUPPORT
MISSION

Evolution of the Mission

A S EMPHASISED in other sections of this book, air warfare as a concept did not exist until 1915. But as early as 1910 aviators were experimenting with firing guns and dropping bombs. In 1911 aircraft began to be used in a sporadic way by the Italians, fighting the Turks in the area around Tripoli, and in 1912 quite large numbers of aircraft were used in the Balkan wars between (mainly) Bulgaria and Turkey. They flew the first CAS (close air support) missions.

This was a time when even flying itself was only just possible. Aircraft were of low performance, so that the ability to fly depended to some degree on the weight of the pilot. There was little "payload" to spare for weapons. Reliability was extremely low, so that, if by luck an aircraft did manage to get airborne at a previously planned time it was quite likely that the engine would stop part-way through the mission, without any interference by the enemy. Missions were impossible except in daylight, and with little or no wind. And when weapons began to be carried, it was left to the people on the spot to decide what to use and how from what was available.

The search for weapons

The only weapons already in existence that could be carried aloft at that time were small arms and grenades. Gradually the concept of the aerial bomb was developed, sometimes by fitting fins to artillery shells or, as in the Balkan wars, by packing explosives into finned canisters. At least one pilot in this war used to carry two such "bombs" hanging from his feet on loops of wire. When he was over the enemy troops he would just kick them off! By late 1914 rather better ideas had begun to take hold, with bombs suspended under the aircraft, or along the side in a kind of pipe-rack, with a string or wire to the cockpit which pulled out the retaining pins.

Another weapon, devised in France in September 1914, was the flèchette, or aerial dart. A plain pointed rod of steel, about 5in (127mm) long, it was carried in boxes of (typically) 250, all released at once. Falling from over 1,000ft (300m), they spread over a wide strip along the line of flight and could pierce a steel helmet.

Right: Almost all CAS missions in World War I were flown by ordinary fighters, usually with no change to armour or armament. These Sopwith Camels of RAF No 73 Sqn in 1918 might at any moment be tasked with "trench strafing", as might the Bristol Fighter.

Of course such random scatter-gun weapons probably had rather low effectiveness, perhaps 90 per cent falling on bare earth. But there was no way of accurately aiming bombs either, unless a pilot was brave or foolhardy enough to dive down right over the heads of the enemy. From the start there was difficulty in deciding at what height to make an attack. Flèchettes demanded a height great enough for the darts to reach near to their terminal velocity, and most pilots considered that 1,650ft (500m) was sufficient. This was not a bad height for bombing either, but it had the disadvantage of putting the aircraft in full view of large numbers of troops at any time, at a height well within effective range of small arms. Specialised AA guns only gradually came into use, but when they were used they tended to make pilots fly either much higher or much lower.

On the Western Front during World War I the initial war of movement was arrested by the Battle of the Marne — a battle largely made possible by accurate aerial reconnaissance — and from that time onwards the ground war was one of essentially static trench warfare. The trench systems became ever deeper and more sophisticated, and though the general "line" of the front might locally be fairly straight, the actual trenches zigzagged in a seemingly random fashion. Increasingly, they offered the infantry protection against mortar and artillery fire, and thus also against light bombs and flèchettes. Had there been any way of accurately aiming heavy bombs these might have caused severe local destruction, perhaps sufficient for the opposing infantry to cross no-man's land and effect a breakthrough. In practice such accurate pinpoint bombing was almost impossible.

The need for armour

As anti-aircraft ground fire became more intense, the possibility of fitting armour to close-support aircraft was studied at length. By late 1916 aircraft were in general much more powerful and able to fly faster and manoeuvre more sharply, even with quite effective loads of weapons. However, the dead weight of armour posed a formidable problem, though in some specially designed aircraft the whole forward fuselage or pusher nacelle was actually made of armour, typically of 6.5mm (about 0.25in) thickness. Thus, the weight of the nor-

Long before anyone had even thought about the possibility of air combat, aircraft had already been used to harass enemy troops in the first "close air support" missions. Today the CAS mission can be flown by fighter-type aircraft, or by dedicated CAS aircraft, or even by helicopters. More than any other mission, it calls for aircraft of totally "stealth" design, able to survive in close proximity to enemy surface forces.

Above: Designed just before the war, the B.E.2 series were by far the most numerous British aircraft on the Western front until 1916. Totally unsuited to the job, they were given various kinds of weapons and used to assist the Army in any way possible.

Below: Typical of World War I armament was the nose gun of the Handley Page O/400. The observer could aim his 0.303in Lewis from a standing position, the drum-fed gun being mounted on a Scarff ring and provided with a canvas bag to collect the spent cases.

mal structure could be subtracted from the weight of armour to give a somewhat reduced overall penalty. Such conceptions were quite quickly arrived at on paper, but very few were actually flown until 1918.

In the meantime the machine gun came to be the dominant air weapon for the mission that was generally called trench strafing. Close-air support aircraft were, in British parlance, often called trench fighters. The general idea, when air support was called for by the local army units, was to fly in Indian file along the enemy trenches raking them with machine-gun fire. Earlier, aircraft with a pusher engine and a gunner in the nose would have been ideal, in that they could have kept their gun(s) aimed reasonably accurately into the enemy trenches for much of the combat portion of each mission. In practice they were too slow and vulnerable. Most of the fast and agile scouts, however, had only fixed forward-firing guns, so their attacks had to undulate: a shallow firing dive until the wheels were only just missing the enemy defences followed by a climb back to perhaps 100ft (30m), followed by another shallow firing dive.

Special CAS armament

Obviously what was needed were guns firing downwards. By mid-1917 many aircraft had been converted, and a few were used in numbers. Remarkably, although a Sopwith Camel was modified into the T.F.1 (Trench Fighter type 1) with two Lewis guns pointing forwards and down at about 60 degrees, the definitive production aircraft, the T.F.2 Salamander, reverted to twin forward-firing Vickers guns, and so had to make its attacks in short dives. Where the Salamander scored was in having 2,000 rounds of ammunition and no less than 656lb (298kg) of armour, proof against all rifle-calibre fire. Even the low-powered B.E.2c appeared with armour. One, fitted with crude slabs weighing 445lb (202kg), was flown by RFC No 15 Sqn through the Battle of the Somme, its pilot Capt Jenkins remaining unscathed while the much-riddled aircraft required 80 new wings in three months, and many other replacement parts!

In Mesopotamia another B.E.2c carried, instead of armour, four Lewis guns firing obliquely down, fastened to the cross-axle of the landing gear. At least one Salamander had no fewer than eight machine guns firing downwards in the same way. Such armament remained the exception, and most trench strafing was carried out with twin forward-firing guns. In 1918 Britain's Royal Aircraft Factory designed the A.E.3 Ram, intended to be the ideal trench strafer. A two-seat pusher, it had a totally armoured nacelle with a nose cockpit for the gunner, who had two Lewis guns which he could aim anywhere ahead. He also had a third Lewis which he could fire upwards to the rear. The only problem with the Ram was that it was a big aircraft, and this made it rather unwieldy and slow, even with a powerful engine.

The Germans were more successful in their procurement of close support aircraft, and to some degree this was because, early on, they identified the need for light and agile two-seaters in a class which they designated as CL. At first these were intended as escorts, but by

the summer of 1917 CL meant ground attack. Though the CL aircraft were usually unarmoured they could take a lot of punishment, and their fixed and pivoted guns and light bomb load proved quite effective. Along with Halberstadt and Hannover, CL types were made by Junkers, notable for their corrugated-skin all-metal construction. But the most remarkable Junkers close support aircraft was known simply as the J.1. Entering service in spring 1917, it was a giant single-engined biplane with a hexagonal-section fuselage clad in steel armour all the way back to aft of the rear cockpit. Known as the *Möbelwagen* (furniture van), it was clumsy but one of the toughest aircraft in the sky. Though specifically designed for close air support, the J.1 often carried a ciné camera.

Amazing prototypes

In 1921 Junkers was prohibited from building in Germany, so he set up factories in the Soviet Union and in Sweden. It was in Sweden that the amazing Junkers-Larsen JL.12 was built, an example of the trench strafer taken to seemingly excessive lengths. A tough all-metal machine, it had a box-like fuselage whose entire lower part was filled with no fewer than 28 machine guns, in seven rows of four, firing obliquely downward! Fortunately there were no infantry-filled trenches against which to try out this awesome 28-gun ship.

At exactly the same time, 1921, the young Boeing company was building its Model 10, known to the US Army as the GA-X. This actually meant Ground-Attack Experimental, but was popularly said to signify guns, armour and the unknown quantity. The GA-X had been designed by the Army's I.M. Laddon (much later the designer of the Catalina and Liberator) on the basis of experience in France in 1918. A massive twin-engined triplane, the GA-X, later redesignated GA-1, carried a heavier weight of armour round the crew and engines than any previous aircraft. The pilot sat as in a tank, looking furtively through armoured shutters. In the front of each pusher engine nacelle was

Above: Take-off by Hawker Harts of RAF No 12 Sqn (where they replaced the Fairey Fox, without which the Hart would probably never have been designed). Similar light bombers saw extensive active service in many parts of the British Empire.

Right: When it entered service, two years before World War II, the Fairey Battle seemed a fantastic advance. It carried more than double the Hart's bomb load further, and at almost 100mph faster but was defenceless against the Messerschmitt Bf 109E.

a gunner, likewise looking through narrow shutters to aim two machine guns. An armour-protected nose gunner aimed a 37mm cannon, plus a machine gun firing up and to the rear, while a fourth gunner in the rear fuselage aimed one machine gun above and two below.

Between the wars

Boeing built ten of these precursors of the Flying Fortress, and followed in 1922 with two slightly smaller GA-2s. These had a single 750hp engine and, because their armour was even thicker, were almost as heavy as the GA-1s. The pilot and two gunners manned a 37mm cannon and six machine guns. These remained oddballs, however, and for most of the 20 years between the World Wars the close support mission, whenever it was needed, was flown by traditional unarmoured machines with two or three machine guns and a few small bombs.

In policing its various Empire and mandated territories Britain's RAF developed a unique kind of deterrent or punitive mission that did not require the presence of ground forces at all. Should warring tribes get out of hand, messages would be dropped warning that their villages would be attacked. Subsequently the villages would indeed be bombed, usually after everyone had retired to a safe distance.

Above: Superficially very similar to the vulnerable Battle, the Soviet Il-2-M3 Stormovik differed in crucial respects. It had devastating anti-tank armament, a hard-hitting rear gun and, most important of all, a tremendous area and thickness of protective armour.

ing the propellant, and a tapering tail with four long curved fins which imparted stabilising spin. Amazingly, when Hitler attacked the Soviet Union on 22 June 1941 the existence of these rockets seems to have surprised both Germany and Britain, although several thousand had been fired in pre-war tests and exercises.

The vital Stormovik

Certainly the vital anti-tank aircraft that first took the RS-82 into action was the Il-2 Stormovik. On paper this was very like the Fairey Battle light bomber, which had been shot down in droves while trying to fly close-support missions in France in 1940. The big difference was that the Il-2 was heavily armoured. Despite great problems the armour was more advanced than in any previous aircraft, a typical weight being about 1,540lb (700kg). The Il-2 also had heavy forward-firing cannon, as well as six or eight rockets and bombs of up to 880lb (400kg), a common load being boxes for 200 PTAB-2.5 anti-armour bombs, which were sophisticated hollow-charge bomblets developed in 1931-34 and yet having no counterpart in other Allied countries until the 1950s.

Despite its conventional appearance, the Il-2 was the biggest single advance in the entire history of close air support. At the start though, things went badly. Glued joints made in winter failed, pilots and ground staff were untrained, and aircraft suffered heavy losses to the Bf 109s. Soon the deficiencies were rectified; a rear gunner was added, engine power was increased, armour was upgraded to 1,985lb (900kg) and the 20mm forward-firing guns were replaced first by the high-velocity

Normally, this quickly restored law and order, and it was extremely rare for major army operations to be necessary.

In the Soviet Union the Red Army was all-important, and air power was almost universally thought of as being in support of it. Several specialised aircraft were developed for attack missions on hostile armies, three during the 1930-32 period being designed by D.P. Grigorovich. All originally stemmed from the ubiquitous R-5, but had armour, more weapons and other features. The TSh-1 had 1,145lb (520kg) of armour, typically of 6mm thickness. Three prototypes were built, one with riveted armour, one with bolted and the third welded. It had two fixed and two pivoted guns, and a box for dispensing 300 grenades. Next came the TSh-2, with four forward-firing guns in each wing. In 1932 the ShON was put into production to crush dissident groups of horsemen in Turkestan. This aircraft was rather lighter, and was designed

for easy transport by road or rail. Other Soviet figher/attack aircraft used the DRP series of large recoilless guns. But what was to prove the most important new development of all was the forward-firing rocket.

Soviet rockets

Simple rockets had been used from 1915, but against balloons and airships. These were little more than big firework-type rockets, but the Soviet designers produced heavier weapons resembling improved versions of the Congreve as used by the British Army from about 1795. By 1933 there were three standard calibres, 75, 82 and 132mm. The RS-82 was by far the most important, at least 2,500,000 being fired from Soviet aircraft in World War II. It was 34in (864mm) long and weighed 15lb (6.82kg). It had a nose warhead with a fuse-arming windmill, a drum central portion hous-

VYa-23 and in 1944 by the NS-OKB-16 of 37mm calibre which could pierce a German Tiger tank.

Big advantages of attack from the air were that the PTABs fell on the relatively thin enemy top armour, while gun attacks could be made from the rear, again where the armour was thin. It became standard for a dozen or so Il-2s to orbit Panzer formations in what the Germans soon called "the circle of death", each aircraft picking a target on each pass. This avoided mid-air collisions and offered better protection against fighters. Attacks could go on for a long time, since each 37mm gun had 32 rounds and a total of 32 RS-82 rockets could be carried. Stalin said, "The Red Army needs Il-2s like it needs air and bread", and the production run of 36,163 exceeds that for any other single type of aircraft in history.

The deadly Stukas

Apart from the Soviet Union the leaders in developing the close-support mission were the Germans. They built up the Luftwaffe as a mighty instrument to support the Wehrmacht (army) in its *blitzkrieg* (lightning war), which was intended to demolish all opposition and sweep across enemy countries without for an instant being bogged down into trench warfare. During 1936-39 the concepts were tried out, particular attention being paid to accurate level bombing of targets a few kilometres ahead of the advancing army, and to dive bombing of individual pockets of resistance. In September 1939 the Ju 87 *Stuka* units became adept at putting down bombs of 550lb (250kg) size only 330ft (100m) from the leading German troops. Their effect was shattering, and with sirens added to the landing gears they often broke the morale of the enemy's hardened fighting men. In France in May 1940 the result was often to turn an opposing army into a terrified mob of refugees. Attempts by Allied aircraft to stem the oncoming Panzers were met by massed Bf 109E fighters and thousands of 20mm and 37mm flak guns which were deadly against low-flying aircraft.

Another type of close air support was pro-vided at the very outset of the campaign in the West by judicious use of gliders and parachute troops. The gliders silently put down small elite forces on strong fortifications and strategic bridges. Much later the Allies took the use of airborne troops much further and used them in far greater numbers, gliding-in light tanks and then resupplying the dropped or landing troops with parachuted containers.

But the RAF and USAAF had no experience of how to use air squadrons to the best advantage in a land battle. By 1942 such fighters as the Hurricane and Kittyhawk had been adapted to carry bombs, and the Hurricane also carried rockets and, in the Mks IID and IV, high-velocity 40mm guns specifically for use against armour. But in the bitter battle for Tunisia, which followed the Allied landings in North Africa in November 1942, the intimate collaboration between the outnumbered Afrika Korps and the outnumbered Luftwaffe was an unpalatable lesson. At the local level the much stronger Allies were time and again

held up or even routed by the highly professional teamwork of the Panzers and their supporting aircraft.

Learning the hard way

Part of the problem lay in the fact that the Allies had little experience in the way of flying close-support missions. Gradually, improved methods were devised, most notably by including specially trained liaison officers (from the army with the local air forces, and from the air force with the local army) who understood how both arms operated and how they could

Below: Though it was undistinguished as a fighter, the Curtiss P-40 Warhawk/ Kittyhawk served on every wartime front in the close-support role. This example was powered by a Packard-built V-1650 Merlin engine, whereas those at upper right were powered by Allison V-1710s.

Above: *Seen here serving with the Italian Regia Aeronautica, the Junkers Ju 87B, "Stuka" caused havoc and panic wherever it went in 1939-40. Only after it had devastated Allied armies and navies was it almost swept from the sky by fighters.*

Above right: *Probably taken in 1942, this photo shows Curtiss P-40 fighter-bombers of the "Flying Tigers" American Volunteer Group on active service in China. The object in the foreground is a drop tank, which was then still quite a new item.*

Right: *A Hawker Hurricane I for the Yugoslav air force on test over Brooklands in 1937. Though by 1941 it was becoming obsolescent in the air-superiority role, the Hurricane became one of the most important Allied close-support and anti-tank aircraft.*

best work together. As far as Britain was concerned there had for many years been Army Co-Operation squadrons, administered by Fighter Command, but formed into a separate command in 1941. They were the only units in the RAF specifically tasked with close-support of ground forces, but after watching the Germans it was recognised that the entire war machine ought to be an integrated whole. All fighters were equipped to carry bombs and rockets, and all were linked by direct telephone (sometimes R/T, radio telephony) with local army units.

If there is one lesson that actual warfare has repeatedly driven home, it is that communications are vital. Lack of them was by far the biggest shortcoming of the huge forces of the Soviet Union. Brave and dedicated, ground soldiers and air pilots strove to help each other in almost total ignorance of the local situation, of the objectives of a mission, of the exact positions of the enemy and of changes that might have taken place since the mission was ordered. Worse, on-the-spot decisions by

Above: *Though it did nothing to delay the programme, the insistence by Adolf Hitler that the Messerschmitt Me 262 should be a "blitz bomber" rather than a fighter certainly removed many of these formidable twin-jets from the air-combat arena in World War II.*

Right: *Differing from the Hawker Typhoon mainly in having a new thinner wing and extra fuel in the forward fuselage, the Tempest V was an outstanding all-round fighter-bomber. By the time it reached the RAF there was little to do but destroy buzz-bombs.*

Above: *Seen here in a false paint scheme in the USA in 1946, the Henschel Hs 129B was one of the first attempts to produce a dedicated aircraft designed to kill tanks. In fact it was a very indifferent machine which suffered from many severe faults.*

Below: *In contrast the Hawker Typhoon IB, originally planned as a high-altitude interceptor, matured as the RAF's most important ground attack and anti-armour aircraft, 3,330 being delivered. The British government did all it could to play down their achievements.*

pilots or local commanders were absolutely forbidden; one almost had to ask Moscow for permission to do anything, and tens of thousands of patriotic Red Army troops were killed by their own aircraft.

In the West the situation was never quite so bad, but there were many occasions when "own goals" were scored. Heavy bombers hated being called upon to give close support. On 18 July 1944 Allied "heavies" caused over 3,300 casualties to the civilian inhabitants of Caen. On 25 July US bombers put down 3,400 tons of bombs near St Lô, almost half falling on American troops waiting to advance. And on 14 August RAF bombers also caused thousands of casualties to Canadian troops north west of Falaise.

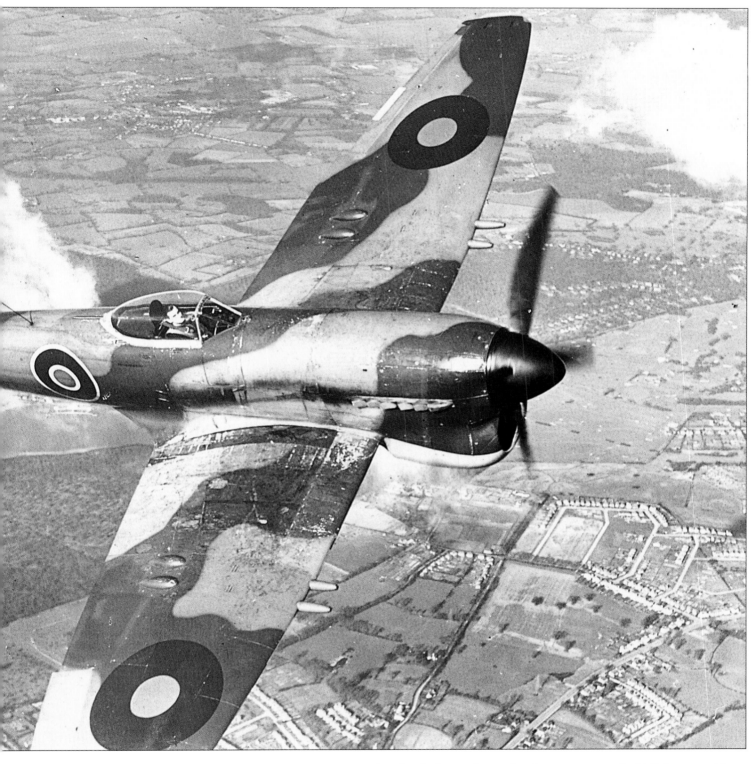

The day of the Typhoon

Nobody wanted such mistakes to be made, and in the end it all came back to the question of good communications. Once command of the air had been gained, which was very much the same with the Allies over Western Europe by 1944, it was possible to use the "cab rank" system in which fully armed fighter-bomber units could be called into action at a few minutes' notice by any local army commander held up by pockets of resistance. The cab rank could be on the ground, with pilots in the cockpits, or with aircraft already in the air waiting for orders and able to respond in a matter of minutes.

On most occasions the pilots had to work to a grid reference on a topographical map. Sometimes they could be directed by ground pyrotechnics, but these could be counterfeited in the wrong place by an alert enemy. Only very rarely, major targets presented themselves in the open. On 7 August 1944 the 2nd SS Panzer Division, supported by two other divisions, was advancing to join battle in Normandy. Despite the intense fire from over 600 flak guns of 20mm and 37mm calibre — to say nothing of many thousands of MG34s, MG42s and MP40s — Typhoons of the 2nd Tactical Air Force decimated the formidable armour in an attack lasting the whole afternoon. Later, on 18 August, the remnants of what had been 16 German divisions, this time

in a desperate state and with little ammunition, were almost sitting ducks in the Falaise pocket.

Oddly, after the war it became official policy to denigrate or even disbelieve these achievements. Rocket attacks were described as inaccurate and a waste of money; there was even an attempt to prove that rockets had never knocked out a tank. What actually happened was rather different. In an attack on the abbey at Carpiquet, for example, entrenched anti-tank and mortar positions all round the abbey moat were completely destroyed by Typhoon rockets, yet only two rockets actually hit the abbey itself. Certainly, by the end of World War II the Allied air forces had at last brought close air support to a fine art, but increasingly this was facilitated by the enjoyment of total command of the air. Though intense and accurate flak was always a great menace, and a deterrent to pressing home an attack, the absence of hostile fighters made the task of close-support squadrons very much easier. Put more forcefully, without local command of the air, close support is impossible.

In Korea the Communist North used 70-knot (80mph, 129km/h) Po-2 biplanes by night mainly to disturb the Allies' sleep (and they were difficult to shoot down, one F-94 jet night fighter stalling and crashing). The Allies used a mixed bag of ex-World War II fighters, the new Douglas AD (later A-1) Skyraider and such jets as the F-80 Shooting Star and F-86 Sabre. The latter was the only aircraft able to engage the enemy's MiG-15 on anything like even terms, but it was soon found that the new breed of jets needed long runways, had limited weapon loads and short endurance, especially at low level. In contrast, the Skyraider was slow, and thus more vulnerable, but it could carry extremely large and diverse loads of weapons and fly missions lasting up to ten hours, after which the fatigued pilot sometimes had to be bodily lifted from the cockpit.

Above: *Take-off by South African F-86 Sabres during the Korean war (1950-53). Alone among Allied fighters, the US-built Sabre had the performance to fight the MiG-15, but these particular Sabres are on an attack mission, loaded with with 1,000lb (454kg) bombs.*

Below: *Here seen in service with USAF Tactical Air Command in early 1956, the Martin B-57B, a version of the British Canberra, proved in the later Vietnam war to have the Skyraider's qualities: reliability, speed, and an unequalled combination of endurance and agility.*

Best of all worlds

Gradually it was realised that what was needed were aircraft able to combine jet speed with heavy ordnance loads, and also equipped with the sensors enabling missions to be flown at night or even in bad weather. The only aircraft with all these qualities was the Martin B-57, an upgraded version of the British Canberra, but this arrived too late for Korea and was never produced in useful numbers.

By 1960 the gradually escalating involvement of the USA in the conflict between North and South Vietnam focused attention on what were called "limited" or "brushfire" wars. It

Below: *The Douglas A-1E served in a multitude of roles with the US Navy, Marines and Air Force. Though powered by a supposedly obsolete piston engine, it combined a tough airframe with good speed and flight endurance, plus a fantastic weapon load.*

was thought that, to fight primitive enemy armies, all that was needed were simple aircraft able to operate from short unpaved airstrips while carrying machine guns or bombs, or even stretcher casualties or front-line supplies.

The US Army (for a time partnered by the Marines, who later pulled out of the project) decided on the Grumman OV-1 Mohawk, an odd twin-turboprop with about the performance of a Spitfire and a crew of two seated side-by-side in the nose in a bug-eye cockpit. Intended primarily for battlefield reconnaissance, using cameras, radar and infra-red linescan, the OV-1 also went into battle in immediate support of ground troops using gun pods, bombs and rockets.

The USAF and Marines decided on an even stranger twin-turboprop, the OV-10 Bronco, with a maximum level speed of 244 knots (281mph, 452km/h) and in some respects a modern-day Fieseler Storch with a superb all-round view from tandem ejection seats. The OV-10 could carry a wide variety of weapons,

Above: This McDonnell Douglas AV-8B
was the first in the Night Attack
programme, with forward-looking infra-red,
night-vision goggles, wide-field HUD,
colour digital moving map and other add-
ons. The RAF have a parallel programme
leading to the Harrier GR.7.

and its agility was impressive, but one of its
chief duties was FAC (Forward Air Control).
FAC pilots could fly anything from a Cessna to
an F-4 Phantom, but in the Vietnam War they
were the crucial link between the close support aircraft and the target. The latter was invariably invisible, being merely something
hidden in the corner of a wood, a river bank or
some other not very obvious place. It was the
FAC's task to use pyrotechnics of different colours to mark with absolute precision where
the next attacking aircraft should aim. Excellent two-way radio was always provided,
and for the first time the attacker not only
knew exactly where to aim but whether he
had hit the target effectively and whether the
skilled and demanding FAC was satisfied.

Getting the act together

This technique was a massive advance in the
close support mission. During the preceding
55 years countless brave and dedicated men
had tried to assist the local ground forces but
had been thwarted by abysmal lack of communications, lack of mutual understanding
and even lack of trust. With the FACs in Vietnam the Air Force (or Navy or Marines) pilots
at last had perfect communications, perfect
trust and understanding and aiming directions
accurate to within a few feet. Of course, this
conflict also saw the maturity of the helicopter.

Today most combat aircraft are, with
unbelievable idiocy — as any impartial
observer would say — parked on huge concrete aprons or inside supposedly protective
hardened shelters on the very places on our
planet that would be obliterated the night
before any major war started. The sole exception is the Harrier, which because of its unique
"jump jet" design can actually operate
without needing an airfield. Special mention
must also be made of the air force of Sweden, a
nation with enough imagination to see the
futility of buying costly aircraft in order to
place them where the enemy's missiles are
targeted. Aircraft costing £40 million and based on comfortable acres of concrete are 1,000
per cent wrong for helping armies win wars.
In contrast, a recent advertisement for the Har-

GR3 Dispersal Site Operation

Above: The blue arrows give a false idea
of exposure to the operations of Harrier II
aircraft in wartime, far from any airfield.
No enemy could blast every motorway
service station or motel, or area of
woodland near a clear pathway. Thus
these aircraft could survive.

rier II claimed a timed actual close-support
mission at just 37 minutes, measured from
when the ground commander called for air
support to the time that the aircraft were back
in their secret hides, refuelled and rearmed,
ready for the next call.

Aircraft of this nature, not just fighting but
also parked in close but hidden proximity to
the ground forces, can fly anything up to 30

missions a day and still have an excellent
chance of survival. Costly Mach-2 fighters
have no chance even of seeing the dawn of
Day 1, because they will never get an opportunity to take off. If by an extraordinary
chance the enemy forgot to eliminate the airfield until after they had taken off, the pilots
would certainly find their airbase a charred
and desolate ruin by the time they returned.

Below: Here about to be catapulted from
a land airfield, the A-4 Skyhawk typifies
the simple kind of close-support attack
platform that might be able to disperse
into the countryside. If airfields were
allowed to survive the A-4 could do a
great job.

The future of CAS

If there is one factor that has dominated all others in the overall field of warfare during the past several decades it is the overwhelming importance of electronics. This term is used in the broadest sense to mean the use of sensors operating at any of a wide range of wavelengths to discover what is going on or where

things are located, secure transmission channels to send back information or pictures in real time without an enemy being able to eavesdrop, and (above all in this context) the launching of air strikes in the most certain knowledge that every unguided bomb will hit exactly where it is intended.

Of course, this paints a very one-sided picture. If it were true, somebody would probably start a war. In the real world there are

likely to be at least an equal number "bad guys" sitting on SAMs and triple-A, absolutely confident that they can hack down 100 per cent. And this is where the importance of electronics comes in. The only way a CAS pilot of the 21st century will be able to fly his mission — in fact, probably the only way he will get as far as retracting his gear on take-off — will be to be seated in an aircraft that does not need an airfield of known location, and which has such

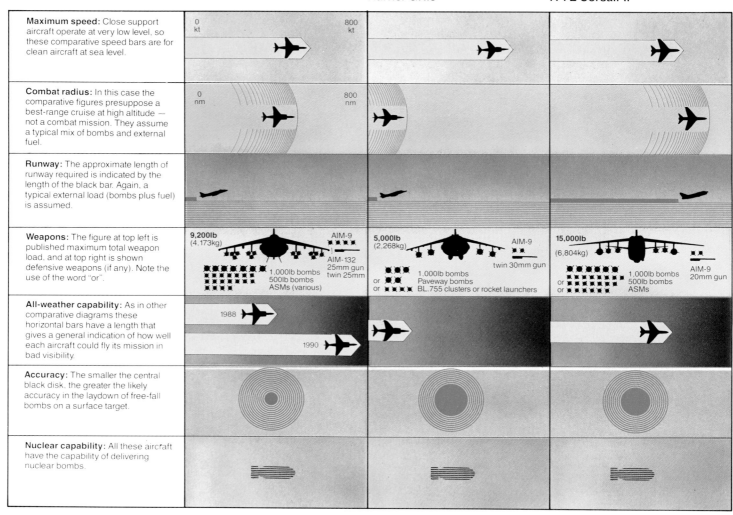

	AV-8B Harrier II	Harrier GR.3	A-7E Corsair II
Maximum speed: Close support aircraft operate at very low level, so these comparative speed bars are for clean aircraft at sea level.	0 kt / 800 kt		
Combat radius: In this case the comparative figures presuppose a best-range cruise at high altitude — not a combat mission. They assume a typical mix of bombs and external fuel.	0 nm / 800 nm		
Runway: The approximate length of runway required is indicated by the length of the black bar. Again, a typical external load (bombs plus fuel) is assumed.			
Weapons: The figure at top left is published maximum total weapon load, and at top right is shown defensive weapons (if any). Note the use of the word "or".	9,200lb (4,173kg) — AIM-9 / AIM-132 25mm gun twin 25mm / 1,000lb bombs 500lb bombs ASMs (various)	5,000lb (2,268kg) — AIM-9 / twin 30mm gun / 1,000lb bombs or Paveway bombs or BL.755 clusters or rocket launchers	15,000lb (6,804kg) — AIM-9 20mm gun / 1,000lb bombs 500lb bombs or ASMs
All-weather capability: As in other comparative diagrams these horizontal bars have a length that gives a general indication of how well each aircraft could fly its mission in bad visibility.	1988 / 1990		
Accuracy: The smaller the central black disk, the greater the likely accuracy in the laydown of free-fall bombs on a surface target.			
Nuclear capability: All these aircraft have the capability of delivering nuclear bombs.			

In these diagrams the contrast in weapon load and delivery accuracy between the Harrier I (GR.3) and Harrier II (AV-8B) is rendered obvious, but what cannot easily be shown is the fact that, should there ever be a war between the superpowers, all Harriers — and no other aircraft whatsoever — would be likely to survive beyond the first day. The only way that other aircraft could survive would be if the Soviet Union omitted, for any reason, to fire their heavy missiles at present targeted on NATO airfields. In a real war it is unlikely that this could happen, so NATO has to reckon on airfield-based airpower vanishing before the conflict starts.

◄ Harrier GR3

Power plant: One RR Pegasus 103 (21,500lb/ 95.6kN)
Span: 25ft 3in (7.7m)
Length: 46ft 10in (14.27m)
Max TO weight: 25,200lb (11,430kg)
Crew: 1

◄ AV-8B Harrier II

Power plant: One RR Pegasus 11-21/Mk 105/ F402-406 (21,750lb/ 96.75kN)
Span: 30ft 4in (9.25m)
Length: 46ft 4in (14.12m)
Max TO weight: 31,000lb (14,061kg)
Crew: 1

◄ A-7E Corsair II

Power plant: One RR/ Allison TF41-2 (15,000lb/ 66.9kN)
Span: 38ft 9in (11.08m)
Length: 46ft 1.5in (14.06m)
Max TO weight: 42,000lb (19,050kg)
Crew: 1

completely "stealth" or low-observables design that the enemy genuinely remains unaware of its presence.

Today the Allied (NATO) air forces are not only about three thousand miles (4,828km) from this situation but they appear not to be even addressing it. We are still bending every sinew to trying to build aircraft which can take off (admittedly in quite a short distance) from a nice paved runway, and which will blast over

their target making a thunderous noise and pumping out megawatts of scorching flames at the back.

One has only to apply one's mind to the problem for about three consecutive seconds to see that such an aircraft is not merely pushing its luck but is sheer nonsense. It does not matter if STOVL design means "penalties". It does not matter if stealth design means "penalties". For penalties of a few per

cent the survivable aircraft does at least have a sporting chance of living to fight another day, whereas the splendid uncompromised 100 per cent aircraft has no chance whatsoever. There is absolutely no way it can even survive to be subjected to the first day's walkaround inspection. If by any chance the enemy overlooked our airfield — how optimistic can we get? — there is no way the enemy can overlook us in the sky.

| MiG-27 | F/A-18A Hornet | Nanchang A-5 | AMX |

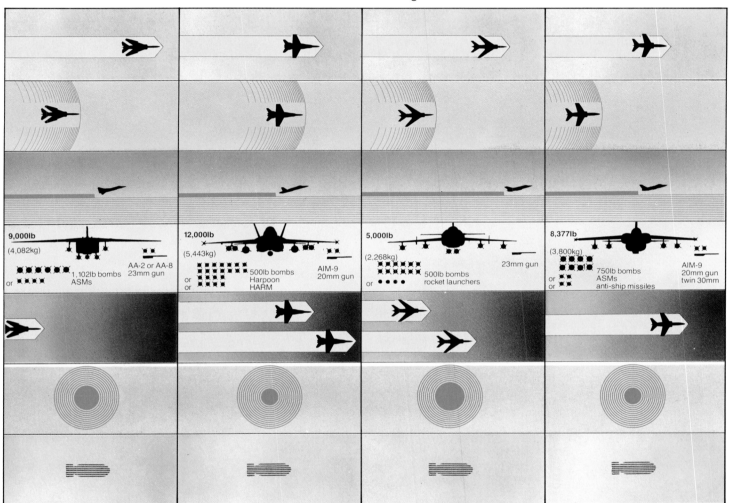

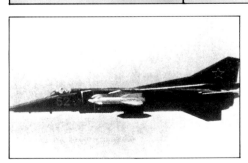

◄ MiG-27

Power plant: One Tumanskii R-29-300 (25,350lb/112.8kN)
Span: (max sweep) 26ft 9.5in (8.17m)
Length: 59ft 6.5in (18.15m)
Max TO weight: 44,313lb (20,100kg)
Crew: 1

◄ Nanchang A-5

Power plant: Two Shenyang WP-6 (7,165lb/ 31.87kN)
Span: 31ft 10in (9.7m)
Length: 53ft 4in (16.255m)
Max TO weight: 26,455lb (12,000kg)
Crew: 1

◄ F/A-18A Hornet

Power plant: Two GE F404-400 (16,000lb/ 71.2kN)
Span: (over missiles) 40ft 4.75in (12.31m)
Length: 56ft 0in (17.07m)
Max TO weight: 49,224lb (22,328kg)
Crew: 1

◄ AMX

Power plant: One RR Spey 807 (11,030lb/ 49.1kN)
Span: (over missiles) 32ft 9.75in (10.0m)
Length: 44ft 6.5in (13.575m)
Max TO weight: 27,558lb (12,500kg)
Crew: 1

The Harrier Mission

L IVING up to the service's hard-earned legend in typically aggressive Marine Corps style, the initial wave of ground troops had stormed ashore shortly after first light. In the few hours that have elapsed since then, heavily armed Bell AH-1T SeaCobra helicopter gunships and McDonnell Douglas AV-8B Harrier II V/STOL fighters have been active almost continually, performing close air support missions at very short notice as forces on the ground at first consolidated and then extended their perimeter from the original beach-head. Harrier operations are still only being conducted from the amphibious assault ship, the USS *Saipan*, which lies well out of harm's way at anchor some several miles offshore. Aboard the *Saipan*'s flight deck, two Harrier pilots while away the time as they sit in their cockpits on "strip alert", ready to launch within a matter of minutes — onshore, Marine ground echelons utilise the command and control communications network to put in an urgent call for an air strike . . .

 1300 hours

It has already been a day of intense activity for the eight AV-8B Harrier IIs operating from the amphibious assault ship USS *Saipan*. Forming part of the complement of composite Marine medium helicopter squadron HMM-264, they continue to share deck space with a mixture of rotary-winged craft that include CH-46F Sea Knights, CH-53E Super Stallions, UH-1N Iroquois and AH-1T SeaCobras, while there are also a couple of OV-10D Bronco forward air control aircraft.

The landing had been a classic assault in true Marine style, with the first troops going ashore on landing craft soon after dawn. By then, the Harriers had already completed a considerable number of sorties, having performed a series of rocket and bomb attacks against the few noteworthy targets situated in the immediate vicinity of the landing area. Having disposed of those, attention then had switched to strafing attacks, half-a-dozen aircraft working in close co-operation with four SeaCobras to lay down suppressive fire as the landing craft moved inshore before ranging further inland to engage the opposing defending forces some several hundred yards from the shore.

Now, with the troops firmly established and with much of their immediately needed equipment having been airlifted ashore by the Sea Knights and Super Stallions, it is time to begin the break out from the beach-head and extend the perimeter. Already, the handful of SeaCobras are much in demand, laying down extremely accurate cannon and rocket fire as the "grunts" (Marine ground troops) advance, the helicopter gunships periodically cycling back to the *Saipan* to refuel and rearm.

Four AV-8Bs are also airborne, with a mixture of bombs and rockets as well as gun armament, while on board the *Saipan* two more Harriers stand at "strip alert", ready to respond to an "immediate" request for air support. From his cockpit, the pilot of the lead aircraft of "Flanker" flight catches a glimpse of

Above: *Marine Corps ground troops storm ashore from landing craft in classic style during a dawn assault. Aerial firepower support for the landing was provided by SeaCobra gunship helicopters and AV-8B Harriers operating from the USS Saipan.*

Left: *Aboard the USS Saipan, deck handling personnel stand by as one of the eight AV-8Bs is brought up from the hangar deck in anticipation of joining in the continuing battle to secure the still vulnerable beach-head. Within an hour, this machine will be airborne.*

aerial activity above the battle zone a couple of miles away as two Harriers deposit a clutch of Mk.82 500lb (227kg) bombs on an unseen target, clouds of dust and smoke hanging in the air for a few minutes after they have gone. He switches radio channels and listens in on the chatter for a few moments, in an attempt to dispel the tedium and ease the discomfort, for he and his colleague have been standing alert now for close to 45 minutes.

 1301 hours

The boredom he can handle by regularly running through a quick check of aircraft systems and by imagining the activity that is going on nearby. The discomfort is rather less easy to tolerate. His bone dome, usually so comfortable, is chafing unpleasantly while the heat of the day is beginning to manifest itself in several unsavoury ways. He is aware that his close-cropped hair is damp, prompting him to make a mental note to try and find a white helmet if he has to stand strip alert again. Between his shoulder blades, where his back presses against the ejector seat, he is aware of a steadily growing patch of moisture and he begins to

Above: *On the flight deck, a pilot runs through pre-departure checks prior to launching on a close air support mission in company with another "strip alert" AV-8B. Their targets lie just a few miles inland and they will be in action within minutes of leaving the ship.*

Below: *Close air support missions in the vicinity of a beach-head can be accomplished by the AV-8B in a number of ways. Operations may be conducted from a sea base. Alternatively, a sea platform close to shore can be used or a forward operating site ashore.*

Harrier Operating Concepts

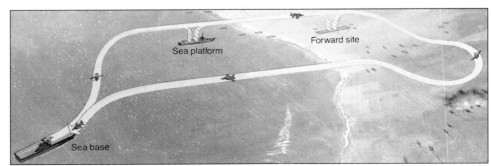

entertain visions of a cooling shower, a change of clothing and a refreshing beer, not necessarily in that order. On this boat, he thinks ruefully, the first two are possible but it certainly looks as though he'll have to wait quite some time for the third.

1302 hours

Switching back to the correct channel, he realises with a start that he is being addressed, "Did you copy that, Flanker lead?"

"Ah, negative, Jawbone (*Saipan*'s air traffic control department). You faded on me. Say again, please," he lies, in response.

1303 hours

A certain amount of testiness is evident in the reply, "Flanker flight cleared to start engines. Contact Cleveland (Tactical Air Control Centre) for brief on orange. Confirm."

"Flanker flight cleared start engines. Orange button for Cleveland. Thanks Jawbone."

Changing frequencies, he hears his wingman speak, "Repeat, two's ready to copy", and he mentally berates himself for allowing his concentration to wander for a few moments.

1304 hours

"Cleveland, Flanker lead, ready to brief."

"Ah, there you are Flanker. So nice of you to call. OK, mission number double alpha 374. Proceed direct Golf, call Bandbox on green when airborne. Confirm."

"Flanker flight, double alpha 374. Direct Golf, Bandbox on green," he reads back from the note pad on his right thigh, running through engine start procedures even as he talks to Cleveland.

1305 hours

"Battery on. APU coming up. Start switch." He recites the litany of actions to himself, his hands busy about the cockpit, hitting switches and buttons in quick succession. Behind him, buried in the Harrier's portly fuselage, the F-402-RR-406A Pegasus turbofan engine whines into life, the noise level rising in intensity as the two Harriers prepare to take flight.

In the cockpit, instruments and displays illuminate, confirming that the AV-8B is in good shape. Lifting his head, the pilot of Flanker lead looks across to his wingman and receives a confirmatory nod that he is now ready to move. Both canopies close as one as he again activates the radio, "Jawbone. Flanker flight request take-off."

"Flanker flight, clear take-off when ready."

Right: *Although the AV-8B Harrier II possesses the ability to operate with belly-mounted cannon pods, on this occasion the primary armament comprises the Mk.82 500lb bomb, each of the 12 that is carried being fitted with "Snakeye" folding fins which delay impact and allow the Harriers to move clear before they detonate.*

Above: *Satisfied that everything is operating satisfactorily, the pilot adds power and quickly accelerates to 90 knots before moving the nozzle vector control lever firmly to the 60-degree setting. Seconds later, he is clear of the ship's bow and climbing to 2,000 feet.*

Below: *Flying low and fast over typical desert terrain, Flanker Leader stays alert for aerial threats even though he has been advised that the risk of being intercepted by enemy fighters is minimal. Beneath the wings are a clutch of Mk.82 500lb bombs.*

Harrier GR.3 Weapons Options

Above: *Weapons which may be carried by Harrier GR.3s of the Royal Air Force.* **1:** *Lepus flare.* **2:** *116M rocket launcher.* **3:** *15S rocket launcher.* **4:** *1,000lb general purpose bomb.* **5:** *30mm cannon (two).* **6:** *Paveway laser guided bomb.* **7:** *BL755 cluster bomb unit.* **8:** *AIM-9L (two).*

 1308 hours

Nudging the throttle, the pilot of Flanker lead rolls forward a few yards before swinging sharply to the right and stopping at the start of the portion of flight deck which is used for take-off. Using vectored thrust with a load of 12 Mk.82 bombs and a 25mm gun pod, he will need no more than 600ft (180m) to get airborne and he quickly runs through pre-departure checks, manipulating the throttle a couple of times to confirm that the fuel control unit is up to speed before coming back to half power and hitting the switch which activates the water injection system. The RPM counter quickly verifies that all is satisfactory and he then selects a ten-degree nozzle setting, at the same time positioning the nozzle vector stop at 60 degrees.

 1310 hours

A last quick scan of the instruments reveals that all is as it should be and he pushes the throttle all the way forward, delaying the moment of brake release until he senses that the Harrier II is beginning to skid. Once free of that restraint and under the impetus of close to 22,000lb (9,980kg) of thrust, the Harrier is no slouch in the acceleration stakes, hitting 90 knots (104mph, 167km/h) in seconds.

 1311 hours

As it passes that speed, the pilot smartly pushes the nozzle vector control lever hard up against the 60-degree detent, an action which instantaneously translates the engine-generated thrust axis to one which literally pushes the Harrier into the sky. Moments later, his colleague follows him down the *Saipan*'s deck, the two aircraft joining up in loose battle formation and climbing steadily to about 2,000ft (600m) as they allow the speed to build up to just over 400 knots (460mph, 740km/h).

Above: *The various stores stations situated beneath the Harrier II's belly and wings are seen to advantage in this view of an aircraft climbing to medium altitude. Also clearly visible are the swivelling nozzles which provide the almost unparalleled agility.*

Below: *Maintaining a gentle dive as he comes up on the target, the last of Flanker Leader's clutch of bombs falls free. Within less than a second, the fins will activate, retarding the bombs and enabling the Harrier to be out of range when detonation occurs.*

 1314 hours

Since the *Saipan* is little more than three miles off shore, it takes no more than a couple of minutes to arrive at point Golf where the pilot of Flanker 28 speaks briefly to his wingman, "Flanker lead. Going to green channel."

"Two, that's green."

 1315 hours

"Er, hallo Bandbox. Flanker flight inbound at Golf."

"Hallo Flanker, Proceed Hotel and contact

Harvest 77 on blue button."

"Direct Hotel, switching to Harvest 77 on blue now."

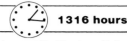
1316 hours

"Harvest 77, Flanker flight checking in, en route Hotel. What've you got for us this afternoon?"

"Hallo, Flanker lead. We've a whole bunch of artillery dug in round a village 'bout five miles east of Hotel on a heading of 275. Most of it's to the right of the road so concentrate on that. If you run in on 275 you shouldn't encounter any AAA. Coming off target, there's high ground a couple of miles beyond through the 11 o'clock to two o'clock quadrant so I'd come hard right once you've pickled."

"Rog, Harvest. We'll proceed straight to Hotel and set up from there. Lead estimates TOT (time on target) at 1324. Flanker two'll be 'bout a minute behind."

" 'kay, Flanker. Cleared in hot. Advise passing Hotel."

1318 hours

Switching his attention to the multi-function CRT display which dominates the left-hand side of the instrument panel, the Flanker lead pilot calls up the weapons configuration presentation and spends a few moments setting up the bomb release pattern, the sequence to be employed phasing jettison so that the weapons will fall in a string of six pairs. In "Snakeye" configuration, folding fins will activate moments after release, slowing the bombs' fall and permitting each AV-8B to be well clear of the target before detonation and out of range of flying fragments.

1321 hours

At 500 knots (576mph, 927km/h) it doesn't take long to cover ground and Flanker lead again activates his radio, "Harvest 77. Flanker lead's passing Hotel." At the same moment, the pilot of Flanker two hauls his aircraft round into a turn designed to introduce the desired separation in order to avoid the risk of being over the target as his leader's bombs strike home. This doesn't entirely eliminate the danger since there is always the possibility of secondary explosions. That, however, is a contingency that cannot adequately be catered for.

1322 hours

A momentary burst of static over the headphones confirms that Harvest 77 has heard the brief transmission. Flashing low over the scrubby desert terrain, Flanker lead is concentrating hard on his head-up display screen and fails to see the clutch of Marine armoured personnel carriers and ground troops as he zips over their heads at little more than 75 feet (23m). One or two soldiers wave half-heartedly at this momentary diversion before preparing to move out and advance on the village which has so far delayed their progress for almost an hour. Just 50 seconds later,

Flanker two also roars overhead but nobody bothers to wave this time . . .

1324 hours

Flanker lead's aircraft climbs rapidly, rolling inverted as it pops up to about 2,000ft (600m), the pilot looking to spot the target which should be dead ahead at a distance of about two miles. He finds the village easily enough, sees the road running through the centre of it and then spots a puff of smoke as one of the artillery pieces is fired. Making a minute correction, he pulls back on the control column to drive his Harrier over the top of the climb and then quickly rolls back right side up as he heads earthwards again in a 10 degree dive. The nearest clutch of enemy artillery slides almost painfully slowly into view on the HUD but another minor rudder input results in the TV cursor on the HUD moving nicely into position over the target. Holding it there, he hits the target designation control switch on the throttle lever to ensure that the system locks on.

His headphones crackle briefly, "Two's at Hotel inbound."

1324:25 hours

Flanker lead continues its dive towards the target, its pilot depressing the weapons release switch on the stick and holding it down even as he concentrates on keeping the TV cursor squarely on target. Inside his aircraft, computers take responsibility for the bomb release sequence, receiving inputs from a variety of sources, processing the constant flow of incoming data and, ultimately, solving the complex weapons release equation. Almost immediately 12 Mk. 82 500lb (227kg) Snakeye

A: Pilot of Flanker Lead begins attack run. **B:** Flanker flight wingman pulls away from target to achieve desired separation. **C:** Flanker Lead deposits Mk.82 500lb bombs on enemy artillery position. **D:** Flanker Lead takes post-attack evasive action and then sets course for the USS *Saipan*. **E:** Bell AH-1T SeaCobras operating from the USS *Saipan* perform fire suppression attacks against forward line of enemy troops. **F:** Forward line of steadily advancing Marine ground troops. **G:** Rockwell OV-10D Bronco forward air control aircraft "Harvest 77".

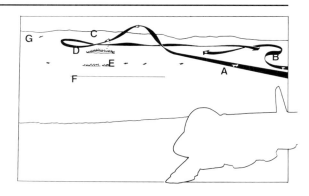

Harrier Viffing Technique

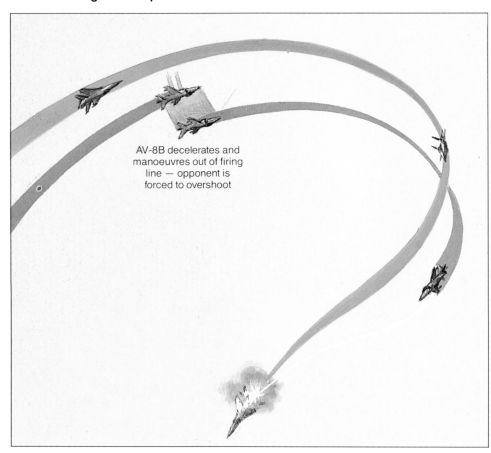

AV-8B decelerates and manoeuvres out of firing line — opponent is forced to overshoot

Above: Use of vectoring in forward flight (VIFF) capability makes the Harrier a hard opponent to beat in aerial combat. In this drawing, a Harrier employs VIFF to force an opponent to overshoot into a position of disadvantage in which the Harrier rapidly becomes the hunter.

Below: Having successfully attacked the enemy artillery emplacements, the two Harriers rejoin in close formation soon after crossing the coast and going "feet wet". On their way out, they will also have reported strike results to the Marine Corps command and control network.

free-fall retarded bombs are released, flicking open as they clear the aircraft. The parachute retarded descent enabling the Harrier 11 to clear the impact area before detonation.

 1324:30 hours

In the cockpit, the pilot feels his aircraft lighten as it is relieved of its burden and immediately initiates a right-hand turn, easing back on the control column so as to level out and leave the area at little more than 50ft (15m). As he goes, he weaves his aircraft from left to right just in case any trigger-happy ground gunner has managed to draw a bead on him. As he withdraws, he calls, "Flanker lead is out on zero-zero-five."

 1325 hours

Behind, the 12 bombs strike home, dust and debris being flung skywards as they detonate among the artillery pieces in quick succession. As he sets up his attack, the pilot of Flanker two is aware of the destruction that has preceded him. He curses briefly as drifting smoke obscures his aim point and looks momentarily like fouling up his bombing pass but it quickly clears and he is once again too intent on positioning his TV cursor on target to pay much attention to the scene.

 1326 hours

Employing identical procedures to his leader, Flanker two uses the mid-point of the artillery line as an aiming point, the bomb pattern slightly overlapping that of his colleague but extending some way further, with the result that the final pair of Mk.82s overshoot to explode harmlessly about 50ft (15m) beyond the last emplacement.

 1326:30 hours

By then, Flanker two is also leaving the area, calling "Two's off on zero-zero-five."

 1327 hours

"Harvest to Flanker flight. Nice work. Very nice work. Don't think we'll be needing you again right now."

"Flanker lead. Thanks Harvest. We'll bug out to rearm if you're through with our services."

"Roger, Flanker. Call Bandbox on green."

"Bandbox on green, G'day Harvest."

"Hallo Bandbox, Flanker flight's off target, heading for Delta."

"Roger, Flanker. Proceed independently to Delta then direct to Jawbone. Call at Delta."

"You hear that, two? Let's rendevous at Delta, confirm."

"Two. See you at Delta."

 1329 hours

"Flanker flight to Cleveland. Inflight report, Mission double alpha 374."

Left: *With the large trailing edge flaps at maximum deflection and the thrust vectoring nozzles fully down, the pilot of Flanker Lead allows his aircraft to gradually overhaul the USS* Saipan *before moving inboard and easing back on the throttle, an action which permits the Harrier to slowly settle into the designated landing area. Once there, he will taxi smartly to a pre-arranged parking spot.*

"Cleveland, Flanker. Ready to copy."

"OK. Target was artillery — 'bout eight pieces, I'd say, five miles east of Hotel. Don't have precise co-ordinates. TOT 1324 slash '26 local. Bomb pattern looked good. On line and on target. Didn't see any sign of continued firing after we hit but the FAC might have more to say about the results. That's Harvest 77 on blue, by the way. Didn't note any defensive activity beyond sporadic small arms fire. No battle damage to report. All bombs expended so we're heading back to rearm."

"Ah, thanks Flanker."

 1330 hours

"Hallo Bandbox. Flanker's at Delta."

"Roger, Flanker. Cleared direct to Jawbone, call them on red."

"Direct Jawbone. Call on red."

 1331 hours

Switching frequencies yet again, Flanker lead notifies the *Saipan*'s air traffic staff that the two Harriers are returning and receives clearance to begin approach. Lead and wingman then break formation to set up in trail for recovery, the lead aircraft flying a standard approach, lowering gear and flaps while still about four miles (6km) from the ship. At about half-a-mile (0.8km) from the landing spot, the pilot of the lead aircraft begins to prepare for landing, calling the tower to request clearance and initiating the transition from conventional flight to vertical flight. Nozzle deflection is first set at 40 degrees, this being maintained while speed bleeds off to roughly 140 knots (161mph, 260km/h) at which point the nozzles are progressively vectored until they reach the hover stop with downwards deflection of 81 degrees.

Above: *Stick-actuated reaction controls permit the pilot of Flanker Lead to hold his attitude and heading as his aircraft gently settles on the deck. Elsewhere aboard the* Saipan, *munitions specialists are busy preparing ordnance for yet another strike.*

Below: *Observed by deck crew, the wingman brings his aircraft safely aboard. On landing, he will reset the nozzle lever fully aft, select nosewheel steering and follow the crew's directions as he moves to a nearby parking spot for re-arming and refuelling.*

 1335 hours

Now, the Harrier is hovering over the sea, adjacent to the landing spot at about 100ft (30m). Moving inboard, the pilot gradually eases back on the throttle and the AV-8B slowly begins to settle, stick-actuated reaction controls allowing heading and attitude to be maintained as the aircraft descends, the pilot quickly moving the throttle lever back to the idle position and shifting the nozzle vector lever to fully aft when he senses that he has arrived on deck. Selecting nose-wheel steering, he blips the throttle slightly and swings sharply right as he taxis to the adjacent parking spot, following directions from deck crew and turning through 180 degrees so as to leave his aircraft ready to fly again when it has been refuelled and rearmed.

The Hornet Mission

WITHIN a matter of hours of the airfield being captured by troops assigned to the Marine Corps expeditionary force, the McDonnell Douglas F/A-18 Hornets of VMFA-333 "Shamrocks" had flown in from their US base at Cherry Point, North Carolina. Deposited by helicopter a few hours earlier, the Marines had unwittingly stumbled upon a real hornet's nest and were now in danger of being decimated by a numerically superior enemy force. In the hours that had followed troop insertion, two attempts at recovery had already failed spectacularly and both time and ammunition were now very much at a premium. For the friendly troops, the pair of F/A-18 Hornets that comprised "Marble Flight" were the "big guns" that would, if all went well, prevent them from being overrun and, at the same time, clear the way for their eventual extraction by a number of Boeing-Vertol CH-46E Sea Knight helicopters that were ready and waiting for the opportunity to go to the rescue.

They had moved in to the airfield within hours of it being taken by Marine ground forces, the dozen Hornets of VMFA-333 being the first tactical jets to arrive and alleviate the burden that thus far had been borne solely by the handful of AV-8B Harriers assigned to the composite helicopter squadron aboard the USS *Saipan*. The long transit flight had been possible only with the aid of several KC-130 Hercules in-flight refuelling tankers but other "trash-haulers" — mostly provided by the Air Force's Military Airlift Command — were now beginning to arrive in considerable numbers, staying on the ground only long enough to offload supplies. At the moment, the defensive perimeter was far from secure, "search and destroy" parties having reported several encounters with enemy forces and the coming night was likely to be "quite exciting" in the words of the squadron commander.

For the pilots who had brought the Hornets, such matters were far from mind for they had been kept exceedingly busy throughout the hours which had elapsed since their arrival. Some Sparrow- and Sidewinder-armed aircraft were undertaking combat air patrol missions but the threat from enemy fighters was considered minimal. As a result, most of the Hornets were operating in the close air support role, bomb-laden aircraft helping the "grunts" to deal with obstacles at half-a-dozen different locations as they fought to subdue the opposition.

Attempts had been made by the enemy to deny use of the airfield, several sustained artillery bombardments forcing personnel to take cover. However, apart from reducing one CH-46E Sea Knight to a burned out hulk and forcing the dispersal of the various assets on hard standings around the airfield, this had achieved little.

The vital runway had thus far suffered only slightly, one shell impacting at its eastern extremity where engineers were hard at work filling in a crater in the overrun. This had had little impact on Hornet operations (and even less on the Harriers), since all departures to date had been made from the western end of the 9,000-foot (2,750m) strip and there was plenty of concrete available for all but the most heavily laden aircraft.

Above: *Pictured shortly after arrival at the freshly captured airfield, a Marine Corps Hornet is silhouetted against the early morning sun as, with canopy ajar, it sits and awaits its first mission. Within hours, it will be a veteran, with several combat sorties to its credit.*

 **1520 hours**

In the office which has been taken over to serve as a temporary briefing room, two pilots gather up their kit and prepare to move out to

Left: *As the day's warmth builds up, so does the pace of activity, VMFA-333's Hornets coming and going with monotonous regularity as they carry the war into the hinterland. Some are employed in the close air support mission while others fly "top cover" for strike elements.*

Below: *With many of the missions calling for ground strafing, armourers are kept particularly busy, servicing cannons and replenishing gun magazines during the all too brief intervals that VMFA-333's F-18 aircraft spend on the ground between succeeding sorties.*

their aircraft. They have been tasked to attack an enemy defensive position about 90 miles (145km) away. There, an element of Marines has come under intense pressure within five minutes of being inserted by helicopter. At least two attempts have been made to get in again and retrieve them but these have been frustrated by accurate ground fire.

On the first occasion, one Iroquois helo had been shot down while the presence of a couple of SeaCobra gunships which laid down suppressive fire during the second attempt some 20 minutes later had not prevented two CH-46s from sustaining damage, one managing to limp a few hundred yards clear of the drop zone before being forced to crash-land when its transmission seized up. Although shaken and bruised, the crew had been retrieved and were even now being brought back to base, but it was clear that heavier metal would be needed to prevent the Marine troops from being overrun.

What was evolving was essentially a holding action and a couple of Harriers had been diverted from a less urgent tasking to work over the area with rocket and gun fire. The Hornets would be the second wave and would go into action with a mixture of Mk.82 500lb (227kg) bombs, cluster bomb units and cannon fire, hopefully working in close co-operation with a pair of SeaCobras in order to lay down sustained counter-air power. It was hoped that this would permit "slick" (unarmed) troop-carrying helicopters to move in and pick up the Marines before nightfall.

As they brief for the mission, ground personnel are busy preparing two Hornets which had returned from another close air support tasking barely 40 minutes earlier. Now, with a fresh load of munitions and with fuel tanks topped off, they are ready to move out again.

 1525 hours

Stowing their few items of kit in the Jeep, the two pilots clamber aboard, taking care to avoid the ferocious looking soldier who sits sprawled in the back, cradling an M60 machine gun in his lap.

"Real glad you're on our side, soldier," says

Right: *In addition to the armourers, ground support technicians are also hard at work, ensuring that a high standard of serviceability is maintained throughout the day. Here, personnel study the upper surfaces of a Hornet that will soon be required to get airborne again.*

one, his attempt at humour meeting no response.

"You *are* on our side, aren't you?" says the other, before reaching forward to tap the driver on his shoulder. "OK driver. Times Square and don't spare the horses. Me and my buddy could use a beer."

"Times Square? Don't say nothin' 'bout Times Square on my requisition," replies the driver.

"Forget it. Just take us to Charlie dispersal, OK?"

"Yessir . . ."

1545 hours

They have completed their pre-flight inspection, signed the acceptance forms for the two aircraft and are now settling into their respective cockpits. A muted whine indicates that the auxiliary power unit is running and they waste little time in activating the BITE (built-in test equipment) programme which quickly verifies that the complex package of avionics is fully operable. Outside, three ground crew wait, one standing near the ever-present fire extinguisher, more in hope than expectation.

1547 hours

Activating his radio, the pilot of the lead aircraft speaks briefly, "Boston, Boston (tower call sign). Marble flight request radio check and start clearance."

Close to a minute elapses before he tries again.

"Ah, Boston. Marble flight request radio check and start clearance."

"Roger, Marble. Strength five, clear start. Call when ready to taxi."

1549 hours

Intense activity ensues, both pilots bringing their aircraft to life before running through a sequence of pre-taxi checks and verifying that the various flight control surfaces are all working satisfactorily. Outside, ground crew scurry back and forth, using hand signals to notify the pilots that all is well and moving the few items of ground equipment clear.

"Boston, Marble flight's ready to roll."

"Roger, Marble. Clear taxi to holding point for 27. Weather as briefed."

Above: A technician removes part of the laser spot tracker pod from a bomb-laden F/A-18A since this item of kit will not be required on the forthcoming sortie. Other ordnance carried by the pair of Hornets that comprise "Marble" flight includes cluster bomb units.

Below: Firmly ensconced in his cockpit, the pilot of "Marble" Lead contacts the tower and requests a radio check and clearance to start engines. In a matter of minutes, he and his wingman will be rolling towards the active runway at the start of another mission.

1553 hours

Signalling to the ground crew to remove the chocks, the pilot of Marble lead waits to receive confirmation from the crew chief that all is well. A hand signal answers his unspoken question and he manipulates the throttle, a touch of power being all that is needed to propel his aircraft on to the taxiway that leads to runway 27. Behind, the second Hornet rolls forward, its nose dipping momentarily as the pilot checks the brakes before swinging right and trundling off in pursuit.

1556 hours

As they hold at the ''last chance'' check point, both pilots have their hands out of the cockpit, resting on the framing while armourers are busy below, pulling safing pins and checking that fusing wires are correctly attached to the ordnance which hangs suspended on the racks. Unable to play any part in this process, both pilots look on almost disinterestedly as a couple of other Hornets whistle in to land, their empty bomb racks providing mute confirmation that they have been in action. A hand signal from one of the armourers indicates that both aircraft have been checked and they roll forward again to the holding point, closing their canopies and arming the ejection seats as they move.

1559 hours

''Boston, Boston. Marble's at holding point, hot to trot.''

''Roger, Marble. Cleared take-off, right turn-out on to 080 once airborne and contact Pyramid (Marine Air Control Squadron call sign) on red.''

''Right turn to 080. Pyramid on red. Marble over and out.''

1600 hours

Rolling forward, the two aircraft take up position on the runway, lead moving to the left with his wingman tucking in slightly astern on his right. Both pilots then run through a quick power check, the familiar routine being well instilled by months of training back in the USA. Cutting back to idle, Marble lead looks to his right, observes a hand signal reporting that all is well with his wingman and then points down the runway.

1601 hours

At the dispersal recently vacated, the ground crew pause from their labours as the roar of engines signals Marble flight's departure. They watch for a few moments as the pair of

Left: Hauling back on the control column as the Hornet hurtles down the runway, the pilot of ''Marble Two'' lifts his F/A-18A into the air right on schedule. Ahead of him lies a 20-minute trip to the combat zone where Marine ground forces await help.

Above: Shortly after getting airborne, the two Hornets adopt battle formation, the wingman splitting away to take up station some 5,000 feet away so as to limit the possibility of being taken by surprise by any enemy fighter aircraft that may be prowling around.

Below: With a clutch of Mk.82 500lb bombs fixed securely beneath the wings, ''Marble'' lead heads towards the battle zone at a cruising speed of around 500 knots. At the same time, he keeps the Marine command and control net informed of the progress he is making.

Hornets roar down the runway in close formation before breaking ground simultaneously. Within seconds, both aircraft have ''cleaned up'' and been lost from view in the haze, the noise of jet engines fading fast as they swing round almost to reverse their course on to the new heading of 080.

1604 hours

Levelling out at 500 feet (150m), Marble lead switches radio channels and speaks, ''Pyramid. Marble flight checking in.''

''Hallo Marble. Continue on 080 to point Golf, then direct Lima. Advise passing Golf.''

''080 to Golf, then direct Lima. Call at Golf.''

Changing frequency yet again, he calls his wingman. ''Lead to Marble two. D'you copy that?''

'' 'firmative skipper.''

'' 'kay, let's open out now.''

1605 hours

The previously tight formation now splits as the two pilots move left and right, taking up new positions with about 5,000ft (1,500m) of lateral separation, so as to reduce the likelihood of their being ''bounced'' by enemy fighters. On this occasion, the risk is perceived as minimal but, as always, it is better to be safe than sorry.

1608 hours

As the two Hornets move further north-east, they pass over evidence of the previous few days of intensive fighting. Here, a clutch of burnt out artillery pieces, there a few wisps of smoke still rise from the remnants of battered villages, punctuation points which mark the path taken by the Marines. Ahead, barely visible in the distance, are the mountains, their presence emphasised by an angry looking bank of cloud.

1611 hours

At 500 knots (576mph, 927km/h), it doesn't take long to reach the first way-point and the pilot of Marble lead thumbs his radio switch, "Pyramid, Pyramid. Marble formation's at Golf, heading for Lima."

"Ahh, roger, Marble. Hold at Lima for instructions."

"Hold at Lima."

Switching channels, he calls, "D'you copy that, two?"

"Rog, Skipper, hold at Lima. Sure looks a mess down below, don't it."

"Yeah. Can't think why anyone'd be prepared to fight for this piece of real estate. It's worse than Nellis . . . and I always thought Nellis was the pits."

"Oh, I dunno . . . there's always Vegas . . . ."

"Yeah, well maybe. Anyway, let's cut the chatter. We've got a job to do and we're coming up on Lima."

1613 hours

Even as Marble flight approaches the next check point, the Marine troops are feeling the pressure of a numerically superior enemy force. Probing attacks on them have been made at several points but these have thus far been repelled, although the number of casualties is beginning to rise to alarming proportions. Worse still, though, is the fact that the Marines are in danger of being encircled, the corridor to the west inexorably shrinking as the defensive perimeter slowly collapses. If the helicopters don't arrive soon, there will be nobody left to rescue.

1614 hours

"Pyramid. Marble's just coming up on Lima. D'you still want us to hold?"

"Ah, negative, Marble. Proceed direct Quebec, contact Touchstone on blue."

"Direct Quebec, Touchstone on blue. Thanks Pyramid."

Changing channels, he talks briefly to his wingman, "OK two. Let's go to blue, shall we?"

"Rog, skipper."

"Touchstone, Touchstone. Marble flight inbound. What've you got for us today?"

1615 hours

On the ground in a dried up river bed a few miles away, the forward air controller attached to the Marine force keeps his head well down as he finishes talking to a solitary SeaCobra which is fighting a losing battle against the constantly pressing enemy. For the past ten minutes or so, it has been the only air power available but it has been instrumental in preventing the friendly troops from being overrun, less than 200 yards (180m) separating the opposing forces in some areas.

Now out of ammunition and perilously low on fuel, the two-man crew of the gunship helicopter almost certainly face the prospect of having to land some way short of base but they will at least be able to fly back to a position of safety. For the ground elements, the picture is rather more ominous but the imminent arrival of the two Hornets looks like offering some respite and the FAC is clearly pleased to learn that they are on their way. "Boy, am I glad to hear you, Marble. We're in a pretty bad way down here. Any news of the choppers?"

"Negative, Touchstone. Suggest you call Pyramid for word of them. In the meantime, where d'you want us to start?"

"OK Marble. We've two main problem areas right now. One north-east and one south-east. What ordnance you toting?"

"Mk.82s and CBUs, Touchstone."

"Ah, good. Well, for openers, how about dumping a few CBUs to the north-east of us. If you run in on a heading of about 095 from Quebec you should get a good visual on the burning Sea Knight. There's a whole bunch of gooks in that area that we'd like taken out."

"OK, that's no problem. What about the other target, Touchstone?"

"I think a few Mk.82s'd be the best idea there. There's a couple of heavy mortars that are pretty well zeroed in on us right now. They're about a thousand yards from our right flank and it'd probably be best to deal with them first. Heading of 110 ought to do it but you'll have to pull hard left when you're coming off target so as to avoid some high ground that lies beyond."

"Thanks, Touchstone."

"Be glad if you could be quick, Marble, we're taking some some heavy casualties down here."

"'kay, Touchstone, we'll call in and out."

A: "Marble" Leader initiates pull up for weapons delivery, before rolling inverted to "eyeball" the target and pulling over the top. **B:** Having rolled right side up again, "Marble" Lead pickles his ordnance. **C:** "Marble" Lead's Mk.82 500lb bombs impact right on target and destroy the enemy mortar battery. **D:** "Marble" Two runs in for laydown attack with cluster bomb units. **E:** Line denotes position of Marine Corps ground troops as they await extraction by CH-46E Sea Knight helicopters.

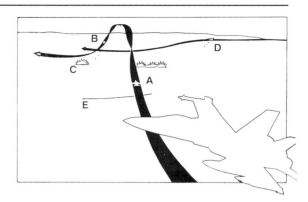

1618 hours

For the next couple of minutes both pilots busy themselves setting up the attack, calling up the ordnance presentation on the master monitor display screen which dominates the left-hand side of the instrument panel and selecting their respective weapons. Marble lead is going for the more difficult target, for Touchstone's instructions were by no means clear as to the precise location of the mortar battery. So as to give himself a better chance of achieving his objective on the first pass, Marble lead opts for a pop-up manoeuvre, rolling inverted as he climbs so as to get a clear look at the general area.

1621 hours

He is fortunate in that a puff of smoke from one of the enemy mortars catches his eye as he rises and he realises that he is more or less directly on track to engage it, only the smallest of corrections being needed as, still inverted, he pulls over the top, rolling right side up a fraction of a second later and seeing the pipper slide neatly into place. Thumbing the target designator control, he continues to hold the pipper on target and hits the "pickle" button, initiating the weapons delivery process, computers performing all the calculations necessary to ensure accurate delivery. Moments later, four Mk.82 "slick" (low drag) bombs slide free of the outer wing racks and begin their brief fall to earth. But even as they plummet downwards, Marble lead is into a brutal left-hand turn, the aircraft skidding slightly as, with afterburner engaged, it accelerates away.

1622 hours

At the same moment as the Mk.82s detonate, some 2,000 yards (1,830m) away, Marble two releases a brace of CBUs in level flight from an altitude of about 500 feet (150m), these falling almost lazily earthwards, before bursting open and disgorging their cargo of deadly bomblets along the line of enemy troops close to the wrecked Sea Knight. Now free to manoeuvre, Marble two dives lower, the pilot also engaging afterburner and reefing into a left-hand turn so as to get clear of the area as quickly as possible.

As he leaves, ahead and off to his left, he sees the dust cloud that marks the spot where lead's bombs impacted and notes a secondary explosion as he flashes past the remains of the mortar battery which has been well and truly put out of action. The CBUs have also done their work well for the intensity of fire originating from that quadrant is now greatly muted.

1623 hours

"Touchstone, Marble lead. How're things down there now?"

"Just dandy, Marble. That was right on the money."

"Anything else we can do for you, Touchstone?"

F/A-18 Radar Navigation and Attack Modes

Above: *One of the great advantages of the Hornet's AN/APG-65 radar is the Doppler beam sharpening facility which permits a pilot to vary the image ratio for navigation and identification or attack. At left is shown the 19:1 ratio while at right can be seen the 67:1 ratio.*

Below: *Even as "Marble" Flight is engaging the enemy ground force, another strike package is setting off to find combat, the pilots and technicians of VMFA-333 being hard-pressed to satisfy all of the claims that they are receiving for close air support.*

"You bet, Marble. How about dumping a few CBUs in our 12 o'clock? We're taking heavy small arms fire from there. I'd say the range is about 600 yards."

"Can do."

1624 hours

Switching frequencies, Marble lead confers briefly with his wingman, telling him to orbit some way off to the south because, since Marble two has expended all his CBUs, it falls to lead to make this pass. Unfortunately, the degree of accuracy is less satisfactory, possibly as a result of the Hornet pilot wishing to make sure that he does not bomb friendly forces. Whatever the reason, most of the bomblets explode harmlessly beyond the opposition but they do at least result in a slight diminution of small arms fire.

1626 hours

"Hallo Marble, Touchstone."

"Yes, Touchstone . . ."

F/A-18 Weapons Options

Above: *1: Rocket pod. 2: Mk.82 500lb bomb. 3: AGM-65 Maverick ASM. 4: "Walleye" ASM. 5: Mk.82 500lb bomb. 6: Rockeye CBU. 7: Mk.83 1,000lb low drag bomb. 8: Vulcan M61A1 20mm gun. 9: Harpoon ASM. 10: AGM-88A HARM. 11: AIM-7F AAM. 12: AIM-9L AAM.*

Left: *With bomb racks now empty, Marble Lead breaks left to set up for his recovery. During the downwind leg, the pilot will lower flaps and landing gear, coming in "hot" so as to present a difficult target for any enemy forces that might still be lurking in the vicinity of the airfield perimeter.*

it bursts into life. Below, dust and dirt flies everywhere as the rounds strike home, the noise of jets and gunfire being overlaid by the metronomic "thwock-thwock-thwock" of the helicopters.

 1634 hours

A final burst of gunfire disappears into the smoke as the last Marines clamber aboard. They barely have time to strap in before the engine note deepens and the Sea Knights lift from the ground, wheeling smartly about and heading off to the south in a nose-down attitude as they accelerate away from the danger zone. Behind them, Marble two lets fly with one final burst of cannon fire, his earphones crackling momentarily with static as he pulls off target, "Lead to two. Looks like the party's over. Rejoin at Quebec."

 1646 hours

Now well clear of the war zone after an uneventful return journey, the two Hornets maintain tight formation as they run in towards the airfield at 800 feet (240m), Marble two breaking to set up his final approach as they pass abeam the control tower. Moments later, Marble lead follows suit, both pilots selecting gear and flaps down during the downwind leg which culminates in a tightly curving final approach that takes them directly over a Hawk surface-to-air missile site on the airfield perimeter. Seconds later, they touch down, rolling to the far end of the runway and turning right onto the parallel taxiway, pausing briefly while weapons specialists insert safing devices into unspent ordnance.

 1650 hours

Back at dispersal, the crew chiefs note the scorch marks on the nose of each aircraft and peer intently at the weapons racks as they direct the Hornets back to their parking spots. For the pilots, another mission is almost over, their next stop being the ready room to check in, since they will probably be airborne again before too long. A quick debriefing will take place but the job of writing up after-action reports will almost certainly have to wait until later, when the level of hectic activity has diminished.

For the ground crews, their work is about to begin, since both Hornets are scheduled to be aloft again in less than an hour. Even as the pilots unbuckle and clamber out of their cockpits, armourers stand by to begin loading another batch of ordnance while a fuel bowser rumbles up to await its turn in the precisely ordered routine of preparing aircraft for combat. Elsewhere, two more pilots are being briefed to go back to war . . .

"Ah've just got word that the choppers should be with us in a couple of minutes. No 'Cobras I'm afraid, though. How's about you guys laying down some suppressive gunfire when they come in to pick us up?"

"Sure thing, Touchstone."

"Okay. Looks as though the major problem s'far as we're concerned is still at 12 o'clock so I guess the best thing would be for you to work over that area."

"Er, Roger."

 1627 hours

Changing channels, Marble lead quickly confers with his colleague over the tactics they will use during the moment of pick-up when the helicopters will be at their most vulnerable. Basically, they will employ adjoining "race-track" patterns with both aircraft flying a clockwise circuit which will result in firing passes being made from opposite directions at intervals of no more than a minute. In this way, target coverage will be maximised, the risk of collision will be virtually non-existent and, since the entire evacuation should take no more than three minutes, the possibility of the enemy forces figuring out Marble flight's tactics and taking effective counter-action will be low. Pattern altitude will be little more than 200 feet, (60m) the Hornets popping up at the last minute to roll in on target.

Even as they engage in laying down suppressive fire, an escorting UH-1N Iroquois helicopter will make a north-south pass at very low level. The Huey's door gunners will also open fire, other crew members flinging out smoke canisters on the narrow strip of land between the opposing groups of troops, this

being intended to screen the two CH-46s that will then move in from the west to evacuate the Marines who will, during the previous few minutes, have retreated to the original landing zone to await collection.

 1630 hours

Despite the fact that it is a hastily-conceived plan, it works almost flawlessly, the only minor setback involving the smoke-laying Huey which comes under quite intense gunfire as it flies between the opposing forces. For a few moments, it looks as though it will escape unscathed but it is hit by a burst of machine gun fire right at the end of its run-by. Most of the half-a-dozen shells that strike the Huey pass harmlessly through the tail boom but one of the door gunners sustains a fairly minor injury, a couple of shell splinters penetrating his right combat boot and embedding themselves in his foot.

 1631 hours

His colleagues go to work to repair the damage as the pair of CH-46Es slide in to the pick-up zone in a nose-high attitude, downwash causing the thick cloud of smoke to swirl and eddy in front of them. A couple of gunners from each Sea Knight rush out of the open rear ramp to direct fire through the smoke at the unseen enemy while others herd the harassed Marines aboard, the withdrawal being accomplished in orderly fashion despite the sense of urgency that prevails.

As they load, a Hornet dives towards the ground, shells spewing from the Vulcan gun which emits its characteristic tearing sound as

THE
INTERDICTION/STRIKE
MISSION

Evolution of the Mission

THE INTERDICTION mission is in general terms intermediate between the close-support attack mission and the strategic bomber mission. It has little to do directly with the ground battlefront, except perhaps to fly straight across it. Its targets are deep in the enemy hinterland, and they ought in principle to be mobile (because otherwise it would be far more sensible to use a missile rather than a manned aircraft). Whereas a strategic bomber may have to fly over intercontinental distances, the interdictor may have to fly perhaps 1,000 miles (1,600km) each way. It may carry nuclear, conventional or various other stores, and may fly its mission alone or in company with other aircraft, in either a tight or very loose formation.

The interdiction/strike (IDS) mission has a rather short history. The term was first used in air warfare to describe the operations of fighter-bombers, in particular Hawker Typhoons, against bridges, rail junctions, canal locks and similar targets in the final few weeks prior to D-day (the invasion of Hitler's Europe on 6 June 1944). Strictly, to interdict means to prohibit or forbid. These interdiction missions were intended to prohibit the easy movement of ground forces and supplies,

not just in the area immediately behind where the Allied landings took place (because that would have given away the location) but in a broad belt along the coast from Brittany to the Low Countries.

The interdiction mission is thus usually concerned with relatively small "point" targets which can be of great importance to a land battle, but (as in the case of these Typhoon missions) they can take place before any land battle has started. In theory the same targets could have been attacked by accurate level bombing by "heavies", but the interdiction mission has from the start been associated with fighter/attack type aircraft flying at low level.

Bearing in mind the actual meaning of the word, the interdiction mission (adding the word strike seems tautological and pointless) has as its objective the prohibition of an act on the part of the enemy. By the 1950s most air staffs distinguished between two forms. BAI, battlefield air interdiction, is concerned with attacks on bridges, junctions, choke points, and similar locations behind the battle area, in order to restrict the enemy's freedom of tactical movement and prevent him from bringing up reserves to reinforce the battle in progress. It can (so the majority of textbooks

Below: *Armed with eight RPs (rocket projectiles) with 60lb warheads, as well as four 20mm cannon, the Hawker Typhoon IB was one of the most important Allied tactical aircraft of World War II, flying both close support and interdiction missions. The close-range flak was deadly.*

While the close air support mission is concerned only with immediate tactical operations, the interdiction mission strikes quite deep behind the front and always involves prolonged penetration of hostile airspace. Obviously, fixed targets such as bridges, road/rail junctions and airfields are best eliminated by missiles, but aircraft are still essential for hitting moving targets.

Above: One of the first Martin B-26 Marauders, in 1941. Later more developed versions served in large numbers, especially with the US 9th Air Force in Europe, flying the medium-altitude level bombing type of interdiction mission. Today such a mission would probably be suicidal.

Below: This McDonnell F-101A Voodoo set a speed record in 1957. The F-101 was planned as an escort fighter to accompany bombers deep into hostile airspace, but later matured in other roles including, as the F-101C, that of interdictor carrying a free-fall nuclear bomb at low level.

have said) be flown by subsonic aircraft with medium range. The last quality is hard to define. In the years after World War II the DC-4 airliner, with a range of 1,500 miles (2,400km) with full payload, was called "long-range"; today the Airbus A-310 is called "medium range" though it can carry full payload 5,700 miles (9,175km). In the BAI context one normally thinks of a combat radius of only about 200 miles (322km).

Air interdiction

The other form, AI, air interdiction, is very similar but goes deeper into enemy territory. Its objectives are to restrict the enemy's freedom of tactical and operational movement, and to neutralise his efforts to bring up forces from his rear areas. Of course, the mission distances depend on the theatre and size of the countries involved, but a combat radius of 1,000 miles (1,600km) might well be possible. Like BAI, air interdiction must be capable of being carried out at night or in bad weather; for 30 years it has been described as "all weather", but the ability to fly such a mission in gales, blizzards and thick fog has been

acquired only quite recently. Unlike BAI, AI is generally held to require supersonic performance, though certainly not with full load at low level.

Before discussing theoretical aspects further it is as well to pick up the historical thread again. During the Korean war the new jets lacked range and weapon load and the B-26 Invader and A-1 Skyraider lacked speed — but it was the latter that had to fly the interdiction missions, often by night. To some degree such US naval jets as the F9F and F2H could fly interdiction missions by being brought nearer to their targets aboard their carrier. Probably the best aircraft in the world for interdiction missions at this time was the Canberra, especially in its B(I).8 and B-57B forms, but the Canberra did not go to Korea. A little later the F-100C/D and F-101A/C brought to the interdiction mission level-supersonic performance, and at the

Below: Designed in 1952 as an uncompromised air-superiority fighter, the Lockheed F-104 found its real niche much later as a low-level attack and tactical reconnaissance aircraft. One of the many users of the later F-104G "Super Starfighter" version was Canada.

Above: These de Havilland Venoms of the Swiss air force will have served half a century in the demanding Alpine tactical attack role when they are finally grounded in the early 1990s. Had Switzerland ever been involved in a war their life might have been measured in hours only.

Below: Designed in 1953, but extensively developed over the next decade, the USAF's Republic F-105 Thunderchief looked like a fighter but could behave like a heavy bomber (as well as a pioneer electronic-warfare aircraft). These big and capable aircraft bore heavy loads in Vietnam.

same time, in the second half of the 1950s, it became normal for tactical fighter wings of the USAF to carry nuclear weapons.

Letting go a "nuke" at low level was not quite like attacking with HE (high explosive). The lethal radius might be several miles, and these nuclear weapons were introduced just at the time that integrated air defences, including reliable surface-to-air missiles, were making it vital for survival to penetrate hostile territory as close to the ground as possible. This in itself presented great problems. It was not uncom-

Below: Planned in the early 1960s as a tactical fighter, the General Dynamics F-111 never served in the air-combat role. Instead it pioneered today's low-level "under the radar" attack mission, using automatic terrain-following. This F-111A was carrying CBU-42 clusters in Thailand.

mon to see in interdiction crew-rooms several posters reminding the crews that "effectiveness of trip-A (anti-aircraft artillery) is 25 per cent, effectiveness of SAMs is maybe 50 per cent, but effectiveness of the ground is always 100 per cent".

With conventional bombs it was possible to make a low-level attack at full throttle just by releasing retarded bombs. Upon release, such bombs immediately deploy airbrakes or a parachute so that, by the time they hit the ground three or four seconds later, the aircraft would be getting on for a mile away. Of course, care had to be taken that there was no wingman following three or four seconds dead astern! But with nuclear weapons (NW) a different procedure was devised.

At first the delivering aircraft adopted the low-altitude bombing system (LABS) manoeuvre, also known as toss bombing.

Above: Taken on 18 December 1968, this photo shows a Douglas A-4 Skyhawk on test from China Lake with a tank, two ECM jammer pods and two precision-guided Walleye glide bombs. The compact A-4 had a run of 26 consecutive years in production, and remains an important type.

Preferably, under pre-programmed autopilot control, the aircraft would enter a very steep climb while approaching the target at maximum speed at low level. The NW would then be released either as the aircraft neared the vertical but still short of the target, to arch high into the sky and eventually fall on the target, or after the aircraft had overflown the target and gone just past the vertical. The latter was known as the over-the-shoulder toss.

In either case, while the aircraft performed the first half of a loop and rolled out wings

level to go back the way it had come, the NW would climb up to perhaps 15,000ft (4,570m) and then fall back, taking around 30 seconds. This was judged ample time for the aircraft to reach a safe distance. By about 1963 many units had adopted LADD, low-angle drogued delivery, which achieves roughly the same result without forcing the aircraft to expose itself at such a high altitude above the ground for such a long period.

Of course, from the 1950s attacking aircraft could use ASMs (air-to-surface missiles), especially when engaging heavily defended targets. Some, such as Walleye, had precision guidance but no propulsion and thus did little to protect the aircraft against the defences. Others had propulsion but only crude command (pilot-controlled) guidance which required a flare on the missile to be kept lined up with the target. This was unquestionably more

dangerous than merely making a fast run with "iron bombs". Gradually, while on the one hand the aircraft got cleverer and better able to aim free-fall bombs, so too did the ASMs get more accurate at much greater ranges. Today the IDS aircraft has a choice of firing a deadly accurate stand-off missile many miles from the target, and then turning back, or of carrying on across the target, at something like Mach 1 in the sure knowledge that any ordinary

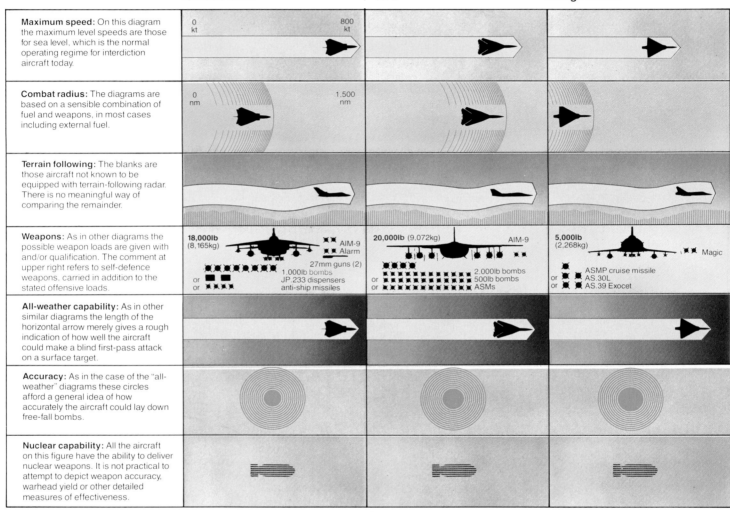

	Tornado GR.1	F-111E	Mirage 2000N
Maximum speed: On this diagram the maximum level speeds are those for sea level, which is the normal operating regime for interdiction aircraft today.	0 kt — 800 kt		
Combat radius: The diagrams are based on a sensible combination of fuel and weapons, in most cases including external fuel.	0 nm — 1,500 nm		
Terrain following: The blanks are those aircraft not known to be equipped with terrain-following radar. There is no meaningful way of comparing the remainder.			
Weapons: As in other diagrams the possible weapon loads are given with and/or qualification. The comment at upper right refers to self-defence weapons, carried in addition to the stated offensive loads.	18,000lb (8,165kg) — AIM-9, Alarm — 27mm guns (2) — 1,000lb bombs — JP.233 dispensers — anti-ship missiles	20,000lb (9,072kg) — AIM-9 — 2,000lb bombs — 500lb bombs — ASMs	5,000lb (2,268kg) — Magic — ASMP cruise missile — AS.30L — AS.39 Exocet
All-weather capability: As in other similar diagrams the length of the horizontal arrow merely gives a rough indication of how well the aircraft could make a blind first-pass attack on a surface target.			
Accuracy: As in the case of the "all-weather" diagrams these circles afford a general idea of how accurately the aircraft could lay down free-fall bombs.			
Nuclear capability: All the aircraft on this figure have the ability to deliver nuclear weapons. It is not practical to attempt to depict weapon accuracy, warhead yield or other detailed measures of effectiveness.			

These diagrams are intended to give a rough overview of how the main types of interdiction aircraft at present in service with the world's air forces compare with each other in all-round capability. It is significant that, for this role, designers have in the past agreed that variable sweep is not merely desirable but essential if the crew are to do any kind of professional job. The rough ride suffered by a Mirage 2000N at sea level cannot be quantified here, but it is the kind of factor that no air force that takes life seriously can gloss over. Likewise the absence of any kind of TFR (terrain-following radar) must be a factor that compromises the capability of the MiG-27 and Buccaneer.

◀ F-111E

Power plant: Two P&W TF30-7 (18,500lb/82.2kN)
Span: (max sweep) 31ft 11.4in (9.74m)
Length: 73ft 6in (22.40m)
Max TO weight: over 91,500lb (41,504.4kg)
Crew: 2

◀ Tornado GR.1

Power plant: Two Turbo-Union RB.199 Mk 103 (16,920lb/75.26kN)
Span: (max sweep) 28ft 2.5in (8.6m)
Length: 54ft 10in (16.72m)
Max TO weight: over 61,000lb (27,700kg)
Crew: 2

◀ Mirage 2000N

Power plant: One SNECMA M53-P2 (21,385lb/95.1kN)
Span: 29ft 11.5in (9.13m)
Length: 47ft 9in (14.55m)
Max TO weight: 37,480lb (17,000kg)
Crew: 2

bombs released will hit in the right place.

Smart aircraft

Clever precision ASMs are often called "smart" (if it has programmable software and can find its way to the target with no outside help at all, it is called "brilliant"). There is a story that when the first F-111As reached the South-East Asia theatre in 1968 someone asked "Do you people have smart munitions?" The F-111 pilot proudly replied, "No, we've got smart airplanes." Unquestionably the F-111A represented a quantum jump in the technology of the interdiction mission, and it is tragic error that it was confused with being a fighter.

Among the requirements of Specific Operational Requirement 183 to which the original F-111 was designed were some that went far beyond anything previously attempted by a "fighter" type aircraft. One was a ferry range of 3,000 nautical miles (3,455 miles, 5,560km). Another was the ability to carry a minimum of 10,000lb (4,536kg) of bombs or attack missiles and fly at low level (say, under 500ft (152m) above the ground) all the way to a target 800 nautical miles (921 miles, 1,482km) away, covering the final 200 nautical miles (230

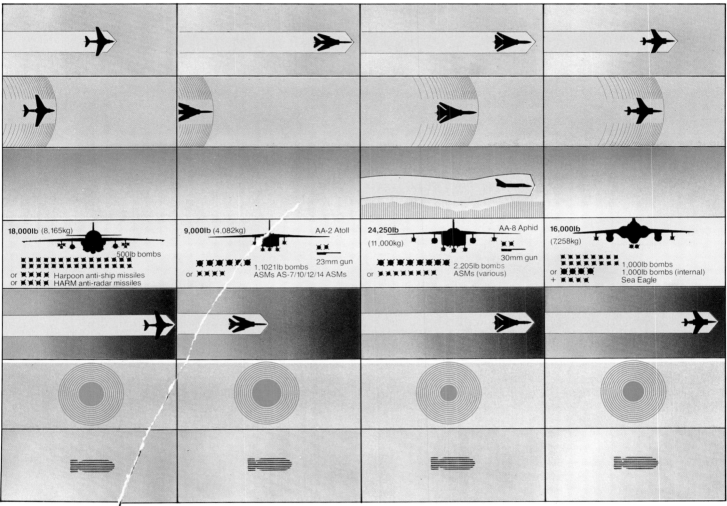

A-6E Intruder	MiG-27	Su-24	Buccaneer S.2B
18,000lb (8,165kg)	9,000lb (4.082kg)	24,250lb (11,000kg)	16,000lb (7,258kg)
500lb bombs	AA-2 Atoll / 23mm gun / 1,1021lb bombs ASMs AS-7/10/12/14 ASMs	AA-8 Aphid / 30mm gun / 2.205lb bombs ASMs (various)	1,000lb bombs / 1,000lb bombs (internal) Sea Eagle
or Harpoon anti-ship missiles or HARM anti-radar missiles			

◀ **A-6E Intruder**

Power plant: Two P&W JT8 (J52-8B) (9,300lb/41.4kN)
Span: 53ft 0in (16.15m)
Length: 54ft 9in (16.69m)
Max TO weight: 60,400lb (27,397kg)
Crew: 2

◀**Su-24**

Power plant: Two (AL-21F?) (about 24,700lb/110kN)
Span: (max sweep) 34ft 5.5in (10.5m)
Length: (excl probe) 69ft 10in (21.29m)
Max TO weight: 90,390lb (41,000kg)
Crew: 2

◀**MiG-27**

Power plant: One Tumanskii R-29-300 (25,350lb/112.8kN)
Span: (max sweep) 26ft 9.5in (8.17m)
Length: 52ft 6in (16.0m)
Max TO weight: 44,313lb (20,100kg)
Crew: 1

◀**Buccaneer S.2B**

Power plant: Two RR Spey 101 (11,030lb/49.1kN)
Span: 44ft 6in (13.59m)
Length: 62ft 5in (19.96m)
Max TO weight: 62,000lb (28,123kg)
Crew: 2

Above: *In every respect the Soviet Union's Su-24 is a "natural", with variable sweep, tremendous engine power, huge fuel capacity and a spectrum of avionic sensors for navigation, self-defence and weapon delivery unrivalled in the West. Its design was certainly influenced by that of the General Dynamics F-111.*

Left: *In many respects the General Dynamics F-111 (photo shows F-111A in Thailand, 1973) failed to meet the requirements for a "fighter", but it led the world into today's era of exciting automatically controlled terrain-following, even in blind conditions, in the run-up to a surface target.*

Minutes of Acceptable Crew Efficiency at Sea Level at Mach 0.9

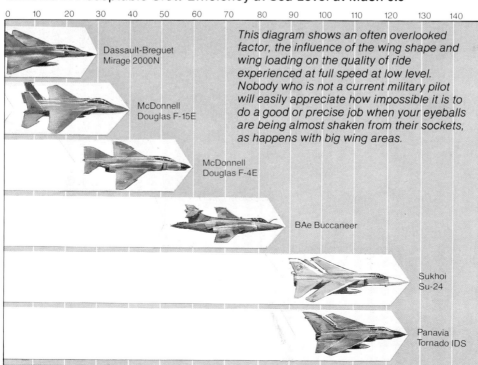

Dassault-Breguet
Mirage 2000N

McDonnell
Douglas F-15E

McDonnell
Douglas F-4E

BAe Buccaneer

Sukhoi
Su-24

Panavia
Tornado IDS

This diagram shows an often overlooked factor, the influence of the wing shape and wing loading on the quality of ride experienced at full speed at low level. Nobody who is not a current military pilot will easily appreciate how impossible it is to do a good or precise job when your eyeballs are being almost shaken from their sockets, as happens with big wing areas.

miles, 370km) to the target at Mach 1.2. Such speed at low level burns fuel at a prodigious rate, and also demands that the ordnance load should be carried internally or at least conformally (recessed into the aircraft). The F-111 was designed with an internal weapon bay, but this was sized to carry two missiles or NWs; there was no way a massive load of conventional bombs could be carried internally.

In fact the F-111 never did meet all the original design objectives, but it emerged as an aircraft of impressive capability — except, perhaps, in the "fighter" role. With a pilot on the left and a WSO (weapon-*system officer)* on the right, in an ejectable capsule, it can carry extremely heavy loads for long distances, which certainly extend beyond the operational radii of B-17s or Lancasters in World War II, and can penetrate hostile airspace at the lowest possible safe height above the ground. Thanks to TFR (terrain-following radar) it can even cross mountain ranges, in dense cloud or at night, at speeds generally faster than other jets (except with maximum bomb load), the crew relying absolutely on the integrity of their electronics. Nearing the target, its already small radar image is further degraded by active countermeasures, while its weapon-delivery systems seek out the target for a precision attack. Some F-111s, for example, carry a Pave Tack belly installation con-

Typical Tornado GR.1 Weapon Loads

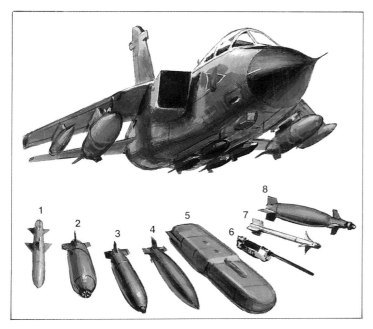

Left: *Most, but not all, of the weapons routinely carried by the RAF's Tornado IDS are illustrated.* **1:** *Alarm anti-radar missile.* **2:** *BL.755 cluster bomblet dispenser;* **3:** *Mk 83 retarded GP bomb.* **4:** *1,000lb GP "slick" bomb.* **5:** *JP.233 airfield-attack cluster munition dispenser.* **6:** *MK27 27mm gun (two).* **7:** *AIM-9L Sidewinder close-range AAM.* **8:** *GBU-13 Paveway II laser-guided bomb. Unlike the F-111 the Tornado can carry a heavy bomb load under the fuselage, leaving the wings free for other stores.*

taining IR and laser sensors for precision lock-on to targets for accurate bombing at night or in bad weather.

Today the main new-generation IDS aircraft are the Tornado, F-15E and Su-24 "Fencer". The Soviet aircraft is virtually a copy of the F-111 with the latter's shortcomings rectified, and the Tornado is a very efficient machine cast in the same mould and doing the same job with a smaller airframe and much smaller engines. The odd man out is the F-15E, converted from an air-superiority fighter designed to the maxim "not a pound for air-to-ground", in other words making no concessions whatever to the IDS mission. One result is that

it has big and thirsty engines (burning fuel at double the rate of a Tornado and seven times the rate of a Harrier II).

At least as serious is the huge wing, which is fine for air combat but extremely unwelcome in a full-throttle attack at treetop height, because the violent turbulence is not just fatiguing to the crew and airframe but seriously degrades the crew's ability to think clearly. So far as is known the USAF does intend to use the F-15E's terrain-following capability, but even at maximum weight the crew will have a rough ride.

A further even more serious shortcoming of all these current aircraft is that they appear to

have no chance of surviving the start of a major war, chiefly because when not in the air they are parked on heavily targeted fixed locations called airfields. A contributory factor is that while penetrating hostile airspace they broadcast their presence with a forward-looking attack radar, terrain-following radar, radar altimeter, FLIR (forward-looking infrared) and laser spot tracker or designator/ranger. Quite apart from the fact that defending sensors naturally get ever-more efficient at detecting and tracking targets, behaving like an aerial lighthouse and broadcasting station is no way to fly the interdiction mission.

Some might say that flying with, or astern of, a dedicated protective EW (electronic warfare) aircraft, such as the EA-6B Prowler or EF-111A Raven, greatly enhances the interdictor's chance of completing its mission. A far better answer is surely total LO (low observables) or "stealth" design, as first seen in service in the Lockheed CSIRS (Covert Survivable Reconnaissance/Strike aircraft). The USAF denies that this is designated the F-19 (one might, however, expect it to be the RF-19 or RA-19), but does not deny that it has long been in operational service. Of course, nothing can be truly invisible, inaudible or (if it burns fuel) at the same temperature as its background, but this elusive Lockheed unquestionably shows how this particular mission should be flown in future. If only it did not come back to park on a known airfield!

Below: *Though it is based on a design first flown 32 years ago the Mirage 2000 is really a completely new aircraft, and the 2000N nuclear low-altitude penetrator is an even more comprehensive update. Shown here in service with the Armee de l'Air 4th Escadre at Luxeil in eastern France, the 2000N force should number 85.*

The Tornado Mission

POSSESSING an all-weather capability that is perhaps only matched by the General Dynamics F-111 and the Grumman A-6E Intruder, the Panavia Tornado is without doubt one of the most important weapons systems currently to be found in the NATO inventory, several hundred examples now serving with Britain's Royal Air Force as well as with the air arms of Italy and West Germany. Able to fly fast at ultra low level in virtually all kinds of weather by both day and night, it incorporates a superlative navigation and attack system which permits it to be piloted with near pin-point accuracy over long distances. In the mission that is examined here, half-a-dozen Tornado GR.1s assigned to RAF Germany's No. 9 Squadron at Bruggen are given the task of penetrating deep behind enemy lines in order to carry out an attack on a Warsaw Pact fighter base. Flying to and from the target at low level, each Tornado carries two examples of the devastatingly effective Hunting JP233 munitions dispenser.

It is uncommonly quiet in the hardened Personnel Briefing Facility (PBF), the usual good humoured and often bawdy badinage that is regularly traded between the aircrews and the operations staff being most notable by its virtual absence, an indication that something is definitely "up".

For RAF Germany's No.9 Squadron, the move to a war footing has obviously not come as a surprise but it is fair to say that events have moved rather faster than anticipated, prompting a hasty recall from Armament Practice Camp at Decimomannu in Sardinia to Bruggen just a few days earlier. Even as they packed hastily to return, so was the squadron's operating area — colloquially known as "Gotham City" in an allusion to the bat motif which forms the centrepiece of No.9's crest — readied for action, ordnance being transferred from the weapons storage facilities to the hardened aircraft shelters (HAS) which would soon be welcoming the homeward-bound Tornados.

Since then, they have been in almost constant action but they have thus far acquitted themselves well, having lost just one Tornado GR.1 in three days and nights of combat. Pilot and navigator succeeded in getting back to the security of allied territory before being forced to abandon their mortally wounded aircraft, but both sustained minor back injuries in the process of ejection and they have not yet returned to Bruggen.

 1132 hours

Now, the degree of tension is again rising as aircrews and ops staff await news of two aircraft and crews that are airborne as part of a six-aircraft package drawn from elements of the Bruggen Wing. The after action in-flight report should have been made a couple of minutes ago and personnel manning the operations desk imminently expect word from the other Bruggen-based squadron which planned the mission.

In the adjacent ready-to-task (RTT) room, a group of pilots and navigators lounge about, one or two conversing softly while a few idly go through the motions of playing darts — but it is fairly clear that they aren't paying much attention to the game.

 1134 hours

The sound of a telephone ringing brings a sudden halt to all activity, most heads turning to watch as an officer of the ops staff picks up the handset and speaks softly into the mouthpiece, nods briefly and terminates the conversation with a terse "Thank you", before returning the receiver to its resting place.

"OK. We've got two aircraft inbound as per schedule," he announces, apparently to no one in particular, before turning to an NCO, "they'll be going to shelters 41 and 47 so you'd better call the ground crew and let them know they're on their way."

Even as he speaks, the Bruggen Wing's combat operations centre receives an urgent signal from 2nd Allied Tactical Air Force's (2 ATAF) Air Task Operations Centre (ATOC) at Maastricht directing an airfield attack by elements of the Wing.

 1137 hours

After a brief conference it is decided to assign this mission to No.9 Squadron, the Air Task Message (ATM) being passed to the PBF via two points. One is the Bramis system, the ATM appearing on a visual display unit in front of the squadron's O/C War (Officer Commanding War, familiarly known as the "Warlord").

In another nearby office, a second terminal notifies the Ground Liaison Officer or "GLO" (pronounced "glow"), an Army officer typically holding the rank of major who is permanently attached to the squadron to assist the "Squinto" (Squadron Intelligence Officer)

Below: Flight in modern high performance combat aircraft such as the Tornado is a physically demanding and fatiguing business, hence the requirement to wear specialised kit. In a brief lull in flight operations, much of No. 9 Squadron's gear hangs ready, waiting for use.

with matters pertaining to intelligence and to co-ordinate the sometimes conflicting interests of air and ground elements.

On receipt of the signal, the GLO immediately begins gathering together such intelligence as exists relating to this particular target. In addition to material relevant to the

Above: *Having already donned their G-suits, personnel involved in the forthcoming airfield attack are briefed shortly before moving out to their aircraft. Tactics, communications and safe corridors are just some of the aspects that will be covered during the briefing.*

Below: *Out at the shelter which houses his Tornado, a pilot clambers aboard after completing a brief external inspection. In the rear cockpit, the navigator will already be at work, programming the computer by means of a cassette tape and readying other key systems for flight.*

target itself, his files contain all known intelligence data on other subjects likely to be of interest to a strike force. Naturally, "threats" such as SAM (surface-to-air missile) sites and AAA (anti-aircraft artillery) batteries figure prominently.

In preparing the intelligence assessment, the Squinto and the GLO also refer to the large "War Map" of the Central European area, plotting and marking the target in anticipation of the forthcoming briefing. Normally screened by curtains in peacetime, this dominates almost an entire wall of the planning room and has been regularly updated as new intelligence filters through, presenting a graphic visual display of "safe" air corridors, the "FLOT" (Forward Line of Own Troops), the "FSCL" (Fire Support Co-ordination Line) and other important data.

 1141 hours

While the GLO and Squinto busy themselves with intelligence-related matters, the "Warlord" studies aircraft and crew availability boards in the operations centre, selecting a lead crew whose task it will be to oversee the mission planning phase. At the same time, engineering staff attached to the squadron operations centre peruse a hard copy of the ATM to ascertain formation strength, allocating the desired number of aircraft and contacting the HASs by land line to set in train the process of preparing those aircraft for the forthcoming action.

 1144 hours

Since this ATM stipulates a six-ship attack using the JP233 airfield denial weapon system, munitions specialists are soon hard at work manoeuvring the bulky dispensers from storage racks inside each HAS into place beneath half-a-dozen Tornados hidden in shelters dotted around No.9's complex, loading AIM-9 Sidewinder heat-seeking air-to-air missiles and checking the integral Mauser 27mm cannon carried by each Tornado. As they work, other ground crew go about their allotted tasks, opening canopies, providing fuel here, switching a defective line replaceable unit there, gathering up "remove before flight" streamers and generally performing the myriad other functions that are necessary to ready their charges for the impending mission.

 1155 hours

Back at the PBF, the designated lead crew — consisting of pilot and navigator — confer briefly with the GLO and Squinto as they study the war map and figure out a fairly broadly defined operational plan. At this stage, there is little point in dealing in specifics (that comes later when detailed planning is under way), but it is advisable to establish a basic routing which avoids known "trouble spots", as well as an attack scenario, taking into account such considerations as the attack axis. This, almost inevitably, is to some extent determined by the type of weaponry and the delivery mode that is to be employed. In the case of bombs, the primary concern is to put them on target but the approach may, if terrain and defences permit, be made from virtually any quadrant, giving the attacking force rather more freedom of action. By its very nature, the Hunting JP23 munitions dispenser requires the use of a rather less flexible approach if the objective of the attack is to be achieved and the lead crew devotes a few moments to studying the fairly limited options that are open to them when they reach their designated target, prior to releasing the sub-munitions.

Today's objective is a fighter base possessing a single runway with an adjacent parallel taxiway, and the lead crew opt for an attack profile which will open with two aircraft flying along the airfield axis, one delivering its sub-munitions against the runway itself while the other goes for the taxiway. The next pair will cut obliquely across the runway/taxiway at the two turn-off points which are located at about the 3,000ft (900m) and 6,000ft (1,830m) markers while the final pair will have the shelter area and its associated complex of taxiways and hard standings as an aiming point. Between them, they should then render the airfield temporarily inoperative.

 1205 hours

"Right, Jim," says the lead pilot to his navigator, "Let's have everybody together for a couple of minutes and put them in the picture before we get down to detail stuff."

 1206 hours

"OK. This is the target," the lead pilot says, pointing it out on the large war map with the aid of a long plastic ruler. "Six-ship attack with two JP233s per aircraft. Jim and I'll lead with Steve as our number two and we'll be going for the runway and taxiway. Mike and Doug'll be three and four respectively and will run in diagonally using the turn-offs as an aiming point. Ken and Pete are five and six and will hit the shelter complex at the western end, again running in diagonally. Three and four'll go through simultaneously with the other two pairs using 20 seconds separation between aircraft. We'll, er, fill you in on defences and so on when we brief later. Right, time check...on my mark, it will be 1206 and 50 seconds ...three...two...one...mark. You got anything to add, Jim?"

"Not a lot, Mac. I think I've figured out a fairly good route, avoiding known hot spots. I'd like John and Ray to concentrate on planning departure and recovery. Then we'll pull it all together."

 1208 hours

With the broad plan defined, attention now switches to the Cassette Preparation Ground Station (CPGS) where detailed planning takes place. Overlaying "half-mil" (1:500,000) maps on the CPGS's electronic map table, they first align the computer by positioning the associated cursor over any two grid intersections and inputting corresponding latitude and longitude references. Thereafter, plotting is relatively easy, the cross-hairs on the movable cursor simply being transferred from waypoint to waypoint around the chosen route and keyed into the computer, data captured in this way being presented on a VDU screen next to the map table. Reference to the screen enables the navigation team to verify that sector times and speeds are satisfactory and they can, of course, "juggle" the figures so as to meet specifics such as time-on-target (TOT).

 1245 hours

In this case, a fairly minor modification is required in order to satisfy the TOT and, with that adjustment made, the lead navigator slots a standard audio cassette into the computer and electronically captures the relevant flight data. Further cassettes are prepared for the other five aircraft while at the same time an associated printer produces the desired number of "hard" copies. These are provided to each navigator as a back-up just in case the tape proves defective. Reference to the print-out will enable him to "load" the flight plan manually into the Tornado's integral computer should it be necessary.

While all that is going on, the pilots are also

busy with maps, working out their respective attack runs. In this case, though, a larger-scale chart (1:50,000) is used, the extra detail that it contains being necessary to permit desired levels of accuracy to be achieved. Attack runs can vary in length depending on circumstances but are seldom less than 10 miles (16km) and rarely exceed 20 miles (32km). Needless to say, the shorter the distance is generally perceived to be the better, since it minimises exposure to enemy counteraction, but that requirement will be subordinate to the need to ensure that ordnance falls squarely on target.

A: Formation leader runs in at low level for airfield attack with JP233 munitions dispensers. **B:** Flying a parallel track, lead's wingman also sets up to strike the airfield with the JP233. **C:** Aircraft three and four employ diagonal approach in order to damage runway intersections. Twenty seconds later, aircraft five and six also run in diagonally with their objectives being the hardened shelter complex. **D:** Target area covered with munitions. Light flak in evidence. **E:** Egress route utilises terrain masking.

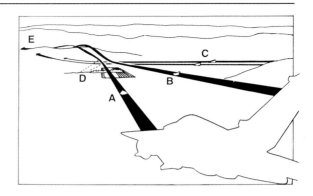

With JP233, there is no initial point (IP) in the generally accepted sense of the term but, regardless of weaponry, three "offsets" are always selected so as to eliminate navigation errors and position the aircraft precisely on track, for even the slightest variation will compromise accuracy and accuracy is a paramount concern with a weapon like JP233.

In this instance, lead and No.2 will begin to set up their attack run some 18 miles (29km) out and their first offset is a large chimney some 15 miles (24km) from the target. This should come up to the left of their track and is intended mainly to check for displacement. Offset two — five miles (8km) from the target — is a cross-roads, again to the left, and should enable them to reduce any track variation to below 100ft (30m). Offset three — just over one mile (1.6km) out — is a radio mast and this should come up on their right, to provide the most accurate positional fix possible. By then, if the navigator has done his job properly and if all the kit works correctly, they should be right on track for their target with only a matter of seconds to go to weapons release — enemy defences permitting.

1255 hours

With all the charts now prepared, a member of the attack force is despatched to a nearby colour photocopier where he spends the next few minutes producing an identical set for each member of the package. These are not strictly necessary since navigation is invariably left to "the system" — however, since no system is yet immune from failure, the back-up charts are taken along as a kind of "insurance" and their presence will enable the mission to be completed in the unlikely event of a major malfunction of the navigation kit.

1325 hours

"OK, guys. Let's brief, shall we?" says Mac, laying the first of a sequence of slides on the projector.

"It's a six-ship airfield attack with JP233. You all have the location... Crews, mission number, aircraft as you see here. Weather... pretty much as per morning briefing. Most of central Europe is still socked-in pretty badly, which is good news for us and we should be on or about cloud base until just before you hit the target. Target weather is supposed to be slightly better so you may get the chance to go VMC (visual meteorological conditions) for delivery.

"Zip lip" naturally, unless we run into a fighter or missile threat or someone wants to declare an emergency, then it's stud eight. IFRep (in-flight report) to Marlin — that'll be number six's responsibility. Autochop (switch automatically) to stud 11 for briefing from Cyclops (NATO E-3A Sentry) at Delta.

"Pairs take-off at 20 second intervals, standard safe corridor departure. Lo-lo-lo profile and we'll be in Card formation until target area, then 20 second separation through the target with rejoin to Card. TF (terrain following) as standard, minimum setting. Standard recovery procedure with advisory call at Mike on stud 6.

"Right, target data," he says, changing slides

Left: With the shelter doors open and both engines running, the Tornado's crew run through a final sequence of pre-departure checks before the pilot adds sufficient power to propel his aircraft clear of its hide and out on to the taxiway that leads to the runway.

Right: Their shapes distorted by the massive amount of vapour generated by the use of afterburner, the last pair of Tornados await their turn to take-off. In the distance, the formation leader's aircraft climbs away steadily and begins to swing round on to a new heading.

Below: Almost simultaneously, the six aircraft involved in this strike mission emerge into the open, falling neatly in line as they move to the runway. Once there, they waste no time in getting airborne since they are at their most vulnerable whilst on the ground.

yet again. "Airfield with SAM and AAA defences. Squinto's got a chart mapping last known dispositions so have a look at that before we walk out. It's JP233 so we'll be using a lay-down attack, speed and height as per slide. Good offsets so there should be no problem in acquisition. Weapons settings — one, two, five and six'll use long pattern, three and four broad pattern. If you foul up the approach, one and two turn left to set up again. Rest of you go right. No re-attack, so look for a target of opportunity. Once off target, rendezvous between Golf and Hotel for transit back to base."

 1340 hours

They have completed the briefing, surrendered all but the few items that they are allowed to take with them (including dog tags and side-arms), been given the latest escape and evasion information as well as a final intelligence update by the GLO and are now in the kit room, suiting up for the impending mission. To date, there has been no indication that either side is employing nuclear, biological and chemical (NBC) weaponry and they are spared the tedious business of donning NBC kit and have no need to carry the portable ventilator units which would provide filtered air once they emerge from the PBF into the open. As a result, with time in hand, they have no need to rush the suiting-up procedure and even have a minute or two to quiz an incoming crew. "How'd it go, Geoff"

"Hi, Mike. Oh, pretty good. We had a clear run in to the target but ran into a bit of interference coming off. The mad Irishman's convinced he got a MiG."

"Reeeally. Christ, if he did he'll be intolerable for weeks. Where is he, by the way?"

"Dunno. I'd have thought he'd have been here by now."

"Oh, you know Liam. He's probably boring the pants off the ground crew right now."

"Them or the Air Marshal. Where are you lot off to?"

"Ahhh, c'mon Geoff. Need to know, need to know...."

"What's the matter, don't you trust me?"

 1400 hours

Leaving the PBF via the airlock and its armoured outer door, the crews hurriedly scramble aboard a couple of armoured personnel carriers to make the short journey to the various HASs in which their aircraft stand. Chat is minimal during the two-minute journey to the first HAS, the lead crew moving quickly to the shelter and notifying their arrival to the personnel inside via a handset situated adjacent to the access door. Inside the HAS, a guard listens briefly and then moves to a spyhole in the door, studying the two figures outside for a few seconds in order to confirm that they are indeed who they say they are.

 1403 hours

Satisfied, the guard opens the door, allowing them to enter. Once inside, the pilot goes first to the office accommodation to attend to the few bits of paperwork which are necessary to make the aircraft "his". At this point, most of the systems have been brought on line by the three ground crew as part of the orderly pre-departure routine and the navigator moves immediately to the access ladder, climbs up and quickly straps in before busying himself with "loading" the computer by inserting the cassette tape into its appointed slot at the front of the right-hand console. He then turns his attention to a series of system checks, commanding a series of built-in test equipment (BITE) programs which soon verify that, from his point of view at least, everything is working satisfactorily.

 1408 hours

In the meantime, the pilot has dealt with the paperwork and set about performing a brief walk-around, checking first that the weapons programming unit (WPU) on the port fuselage side directly ahead of the air intake has been set correctly so as to permit the two massive JP233 pods beneath the belly to disgorge their contents in a long thin swathe down the run-

way and taxiway. Similar settings will be used by his wingman and by Nos.5 and 6 against the shelter complex while the other two aircraft in the formation will employ a "short fat" pattern when they hit the runway turn-off areas. Having ascertained that the WPU is indeed correctly set, the pilot then devotes a few seconds to the dispensers themselves, checking that they are secure. He also looks briefly at the two Sidewinder AAMs and makes a rapid check of control surfaces, underwing fuel tanks and tyres, being momentarily distracted by a rumbling sound as the two steel doors at the rear of the HAS are slid open.

 1413 hours

Then, satisfied, he climbs the ladder to the cockpit, straps in and dons his helmet. "Radio check, Jim."

"'kay, Mac."

A horn blares momentarily as the canopy is lowered and locked. Then, once again, the computer is called upon to facilitate the predeparture procedure, the pilot running through his own sequence of BITE programs. Outside the aircraft, but plugged in to the Tornado's intercom system, ground crew watch to confirm that all is normal. Flaps cycle in and out, air brakes pop up and down, stabilators swivel and inlet control systems activate automatically in response to computer-generated signals, the whole performance being overlaid by the shrill whine of the APU.

 1423 hours

"Okay, it's time to start. Let's have the main doors open," says the pilot. Below, one of the shelter's occupants moves quickly to a control panel and activates the motors which drive the massive blast-proof doors. Even as daylight begins to flood in, the pilot initiates the engine start procedure, power supplied by the APU being used to fire up No.1 engine via a gearbox torque converter. With that engine idling satisfactorily, the APU shuts down automatically, a cross shaft thereafter transferring power to the second gearbox and permitting the No.2 engine to be brought to life.

In five other shelters, the same process is re-enacted but apart from those who are directly involved and one or two patrolling guards the activity goes unnoticed. In the distance, a trolley laden with a clutch of eight 1,000lb (454kg) bombs trundles around the perimeter track, heading towards the dispersal area of another Bruggen-based squadron, but the casual observer (had there been one) might well be excused for thinking that the station was virtually deserted. Certainly, many personnel had taken up war stations off-base, these being epitomised by the Rapier surface-to-air missile batteries positioned some distance from the perimeter along anticipated lines of approach.

On-base, the apparent lack of humanity is deceptive. Armed guards are situated in each squadron dispersal area, but one has to know where to look for them and even then their presence is not always obvious until they move. Some occupy carefully positioned slit trenches overlooking the various facilities while others find cover in the shadows surrounding the HASs and the PBF building. Elsewhere, more guards protect fuel and weapons storage areas with yet more monitoring the station perimeter in case of attack by Spetznaz personnel (Soviet special sabotage forces) or fifth columnists.

 1433 hours

Precisely on schedule, the pilot of the lead Tornado manipulates the throttle, adding just sufficient power to get his aircraft moving clear of the shelter before turning right on to the taxiway. Five other Tornados also emerge into the open and begin to head towards the active runway which lies just a few hundred yards from No.9's dispersal area, lead and wing elements falling nicely into formation as they roll out. As the roar and reverberation of the engines increases, guards in trenches and around the shelters, increase their already high degree of alertness, for now is an ideal moment for an enemy to strike.

 1436 hours

Fortuitously, the Tornados will depart on runway 09, permitting them to set course direct for the first waypoint. Lead moves straight out to take up position on the right-hand side of the runway. Seconds later, his wingman taxis alongside on the left, both aircraft performing a quick power check, before the lead pilot switches his attention to the runway caravan nearby to await the steady green signal which will clear them to begin their take-off roll.

Below: Moving fast at low level, munitions spill from the JP233 dispensers of a Tornado as it flashes across the enemy airfield. The larger devices are cratering bombs while the smaller items are anti-personnel mines designed to impede engineers from beginning repair work.

Tornado Terrain Following

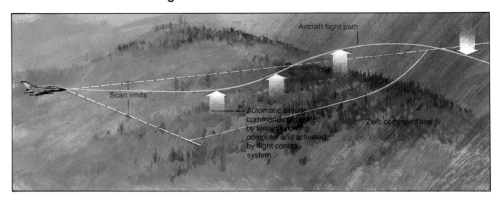

Above: One of the great merits of the Tornado is its terrain following capability, which allows it to be flown "hands off" at altitudes down to around the 200ft mark. "Ride quality" may also be varied, from "hard" to "soft", the latter being much more comfortable for crew members.

Below: The HB876 area denial munition. Each JP233 dispenser contains no fewer than 215 of these anti-personnel mines in addition to 30 examples of the larger SG357 cratering sub-munitions. Between them, they can render an airfield untenable for a prolonged period of time.

1437 hours

It comes right on time. Pausing only long enough to pass a hand signal to his wingman, he pushes the throttle levers forward, holding the aircraft on the brakes while power increases to maximum dry thrust rating. Then, releasing the brakes, he moves the throttles further forward, engaging afterburner. Pilot and nav are pushed back into their seats as, free from restraint, the two Tornados quickly accelerate away down the runway in an eardrum-splitting display of awesome power. Behind them, two more aircraft taxi smartly into place, wind up to full power and begin their thunderous journey down the concrete strip. Barely 20 seconds after that, the last pair are rolling, the guards back at dispersal relaxing their vigilance slightly as the noise level fades and the six aircraft head off eastwards. However, aware of the ever present danger, the guards soon resume the usual high level of necessary vigilance.

Above: Delivery of the HB876 area denial sub-munition is by parachute. Variable settings on the JP233 dispenser system permit the spread of sub-munitions to be either "long and thin" or "short and fat", the choice naturally depending on the target being attacked.

1506 hours

Thus far, the mission is proceeding like clockwork, all six aircraft having negotiated the safe corridor after getting airborne from Bruggen, and they are now approaching the narrow strip of the forward line of troops and fire support co-ordinating line (FLOT and FSCL). As forecast, the weather is really abysmal and even from a very low level they catch only occasional glimpses of the ground over which they pass as they continue eastward at a fairly modest speed at which they are flying. Just before the FLOT/FSCL, speed is increased, since it is desirable to minimise the length of time spent over enemy territory for obvious reasons.

At this point, they "autochop" to "Cyclops" for a short briefing on enemy air activity. Above and behind, a NATO E-3A Sentry (AWACS) electronically scans the area through which the Tornados will pass, its radar displays clearly showing the presence of six aircraft heading eastwards. Automatic IFF (identification friend or foe) equipment "interrogates" the six Tornados and the formation is very quickly verified as friendly. The ensuing briefing is concise, is broadcast on a secure voice channel virtually immune to jamming and includes certain passages which permit the Tornado crews to confirm that they are indeed in contact with Cyclops. What they learn is reassuring: there is apparently little in the way of air activity in the area to which they are going, most of the opposition's all-weather fighters evidently having gone north to engage a larger force that is also en route to its target.

1507 hours

All six aircraft are in terrain following mode, the Texas Instruments radar package working in conjunction with the computer to generate symbology which is presented to the pilot via the E-scope radar display and the head-up display (HUD). Pull-up and push-over commands appear on the latter but all six pilots have engaged autopilot and are content to leave the job of actually flying the aircraft to "the system".

Relieved of this responsibility, the crews devote their attention to other no less important matters. Engine instruments are regularly scanned as are fuel indicators and the moving map display.

In the rear cockpit, the nav is perhaps somewhat busier, checking their progress by means of the combined radar and projected map display (CRPMD) which dominates the centre of his instrument panel and by the two "TV Tabs" or Cathode Ray Tubes (CRTs) positioned left and right of the CRPMD. The latter are, in essence, little more than miniaturised computer terminals and they can be used to present mission-related data in a number of formats, associated switches permitting the main computer to be re-programmed.

Navigation is accomplished by a mix of systems, including the prime Ferranti FIN 1010 digital three-axis inertial package, Decca Type 72 Doppler radar, a secondary attitude and heading reference set and an air data computer. Data originating from these is "averaged" by the Litef Spirit 3 main computer to present a more accurate picture.

In war, of course, a prime concern is that of not betraying one's presence and that is certainly true of this strike formation. In consequence, strict radio silence procedures are observed, while other electronic emissions are minimised as much as possible so as to reduce the risk of detection by enemy radar warning receivers. For the navigator, however, this poses problems in ensuring that they are on track, since the primary INS is not immune from error and even the smallest variation can result in the attack failing to achieve its objective.

Use of the Texas Instruments ground mapping radar (GMR) permits him to update the evolving navigation equation and "take out" track errors but may also be described as being akin to firing off flares to advertise one's position. As a result, the GMR is employed only briefly while en route to identify and mark fixpoints for which precise positional information is known. This permits navigational errors to be eliminated.

1508 hours

Thus far, track is good and the formation crosses the FLOT right on course, running through the narrow safe channel. In the six aircraft, six pilots adjust the throttles, speed quickly rising to reduce the amount of exposure time to enemy ground threats. When they begin the final leg that will take them to the target, their speed will again increase.

Below, a company of American soldiers hear but do not see their passage.

"Sounds like a bunch of One-Elevens heading east..." remarks one, to nobody in particular.

1518 hours

They have been over enemy territory for a few minutes now and are closing rapidly on the target. In the rear cockpit of the lead aircraft, the nav switches his attention from course considerations to study the radar warning receiver display on the right-hand side of the instrument panel. He observes a strong strobe indicative of a SAM site a few miles ahead, at about their two o'clock position. The adjacent data panel identifies it as an SA-8. He makes up his mind to speak but before he can utter anything, the strobe disappears, its line-of-sight radar being blanketed by high ground which suddenly interposes itself between the Tornado and the site. He makes a brief note of the site and is interrupted by his pilot's voice over the intercom.

"You still awake back there, Jim"

"Yeah, Mac. D'you see that strobe just now?"

"Hmmm. We should be well clear when they acquire us again."

1521 hours

They are now some 90 miles (145km) into enemy territory and, with 35 miles (56km) still to run, they approach their final fix-point, a radar-significant feature (in this instance, a mast) that has been extremely accurately surveyed with regard to position and height. Using their own ground mapping radar briefly to "paint" the mast, the nav employs his hand controller to slew the display marker cross directly over it before hitting the "capture" button, an action which instantly updates the navigational equipment. They are still on track but are running five seconds early so the pilot judiciously manipulates the throttle levers so as to take out the time variation.

1521:30 hours

In the front cockpit, the pilot continues to divide his time between monitoring the HUD and other key instruments and it is a couple of seconds before he realises that they have emerged from cloud and are threading their way along a broad valley. Off to the right he sees a small village, but there is little sign of life, save for a herd of cattle being driven along a narrow track towards what he assumes to be a milking shed. On the ground, the herdsman looks up to catch a glimpse of the speeding Tornado as it heads away from him, its noise still being audible as a second aircraft flashes overhead, precisely 20 seconds later, followed by a third at which he waves before turning to devote his attention to a recalcitrant cow.

By then, the lead aircraft is several miles away and has begun an exaggeratedly wide final turn for the run-in to the target, so as to maintain the desired degree of separation between elements as they pass over the enemy airfield. Speed is now in excess of 500 knots (576mph, 927 km/h) but the ride quality is surprisingly smooth, pilots and navs experiencing only the occasional "bump" as they hit a patch of turbulence. Lead's wingman times his turn so as to fall into trail at the pre-determined 20 second interval. The remaining four aircraft continue on the original heading for a few seconds longer, before they, too, turn to set up their respective attacks.

1523 hours

In the lead aircraft, the first offset stands out clearly on the radar presentation, more or less where it should be and only the minutest of corrections is necessary. A strong strobe on the RWR notifies them of the presence of a missile control radar directly ahead, but there are no launch indications, so they press on, content to leave the task of countermeasures to the Sky Shadow pod which has noted the radar's presence and which is now actively jamming it. In the rear cockpit, the nav per-

forms the few actions necessary to prepare the BOZ-107 pod but does not yet activate it, preferring to wait until they are into the target area before commanding it to eject flares and chaff to saturate the airfield defences.

1523:55 hours

As they come up on the second offset, the pilot disengages the autopilot and begins to fly the aircraft manually as per the cues on the HUD. Like most pilots, he prefers to be "in control" at this critical time. He cannot yet see

the target but all the indications are that they are right on track and in good shape to execute a copybook attack. More strobes indicate the presence of other radars, Sky Shadow automatically detecting, identifying and prioritising the "threats", and taking the necessary countermeasures to negate them.

 **1524:18 hours**

Only the smallest of corrections is needed at the third and last offset. On the HUD, the Bomb Fall Line (BFL) is positioned nicely over

A: Tornado's BOZ107 pod ejects chaff cloud to decoy a radar-guided surface-to-air missile which has been launched. **B:** Chaff "bloom" succeeds in confusing the SAM which homes harmlessly on the expanding cloud. **C:** BOZ107 dispenser carried by second Tornado ejects infra-red flares as a defensive measure against heat-seeking missiles. **D:** Following flare ejection, the Tornado employs terrain masking as an additional self-defence measure by rolling inverted and utilising a ridge line for cover.

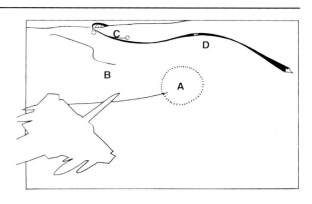

the runway centreline. The target bar marker also stands out clearly, in just about the optimum position, a little way beyond the threshhold while the far end of stick (FEOS) cross marker is also nicely aligned. The circular time-to-go indicator which surrounds the aircraft position marker unwinds almost agonisingly slowly while, in distinct contrast, the Continuously Computed Impact Point (CCIP) marker seems to rush along the BFL.

In the front cockpit, the pilot flicks aside the cover of the "commit" button, pauses momentarily for one last check that everything is looking good and briefly depresses it. The "system" takes over...

1524:25 hours

As the CCIP marker comes astride the target bar, electrical impulses command the pair of JP233s to dispense their munitions. In a matter of moments, each dispenser spews cratering bombs and hundreds of area denial mines, each of which is stabilised and lowered to the ground by a small parachute. Most of the craterers impact on the runway. An initial directional charge in each blasts a small hole in the concrete so as to clear a path for a second charge which detonates beneath the surface.

It is this second charge which really causes the damage, the "heave" effect arising from the explosion resulting in slabs of cracked and broken concrete being driven upwards by the blast. At the same time, area denial mines rain down, some landing in craters while others litter the runway surface and the adjacent grass. Random timing devices in the HB876 mines will cause some to detonate at irregular intervals so as to dissuade repair teams from coming too close, the task of clearance being very much a long-term job for specialist mine disposal personnel.

1524:31 hours

Surprise is evidently near-complete and only a couple of anti-aircraft artillery pieces burst into action as the JP233 pods disgorge their deadly contents. The pilot of the lead aircraft is momentarily disconcerted when he observes one or two puffs of angry-looking black smoke as the shells detonate but the fire is inaccurate and the gunners make the mistake of continuing to track him as he comes off target.

1524:35 hours

For a couple of moments the AAA team believe they have hit the Tornado, since they see several large pieces fall clear from its belly, as, now jinking from left to right and with chaff and flares being ejected by the BOZ-107 pod, it quickly heads away from them. Their jubilation is destined to be short-lived, for it is only empty JP233 dispensers being jettisoned. The front mine containers leave first at fractional intervals before they are followed by the cratering containers.

Even as the aircraft disappears from view and the AAA team realign their guns, the second Tornado is upon them, depositing its munitions in a neat line down the taxiway which is quickly reduced to the same sorry

Above: An SG357 cratering bomb detonates at the same moment as another is lowered to the ground by parachute. Between them, the 360 cratering submunitions deposited by the six Tornados cause serious damage to the airfield's runways, taxiways and shelter complex.

Below: Several hours later, when some of the area denial mines have been cleared, airfield repair specialists study the after effects of just one cratering bomb. Ahead of them lies a long and massive repair job for the Tornados have done their work well and accurately.

state as the adjacent runway. Again, only a few shells are directed at this aircraft which makes its escape more or less unhindered, the crew feeling a slight jolt as they flash through disturbed air left by a detonation some way ahead of them.

1526:20 hours

Succeeding waves meet with slightly stiffer opposition, but the varied lines of approach evidently achieve the objective of confusing

the defences and they run through more or less unscathed. The crew of number five experience a few anxious moments when they sustain minor damage to a wing-tip and part of the fin from shell fragments, but the aircraft's handling qualities appear unaffected and they also make good their escape from the area.

1529 hours

Behind, when it is clear that the attack is over, the gunners begin to take stock of their surroundings. The runway and taxiway are clearly severely damaged, especially in the area of the intersections. The two Tornados which had these as their targets have obviously delivered their weapons extremely accurately. A sudden detonation as one of the mines explodes causes several gunners to drop to cover while another trigger-happy gun crew pumps two or three rounds skywards before realising that they are simply wasting ammunition.

In and around the shelter complex, the devastation is no less impressive. Access from the taxiway to most of the shelters has been cut, effectively penning the aircraft inside their concrete containers. Smoke from a burning fuel bowser which has been hit by a cratering device blankets much of the airfield and prevents those in command from immediately assessing the degree of damage, but contact with other base facilities soon reveals that the Tornados have done their work well and that it will be many hours before the field is able to resume operations.

By then, the six aircraft have rejoined into the parallel track "card" formation and are again in cloud, well on their way home to Bruggen. The pilot of number five contemplates breaking radio silence for a few seconds to report his aircraft is damaged but since everything seems to be working satisfactorily he opts to remain "zip lip" until they cross the FLOT/FSCL.

 1545 hours

They are back on the right side of the battle line and "Marlin" has been given a brief summary of the results by the pilot of number six, who is of the opinion that the target airfield has been rendered inoperative for at least the near term future. In addition, number five has informed lead of the fact that his Tornado has sustained some battle damage.

On hearing this, number six takes advantage of a clearer patch of sky to move across for a few moments to study the damaged airframe. His perusal reveals one or two punctures on the upper wing surface and a small hole in the fin. Fortunately, none of the punctures seem to be in critical areas and after a rapid exchange of hand signals confirming that all appears to be well, number six slides away to take up battle station again.

 1604 hours

Using safe corridors again, the formation is now about 30 miles (48km) from Bruggen. In the lead aircraft, the pilot switches channels and activates the radio, transmitting a brief cryptic message which notifies the Bruggen command post that they are returning and should be back on the ground within a few minutes. He receives an even briefer response, which informs him (and his colleagues, who are also listening in) that there has been no change in airfield status since they departed.

 1606 hours

In No.9's PBF, operations personnel set in train the recovery procedure, communicating with the various shelters by land line to notify

Above: Back at Bruggen, the Tornado flown by the strike leader is well established on final approach to land. Gear and flaps are down and wings are spread as it whistles over the boundary fence. Within moments, thrust reversal will be employed to bring it to a halt.

Below: Bruggen's runway lights shine brightly as the last of the six Tornados settles towards the runway, its part in this mission almost complete. For the crew, however, there is still the job of debriefing to face before they can think about taking a well-earned rest.

them that the aircraft are on the way back and directing a battle damage repair team to move to No.5's HAS so as to begin remedial work with the minimum of delay.

1609 hours

In the lead Tornado, the pilot continues to monitor the HUD as he lets down through the murk, the rain dispersal system doing a good job of keeping the windscreen clear, but there is still nothing to be seen save for an opaque wall of cloud. Autopilot is still engaged and the navigator has "marked" the runway with the radar, since this recovery is being made without benefit of external aids.

1611 hours

Wings are at maximum spread and speed has diminished to less than 200 knots (230mph, 370km/h) as the pilot sets up his aircraft for landing, lowering flaps, selecting undercarriage down and "arming" the thrust reverser system so that the bucket doors will operate as soon as the main wheels touch down. Moments after the indicators confirm that the gear is down and locked, the Tornado emerges from cloud and the pilot immediately spots the runway dead ahead. He has little more than a mile to run and he quickly disengages the autopilot and nudges the rudder pedals to kill off a slight amount of drift.

1612 hours

With minimal flare, the Tornado meets the runway firmly at about 135 knots (155mph, 250km/h) and the hydraulically-actuated bucket doors deploy a fraction of a second later, the pilot allowing the nose to settle quickly so as to obtain maximum benefit from thrust reversal. As the nosewheel touches down, he pushes the throttles smartly forward. Black exhaust gases blossom around the aft fuselage as the engines make their contribution to slowing the Tornado. Within seconds, it has decelerated to a speed at which more conventional forms of braking can be employed and the pilot throttles back and commands retraction of the doors. He taxies straight ahead for a few moments before turning right at the first intersection.

As he clears the runway, the second aircraft in the formation is just moments from landing, its wings waggling slightly as the pilot makes a minor correction. Then it, too, is down safely, the roar of thrust reversal echoing across the seemingly deserted airfield. It is a sound that is repeated four times in the next couple of minutes as the remaining elements of the flight return to Bruggen.

1614 hours

As the last Tornado vacates the runway, the lead aircraft is just entering the shelter complex, moving quickly to its designated HAS where the pilot swings it smartly round under the directions of a ground crew member so as to position it facing outwards. Pilot and navigator relocate ejector seat and detonating

Above: Back at the dispersal area, each Tornado will turn and taxi through 180 degrees so as to face outwards from the hardened aircraft shelter. Once in that position, it can quickly be manoeuvred back into the protection offered by the reinforced concrete structure.

Below: Ground crew assist as one of the six Tornados which took part in the raid is hauled back into its shelter by means of a cable attached to a winch. Only when it is inside again will the engines be shut-down and the crew disembark to make a brief post-strike report.

cord safety pins to their rightful positions, while another ground crewman couples up the winching cable to the anchor point at the rear of the aircraft, moving in from the side since both engines are still running. A hand signal from the crew chief advises the pilot to release the brakes so that the aircraft can be hauled back into the HAS, and in little more than a minute it has disappeared from view. The pilot runs through the shut-down drill, a task he completes just in time to see the shelter doors close.

1618 hours

The pilot is first to disembark, clambering down the ladder and stretching for a few moments to relieve cramped muscles as the navigator retrieves his tape cassette, gathers up other mission-related paperwork, unstraps and climbs down.

Seeing the pilot and navigator have disembarked, the crew chief takes a few seconds out from his duties to converse briefly with them.

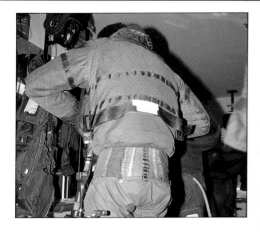

Above: Having returned to the personnel briefing facility, pilots and navigators discard most of their specialised flight kit in the life support section before entering into a comprehensive debriefing which examines all aspects of the mission recently completed.

Below: Although the Tornado is able to fly and fight in all kinds of weather, night is often the busiest time for support personnel since the cover of darkness offers a good opportunity to renew ordnance stocks held in each of the squadron's hardened shelters.

"Good trip, sir?"

"Oh, yes, sergeant. Very good."

"Any snags to report, sir?"

"No...no...she was just fine, chief. Look, I'd better check in with GLO before I sort out the paperwork, OK?"

"Yes, sir..."

 1620 hours

Picking up the phone in the adjacent office, the pilot listens, dials and waits for a few seconds before speaking. "Hallo, GLO. Got your notebook handy? OK, well I think you can cross that target off your list for a few days."

He listens again for a few seconds, before looking up and grinning at his navigator who chooses that moment to walk in to the office and dump his few belongings on a nearby table.

"Yes...yes...bang on the centreline. It was right out of the manual...you should've been there. You'd have been proud of us."

More tinny squawks emanate from the earpiece, but the navigator is unable to discern more than the occasional word.

"Gun sites? No, I didn't really notice....I had other things on my mind. Nav might have spotted a few though. D'you want to speak to him? No...OK...yes, right, see you in a few minutes."

Replacing the receiver, he turns to the navigator and speaks again. "Apparently we went through while they had a load of aircraft up. Listening post said it was chaos afterwards with all these pilots screaming for a divert field. Couple of them were forced to punch out, they reckon. GLO seems to have a bee in his bonnet about gun sites as well...d'you spot any?"

"Yeah, one or two...."

 1655 hours

They have been back at the PBF for some time now. Flight kit once again hangs on its appointed peg in the suiting-up room and the task of debriefing is all but wrapped up. Post-mission discussion pursues two broad strands. The squadron Intelligence Officer's concerns are more with the attack itself and particularly the tactical considerations, while his Army counterpart, the GLO, is anxious to update his intelligence files, questioning all crew members closely about airfield defences and other observations made while aloft.

As each crew completes the process of post-attack assessment, pilots and navigators move out of the briefing and planning area back to the RTT room. Some of them resume the game of darts which was interrupted earlier.

The'Aardvark' Mission

FOLLOWING a long period of steadily deteriorating relationships between Colonel Gadaffi's Libya and President Ronald Reagan's America, the USA successfully demonstrated its resolve to respond firmly to terrorist activities when General Dynamics F-111F strike aircraft from the 48th Tactical Fighter Wing at RAF Lakenheath performed a several thousand mile round trip to join carrier-borne Grumman A-6E Intruders operating from the USS *Coral Sea* and the USS *America* in a

series of attacks on key military targets in Libya. The build-up to this unexpected attack is covered in some detail in the accompanying text, as, indeed, are the events that took place on the night in question, when Libya was at last forced to face up to the fact that it would no longer be able to conduct a campaign of terror and hope to escape unpunished. Following the attack, post-strike photographic coverage of the target areas was obtained by a pair of UK-based Strategic Reconnaissance Wing SR-71A Blackbirds.

A persistent thorn in the side of the USA, Colonel Gadaffi undoubtedly precipitated the American attack on Libya, the already bad relations between that country and the USA deteriorating still further in January 1986. It was in that month that Gadaffi invoked the so-called "line of death" across the Gulf of Sidra, in the process seemingly challenging the USA to open confrontation by an action which clearly transgressed international law.

The response was not long in coming. US warships crossed the "line" in order to stage a major military exercise and, at the same time, assert their right to freedom of manoeuvre in international waters. If they expected a Libyan reply, they were not to be disappointed. Soviet-supplied surface-to-air missiles (SAMs) were directed against US aircraft flying over the Gulf while the fleet itself came under threat from fast-moving surface vessels equipped with anti-shipping missiles.

Early operations

In three days of operations, the Navy sustained no casualties despite frequent altercations with Libyan forces during which they meted out fairly heavy punishment. Rocket and bomb attacks devastated at least one Libyan missile site while a number of enemy attack craft were destroyed by air power.

It was against this background that Libya evidently elected to unleash its terrorist forces. Elements of the US intelligence community intercepted signals which seemed to indicate that Gadaffi had decided to employ other, covert, means. On 25 March, an order apparently passed from Tripoli to the Libyan People's Bureau in East Berlin directing them to mount a terrorist attack, a reciprocal signal on 4 April reporting that this would take place on the following day.

On 5 April, the "La Belle" discotheque in West Berlin was laid waste by a time bomb. A Turkish woman and a US soldier were killed while no fewer than 230 others sustained in-

Left: Munitions expended by the F-111Fs were withdrawn from the weapons storage facilities at Lakenheath and loaded in the hours immediately preceding the strike. Of the 13 aircraft which attacked, eight delivered Mk.84 laser-guided bombs with the rest dropping Mk.82 bombs.

The Build Up — 8-9 April

An RC-135V and an RC-135W from the 55th Strategic Reconnaissance Wing (SRW) at Offutt AFB, Omaha, Nebraska, stage through Mildenhall en route to an unknown destination. They are almost certainly employed as "ferrets", gathering electronic intelligence pertaining to Libya's defences.

11 April

Expansion in size of European Tanker Task Force (ETTF) begins in mid-afternoon with the transfer of four KC-10A Extenders from Zaragoza, Spain to Fairford, England. These were drawn from the 2nd Bomb Wing (BW) and the 22nd Air Refuelling Wing (ARW).

Additional tanker assets begin arriving at Mildenhall later that same afternoon when single KC-10As from the 22nd ARW and the 68th Air Refuelling Group (ARG) move from Sigonella, Sicily. They are followed in the evening by five more which deploy direct from the USA, two coming from Barksdale AFB, Louisiana (2nd BW) and three from Seymour-Johnson AFB, North Carolina (68th ARG).

USAF Chief-of-Staff General Gabriel also reaches Mildenhall, flying in aboard an Air Force Systems Command (AFSC) C-135C which stages from Brussels via London (Heathrow) Airport.

In addition, elements of the Woodbridge-based 67th Aerospace Rescue and Recovery Squadron (ARRS) prepare to move to Italy.

12 April

Another 2nd BW KC-10A arrives at Mildenhall direct from Barksdale in mid-afternoon.

Three 67th ARRS HH-53Cs depart Woodbridge for Naples, Italy, in the morning, staging via Lyon-Satolas where they refuel. They are followed in the afternoon by two 67th ARRS HC-130Ns, these proceeding direct to Naples.

Two 17th RW TR-1As apparently depart Alconbury for Ramstein, West Germany (and, perhaps, beyond).

Evening activity observed at Lakenheath includes several 48th Tactical Fighter Wing (TFW) F-111Fs performing engine runs while many of the TAB-V shelters are open.

13 April

The European Tanker Task Force (ETTF) continues to expand. More KC-10A Extenders arrive, with most, if not all, coming directly from the USA. Fairford receives three aircraft from the 22nd ARW at March AFB, California, while Mildenhall welcomes four from the 2nd BW and three from the 22nd ARW.

Above: With afterburner flames spearing out from the twin TF30 turbofan engines, a General Dynamics F-111F of the 48th Tactical Fighter Wing at RAF Lakenheath rotates for take-off. Flying from their British base, some 18 "Aardvarks" took part in "El Dorado Canyon".

Above left: In TAB-V hardened shelters scattered around RAF Lakenheath, ground crews and weapons specialists worked hard to prepare two dozen aircraft for the raid on Libya, a figure which included six "air spares" to fill in if any of the prime mission F-111Fs aborted.

Left: Helmets and oxygen masks used by personnel assigned to one of the 48th TFW squadrons. Aircrew which took part in operation "El Dorado Canyon" were drawn from all four of the "Statue of Liberty" Wing squadrons, other strike elements coming from the 6th Fleet.

juries of varying degrees of seriousness. For the USA, it was now clear that the time had come to take fresh action.

The US President acts

On the diplomatic front, attempts were made to persuade European nations to join in condemning Gaddafi and Libya and to undertake joint action — these were largely unsuccessful, most nations being reluctant to be seen to take much in the way of overt action for fear of inviting reprisal attacks. On the military front, contingency plans were drawn up, the US Sixth Fleet in the Mediterranean was directed to move towards Libya and US air bases in the European theatre were brought to a heightened alert state.

Finally, on 14 April, President Reagan, acting in his capacity as the Commander-in-Chief US Armed Forces, issued the executive order committing his forces to combat.

14 April

Expansion of the ETTF is completed with the appearance of two more 2nd BW KC-10As. One moves direct from the USA to Mildenhall while the other transfers from Aviano, Italy, to Fairford. Relocation of one 22nd ARW Extender from Mildenhall to Fairford during the day results in nine KC-10As being present at Fairford while Mildenhall is temporarily home to no fewer than 15. In addition, in-place Stratotanker assets comprise 10 examples of the KC-135A at Fairford with 12 KC-135As, one KC-135E and seven KC-135Qs at Mildenhall. These 30 ETTF tankers are drawn from 14 regular SAC units and one Air National Guard squadron.

 1745Z hours

Six KC-135A/Qs depart Mildenhall in quick succession. These are used to top-up the Extenders and recover to Mildenhall in late evening. Fifteen minutes later ten KC-10A Extenders depart Mildenhall, being followed soon afterwards by a seventh KC-135A.

 ca 1800Z hours

Fighter elements begin to get airborne from Lakenheath and Upper Heyford. At Lakenheath, 24 F-111Fs depart, these being drawn from the 48th TFW's four squadrons. Broken down into six cells of four aircraft, each of which includes an ''air spare'', they begin to format with the KC-10As, some being observed over Mildenhall as they set off on the circuitous route to Libya.

With overflight rights denied by France and Spain, the track they pursue takes them over Land's End, across the Bay of Biscay, down around the Iberian peninsula and along the Mediterranean. It also entails four in-flight refuellings during the outbound journey with two more being completed on the way home.

At Upper Heyford, five EF-111A Ravens of the 42nd Electronic Combat Squadron (ECS) take-off. Only three of these are prime mission aircraft, one returning fairly soon afterwards while another accompanies the strike package to the operating area where it is held in reserve for the duration of the attack.

 1812Z hours

The first KC-10A gets airborne from Fairford, being followed during the next 30 minutes by three more Extenders and two KC-135As. These soon link up with the EF-111As. Twenty-two minutes later a further KC-10A leaves Fairford.

 2030Z-2130Z hours

Six F-111F ''air spares'' recover at Lakenheath; two more KC-10As leave Fairford; the two KC-135As which had flown from Fairford return, having presumably been used to refuel some of the KC-10As.

 2220Z-2320Z hours

Eight A-6E Intruders and six F-18A Hornets launch from the USS *Coral Sea* (CV-43); six

A-6E Intruders and six A-7E Corsairs launch from the USS *America* (CV-66). These 26 aircraft comprise the Navy strike contribution to El Dorado Canyon but other Navy aircraft are also launched to provide CAP cover (F-14As from USS *America* and F-18As from USS *Coral Sea*), airborne early warning (E-2Cs), ECM (EA-6Bs) and in-flight refuelling (KA-6Ds).

 2300Z hours

One KC-10A recovers at Fairford. This was also evidently used to top-off other tankers ac-

companying the F-111Fs. By 0015Z (15 April) a KC-10A, three more Extenders and a solitary KC-135A return to Mildenhall.

2354Z hours

EF-111As begin emitting jamming signals in order to suppress defences in the vicinity of Tripoli. At the same time, Navy A-7Es and F-18As engage enemy radar installations in Benghazi area. A-7Es launch a dozen AGM-45 Shrikes while the F-18As fire no fewer than 36 AGM-88A HARM anti-radiation missiles.

A: First wave of eight F-111Fs deliver Mk.84 2,000lb laser-guided bombs on Al Azziziyah Barracks and Sidi Bilal training area with "Pave Tack" system being used to designate targets. **B:** Second wave of five F-111Fs deposit Mk.82 500lb "Snakeye" retarded bombs on Tripoli airport, each aircraft carrying a dozen of these weapons. **C:** Libyan defences react with indiscriminate anti-aircraft artillery fire which is evidently largely inaccurate. **D:** General Dynamics EF-111A Raven emits jamming signals to suppress defensive networks.

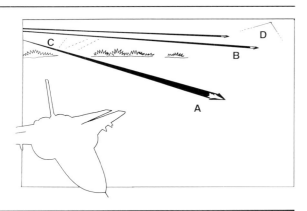

15 April 0001Z hours

Single-pass attacks are made by eight F-111Fs on barracks at Al Azziziyah and Sidi Bilal training area. Weaponry delivered evidently comprises Mk.84 2,000lb (907kg) laser-guided bombs, the F-111F's "Pave Tack" laser designator/rangefinder package being used as a delivery aid.

A dozen A-6Es also execute simultaneous attacks on Benina air base near Benghazi and the Al Jumahiriya barracks.

0007Z-0011Z hours

Tripoli airport is hit by five F-111Fs, each of which carries 12 Mk.82 500lb "Snakeye" retarded bombs.

0013Z hours

All the Navy aircraft report "feet wet" and safely clear of target area, two of the Intruders having been forced to abort by system malfunctions, it being decreed in advance that any aircraft which experienced weapons system failure should not press home its attack. This ruling resulted in five F-111Fs having to abort

Below: Ilyushin Il-76 cargo aircraft parked on the military ramp at Tripoli airport were amongst the targets hit by the F-111Fs from Lakenheath. The nine dark objects visible at mid-right are Mk.82 bombs falling towards the target, weapons delivery being aided by the "Pave Tack" systems.

and of the 13 "Aardvarks" which did attack, one subsequently failed to check-in.

0015Z hours

Search and rescue forces are alerted to look for missing 48th TFW F-111F, and one KC-10A leaves Mildenhall.

0046Z-0053Z hours

All aircraft from the USS *Coral Sea* safely recovered; all aircraft from the USS *America* safely recovered.

c0100Z hours

One KC-10A leaves Mildenhall.

0114Z hours

Post-strike refuelling of F-111Fs reveals that one aircraft is indeed missing in action. Search activities continue until 0300Z on 16 April when crew is declared lost.

c0115Z-0130Z hours

One KC-135A returns to Mildenhall; one KC-135Q and one KC-10A depart Mildenhall. These are operating in support of the SR-71As of the 9th Strategic Reconnaissance Wing's (SRW) Detachment Four, which will perform post-strike photographic reconnaissance.

0300Z-0320Z hours

Two more KC-135Qs and one KC-10A leave Mildenhall in conjunction with SR-71A operations. Engine overheating problem results in one F-111F having to divert.

0400Z-0424Z hours

One 9th SRW Det.4 SR-71A leaves Mildenhall; one KC-10A recovers at Fairford. The diverted F-111F lands safely at Rota, Spain. It eventually returns to Lakenheath on 16 April.

0515Z hours

A second 9th SRW Det.4 SR-71A leaves Mildenhall. Five minutes later a KC-10A recovers at Fairford.

0630Z hours

First of 16 remaining F-111Fs recovers at Lakenheath. At Mildenhall, eight accompanying KC-10As also begin landing, while nine minutes later a KC-10A departs Mildenhall in connection with post-strike photographic reconnaissance mission.

c0700Z hours

Two KC-10As recover at Fairford. Four EF-111As return safely to Upper Heyford, and at 0752Z the last F-111F lands at Lakenheath.

0835Z hours

First 9th SRW Det.4 SR-71A returns to Mildenhall, and the second lands thirteen minutes after.

By 1000Z hours

Last two Extenders return to Fairford.

1152Z hours

General Gabriel leaves Mildenhall for Andrews AFB, Washington, aboard AFSC C-135C. He almost certainly takes with him the results of the SR-71A reconnaissance missions.

Subsequent events

Another post-attack reconnaissance mission is performed on 16 April by the SR-71As of Det.4 from Mildenhall. This is apparently deemed necessary as a result of weather problems encountered on the previous day.

Study of reconnaissance material reveals that all five of the assigned targets were hit successfully although the amount of damage varied, the Sidi Bilal training area escaping relatively lightly. Department of Defense officials subsequently confirm that three bombs hit civilian areas in Tripoli, some damage being caused to the French Embassy. They attribute these weapons to the missing F-111F. Navy bombing also suffered from its share of inaccuracy, two bombs falling on civilian areas.

On the plus side, several Libyan aircraft were destroyed: at Tripoli airport, F-111Fs accounted for at least one Il-76 with several more being damaged, while at Benina A-6Es definitely destroyed four MiG-23 Flogger fighters, two Mil-8 Hip helicopters and one F-27 Friendship. Extensive damage was also inflicted on other MiG-23s, Mi-8s and a Libyan Arab Airlines Boeing 727.

The decision not to initiate further action was evidently reached on 22 April, for it was on that date that the Extenders began returning home. Fairford's tanker fleet was despatched first, three Extenders departing on 22 April. Another KC-10A left on the following day, with the remaining six disappearing from the base on 25 April.

In the meantime, three unusual KC-135As had also reached Fairford. All were from the 305th ARW at Grissom AFB, Indiana, and they evidently played some part in El Dorado Canyon, operating from another (still unknown) European air base. Two of them landed at Fairford on 15 April with the third arriving on the 22nd. All three then left for Grissom on 25 April. Since the 305th ARW forms part of SAC's Post Attack Command Control System, it is possible that these three aircraft functioned in a radio relay capacity.

Returning to the Extender fleet, attention then switched to Mildenhall, where some reshuffling of assets had occurred, two more aircraft having arrived by 26 April to replace two others that had returned to the USA. Of the 15 aircraft that remained in place, four left on 26 April with three more following on 27 April. By May, only two were still present.

Below: *Naval strike aircraft from the USS* Coral Sea *and the USS* America *hit a number of objectives which included the air base at Benina. In this post-strike photograph, probably taken by an SR-71A, it is possible to see the wreckage of several Libyan "Floggers".*

Above: *The rather tortuous route taken by F-111s flying from air bases in the UK is shown on this map. Air refuelling areas are also indicated, the F-111s accomplishing four in-flight "hook-ups" on the outbound leg as well as two more during the equally long homeward flight.*

BENINA AIRFIELD
15 APR 86

DESTROYED MIG-23/FLOGGER

MIG-23/FLOGGER PIECES

THE DEFENCE SUPPRESSION MISSION

Evolution of the Mission

Soviet Tactical AA Systems

Straight Flush radar

Flat Face radar

SA-6 Gainful SAM system

SA-4B Ganef long-range ramjet SAM system

Pat Hand engagement radar

SA-8B Gecko SAM system

ZSU-23-4 flak (AAA) system

T
HE TASK of defence suppression is by no means new. Indeed, such operations were almost certainly undertaken as long ago as World War 1 when primitive "stick-and-string" biplanes of both sides attempted to bomb enemy artillery emplacements. For the most part, though, such attacks had little more than nuisance value and it was not until World War II that defence suppression began to assume greater — indeed vital significance.

At the start of that conflict, radar was still very much in its infancy but even as the efficacy of this new aid to aerial warfare was developed so too was its candidacy and legitimacy as a target. The first recorded raids on radar sites were actually conducted by Germany's Luftwaffe, which devoted a fair amount of attention to Britain's "Chain Home" system during the opening phases of the Battle of Britain in the summer of 1940.

Action and counter-action

In the fertile breeding ground of World War II, it was almost inevitable that rapid progress would be made in developing the potential of radar, this progress being matched by determined efforts on the part of most of the major combatants to conceive and implement effective countermeasures. As they do today, these fell into two broad categories, it very quickly being acknowledged that it wasn't always necessary physically to destroy a radar site in order to render it inoperative. Jamming the radar beam was one variation on the countermeasures theme, the aluminium strips known as "window" (later more universally referred to as "chaff", a term and device which is still used today) being employed by

Above: The very first dedicated anti-radar aircraft were Hawker Typhoon IBs of the RAF. Fitted with pre-tuned receivers, their task was to fire marker rockets, at operating hostile radars. Because they "smoked" their code-name was "Abdulla", a popular brand of cigarette.

Right: This illustration shows major features of some of the vast array of anti-aircraft weapon systems that can roll across country and across rivers and lakes with the Soviet Ground Forces. All these have been in service for many years; replacements are less familiar.

RAF bombers to blind German radar with considerable success. So, too, were jamming transmitters, "Carpet" and "Mandrel" being two examples configured to disrupt Germany's "Freya" and "Wurzburg" radars.

Both of these techniques were what might be described as "passive" but they were accompanied by a number of "active" measures, perhaps best epitomised by the Hawker Typhoons that were fitted with homing receivers. These began operations, code-named "Abdullah", in the summer of 1944 and they could fairly lay claim to being the progenitors of today's generation of "Wild Weasels" in that they were intended first to detect the radar energy emitted by a radar site and then track it to its source, marking the target with smoke rockets for attention by accompanying fighter-bomber aircraft.

"Abdullah" was, however, somewhat primitive and possessed a number of noteworthy drawbacks. Perhaps the most serious was the fact that the detector equipment had to be pre-set to a specific frequency on the ground before take-off — as a counter-coun-

termeasure, all the Germans had to do was switch frequency, an action which rendered the Typhoon more or less useless. In addition, it was also necessary for the Typhoon literally to fly down the beam if it was to "eyeball" the radar site and the Germans soon learned that the best way to negate this was to switch off while "Abdullah"-configured aircraft were in the vicinity. That, of course, could be described as a victory of sorts for the Typhoon, for,

The task of hampering or crippling an enemy's anti-aircraft defences has grown to become a mission in its own right. Far more than any other, it embraces what the Soviet Union long ago recognised by the descriptive term "electronic combat". Though suppression of enemy air defences (SEAD) certainly includes things that explode with a bang, much of the task comprises what the West calls Elint, ECM and ECCM.

while the radar was off the air, it was quite clearly unable to fulfil its function of detecting Allied aircraft.

The Korean War

In the years which immediately followed the Allied victory, a considerable amount of attention was devoted to perfecting radar. By the time of the Korean War, its use had expanded to anti-aircraft artillery and searchlights, both of which devices had been employed with considerable success against USAF B-29s. In distinct contrast, little effort had been devoted to improving anti-radar capability and the United Nations forces were thus largely dependent upon equipment and techniques which had been formulated in World War II. Active measures at the time included the use of "ferret" aircraft like the TB-25J Mitchell to detect radar sites which were then attacked by B-26B Invaders armed with guns, rockets and bombs.

Following the ceasefire in Korea, electronic warfare was again largely relegated to the "back burner" and it did not begin to assume greater importance until the discovery that the

Above: The last version of the McDonnell Phantom to enter USAF service was the F-4G Advanced Wild Weasel. This is a platform for the APR-38 EW system, which uses 52 antennas, the most obvious of which are pods facing forward under the nose and aft at the top of the fin.

Above: AGM-78A Standard ARM was one of the earliest and biggest American anti-radar missiles. Derived from a ship-to-air missile, it was not as reliable as more recent weapons. The carrier here is an F-105G Wild Weasel, which bridged the gap between the F-100 and the F-4G.

Below: Among the last to fly the mighty "Thud" (Republic F-105 Thunderchief) was the 128th Tactical Fighter Squadron of the Georgia Air National Guard. Their F-105G Wild Weasels had ECM pods scabbed to the sides of the fuselage; under each wing are blue ARM simulators.

Soviet Union had succeeded in developing surface-to-air missile capability in the shape of the radar-guided SA-2 "Guideline". This weapon gained its first confirmed kill in October 1962 when it was used to shoot down a U-2 during the Cuban missile crisis. Earlier, the SA-2 had been linked with the loss of Gary Powers' U-2 over the Soviet Union in 1960. This was later proved conclusively.

The spur of Vietnam

These events undoubtedly pointed up the requirement for dedicated defence suppression resources. The US Navy was one of the first to address this matter seriously by moving ahead with the development of the Texas Instruments AGM-45 Shrike anti-radiation missile. As is so often the case, though, it was to take another war to transform defence suppression into the near art form that it is today. The Southeast Asia conflict in the 1960s witnessed the evolution of a number of sophisticated weapons and systems intended specifically to counter the threats posed by ground-controlled intercept radar, surface-to-air missiles and radar-directed anti-aircraft artillery system.

Above: The massive ZUR-3M8M family of ramjet-powered SAMs are just one of the major weapon systems that depend totally upon radars, both for target detection/tracking and missile guidance. With a range exceeding 45 miles (72km) ECM must be exceptionally powerful.

Arguably the best known manifestation is the so-called "Wild Weasel", this generic term describing the family of aircraft which have been employed to detect, locate, classify and, ultimately, destroy enemy radars. Weapons like the AGM-45 Shrike and AGM-78 Standard ARM (Anti-Radiation Missile) were developed specifically for use against such sites.

The first true "Weasel" to enter combat in Southeast Asia was a variation of the F-100F Super Sabre, a handful of aircraft being deployed to Korat, Thailand in November 1965, from where the first (and, incidentally, uneventful) "Iron Hand" mission was flown on 1 December. As it transpired, the Super Sabre was employed only briefly as a "Weasel", being supplanted in the summer of 1966 by the rather more suitable F-105F.

This two-seat derivative of the Republic Thunderchief very soon proved itself to be a near-ideal vehicle for SAM suppression and bore the brunt of USAF activity in this often-hazardous arena for the next few years. It eventually gave way to the ultimate "Weasel Thud" in the shape of the F-105G which introduced a number of improvements and which possessed a greater weapons payload.

Improved "Weasels"

Between 1966 and the ceasefire in January 1973, these two Thunderchief models constituted virtually the entire active USAF defence suppression force in Vietnam although they were augmented by some suitably-modified F-4C Phantoms which played an important part in the "Linebacker II" campaign of December 1972. US Navy air-

craft which were utilised as "Weasels" included the A-4 Skyhawk, A-6 Intruder and A-7 Corsair II, carrying special equipment. In this operation the USAF delivered massive blows north of the 20th parallel inducing the North Vietnamese to negotiate a truce.

Following the progressive phase-out of the F-105G during the late 1970s and early 1980s, the USAF's "Wild Weasel" force has been entirely equipped with the F-4G Phantom. The type is presently active with elements of Tactical Air Command (TAC), Pacific Air Forces (PACAF) and United States Air Forces in Europe (USAFE).

Kfir attack: The effectiveness of tactical air operations can be vastly enhanced by the presence of a friendly AWACS-type surveillance and direction platform. Here two Israeli Kfirs run in to attack a surface-to-air missile (SAM) site, one (A) along an escarpment and the other (B) on the desert floor, pulling up to release its weapons to destroy the SAM site (C). At (D) some F-15s provide high cover, while (E) is an F-4 strike force. The vital E-2C Hawkeye is at (F) coordinating the operation from afar.

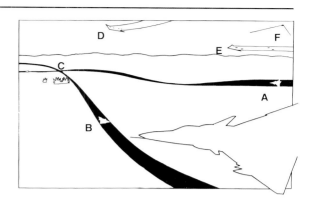

Other air arms, with less in the way of financial resources available, have been slower to implement the "Weasel" concept. The RAF was forced to rely on elderly Shrike-armed Vulcan B.2 bombers to undertake defence suppression tasks during the Falklands War. Even here, however, change is in prospect,

Above: *One of the Douglas EB-66C ECM jammer aircraft used by the 39th TEWS at Spangdahlem in the early 1970s. Similar aircraft, and Elint EB-66Es, served in Vietnam in support of tactical attack and reconnaissance missions. They were the first dedicated EW aircraft in the USAF.*

Germany, for example, forging ahead with development of a "Wild Weasel" variation of the Panavia Tornado.

In addition to the celebrated "Weasels", Vietnam also served as a catalyst for improvement in other areas of defence suppression, in particular the task of jamming, for which a number of Douglas Destroyers were modified. Some — such as the RB-66B (later EB-66B) and the RB-66C (later EB-66C) — actually predated that conflict but the EB-66E was a true child of the war, making its debut during the latter half of the 1960s. Between them, these three derivatives were the only dedicated "jammers" available to PACAF, additional capability being provided by pods fitted to most tactical aircraft and by a trio of specialised Navy machines, namely the EA-1F Skyraider, the EKA-3B Skywarrior and the EA-6B Prowler. The US Marine Corps also maintained a modest electronic warfare capability in Vietnam, initially employing the vintage Douglas EF-10B Skyknight as a "jammer" and, with effect from October 1966, the Grumman EA-6A Intruder.

Age finally caught up with the Destroyer in 1974 and for a few years the USAF had to

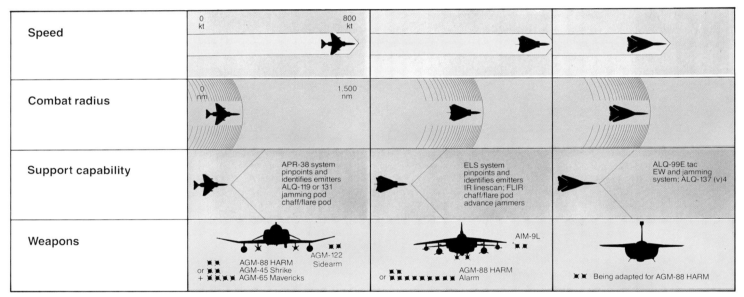

	F-4G Phantom II	Tornado ECR	EF-111A Raven
Speed	0 kt — 800 kt		
Combat radius	0 nm — 1,500 nm		
Support capability	APR-38 system pinpoints and identifies emitters ALQ-119 or 131 jamming pod chaff/flare pod	ELS system pinpoints and identifies emitters IR linescan; FLIR chaff/flare pod advance jammers	ALQ-99E tac EW and jamming system; ALQ-137 (v)4
Weapons	AGM-122 Sidearm / AGM-88 HARM or AGM-45 Shrike + AGM-65 Mavericks	AIM-9L / AGM-88 HARM or Alarm	Being adapted for AGM-88 HARM

It is particularly difficult to assess and compare defence-suppression and EW aircraft, if only for the fact that the crucial aspect of their performance is electronic, and thus not amenable to slick numerical measures (Much, if not all, of this information is classified in any case.). There is little point in comparing such measures as speed or altitude performance, though combat radius can be important, as can the ability to fly to a target in company with attacking aircraft. The first aircraft in the world to fly EW/ECM defence suppression missions was the US Navy EF-10B Skyknight, a converted night fighter, and ever since most aircraft in this category have been conversions, variants or rebuilds of fighter or attack aircraft (It is interesting to note that the EF-10B ECM jamming and dispensing aircraft was the only fully suitable and available EW platform in Vietnam. These aircraft had previously obtained the first signatures of Soviet surveillance and SAM radars in China and Cuba.). In future such lo-observable "stealth" aircraft as the Lockheed CSIRS (Covert Survivable In-Weather Reconnaissance Strike Aircraft) are bound to be the most important candidates for the defence-suppression role, because, employing increasingly comprehensive ECM and other defence systems, (not to mention the use of exotic composites and careful shaping of the airframe to reduce the radar cross-section) they are much more likely to be able to return to fly another day.

◀ **F-4G Phantom II**

Power plant: Two General Electric J79-17 (17,900lb/80kN)
Span: 38ft 5in (11.7m)
Length: 63ft 0in (19.2m)
Max TO weight: 60,360lb (27,379kg)
Crew: 2

◀ **Tornado ECR**

Power plant: Two Turbo-Union RB.199 Mk 105 (18,100lb/80.5kN)
Span: (max sweep) 28ft 2.5in (8.6m)
Length: 54ft 10in (16.72m)
Max TO weight: about 60,000lb (27,215.4kg)
Crew: 2

Above: *Produced by totally rebuilding F-111A attack aircraft, the GD/Grumman EF-111A Raven is today's USAF EW jammer, serving at Mountain Home, USA, and Upper Heyford, England. The advanced ALQ-99E system does not need the two extra human operators carried by the EA-6B.*

many air arms it was the only option and the benefits in the area of enhanced survivability were felt by far to outweigh the disadvantages of reduced payload.

For the USAF, the situation was less than satisfactory but the gap was not filled until the advent of the EF-111A Raven derivative of the controversial General Dynamics warplane. Entering service with the 366th TFW at Mountain Home AFB, Idaho in late 1981, the EF-111A incorporates the AN/ALQ-99E Tactical Jamming System and a total of 42 examples of the Raven was eventually "produced" by conversion of existing F-111As. The lion's share of these are presently assigned to TAC's 366th TFW which controls one fully operational squadron (390th ECS) but 13 have found their way overseas, greatly boosting USAFE EW capability in the process.

Presently equipping the 66th Electronic Combat Wing's 42nd ECS at RAF Upper Heyford, in England, five of these aircraft were despatched to provide support for F-111Fs participating in the US raid on Libya during April 1986 although only three were actually involved in the attack phase of that operation, "El Dorado Canyon".

manage without a dedicated jamming platform. For air arms with tighter budgetary limitations such capability as did exist was in many ways a compromise, provision of jamming pods on tactical aircraft being possible only at the expense of weapons payload. While this may have been undesirable, for

EA-6B Prowler   **MiG-25 FR**   **F-16 FOW**

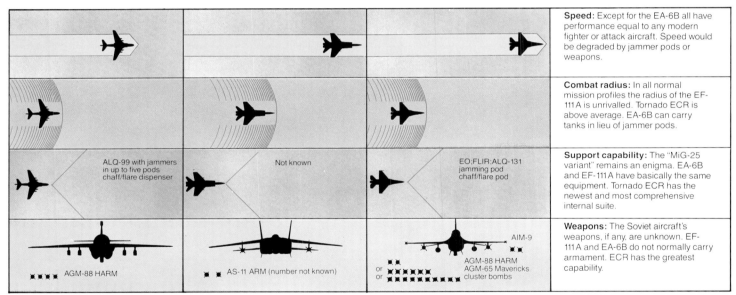

			Speed: Except for the EA-6B all have performance equal to any modern fighter or attack aircraft. Speed would be degraded by jammer pods or weapons.
			Combat radius: In all normal mission profiles the radius of the EF-111A is unrivalled. Tornado ECR is above average. EA-6B can carry tanks in lieu of jammer pods.
ALQ-99 with jammers in up to five pods chaff/flare dispenser	Not known	EO;FLIR;ALQ-131 jamming pod chaff/flare pod	**Support capability:** The "MiG-25 variant" remains an enigma. EA-6B and EF-111A have basically the same equipment. Tornado ECR has the newest and most comprehensive internal suite.
AGM-88 HARM	AS-11 ARM (number not known)	AIM-9 / or AGM-88 HARM AGM-65 Mavericks / or cluster bombs	**Weapons:** The Soviet aircraft's weapons, if any, are unknown. EF-111A and EA-6B do not normally carry armament. ECR has the greatest capability.

◄ EF-111A Raven

Power plant: Two Pratt & Whitney TF30-3 (18,500lb/88.28kN)
Span: (max sweep) 31ft 11.5in (9.74m)
Length: 77ft 2in (23.53m)
Max TO weight: 87,478lb (39,680kg)
Crew: 2

◄ MiG-25FR

Power plant: Two Tumanskii R-31F (30,865lb/137.3kN)
Span: 45ft 9in (13.95m)
Length: 78ft 2in (23.83m)
Max TO weight: (approx) 82,500lb (37,425kg)
Crew: 2

◄ EA-6B Prowler

Power plant: Two Pratt & Whitney J52-408 (11,200lb/49.8kN)
Span: 53ft 0in (16.15m)
Length: 59ft 10in (18.24m)
Max TO weight: 65,000lb (29,483kg)
Crew: 4

◄ F-16 FOW

Power plant: One P&W F100-229 or GE F110-IPE (each 29,000lb/129kN)
Span: (over missiles) 32ft 9.75n (10.0m)
Length: 49ft 4in (15.03m)
Max TO weight: 37,500lb (17,010kg)
Crew: probably 1

The Raven Mission

I N PURELY monetary terms, the Grumman/ General Dynamics EF-111A Raven must surely rank as one of the most expensive warplanes around and yet it lacks the ability to deliver even the most rudimentary weapon. Be that as it may, its deficiency in sheer offensive capability is more than compensated for by its unparalleled potential as a "force multiplier", for the presence of even a single fully mission capable Raven is almost guaranteed to ensure the survival of far less costly but no less valuable strike aircraft. Almost literally stuffed from nose to tail with a sophisticated array of electronic equipment and tasked with the jamming of enemy defensive networks, as is related in the accompanying account, the Raven will spend much of its time far from the thick of the action, on the friendly side of the front line. From that reasonably secure position, it will detect, identify, locate, record and aim powerful but unseen electronic emissions, from its jammer installation, at distant enemy radars.

 1030 hours

At RAF Upper Heyford, a few miles to the north of the university town of Oxford in England ground crews and armourers perspire heavily as they prepare the F-111Es of the 20th Tactical Fighter Wing for combat duty. Not too far away, more 20th TFW personnel go through the motions of preparation, but their work is more cerebral in nature and the flight planning room is fairly hushed as some 20 crews — each comprising a pilot and weapons system officer or "wizzo" — ready themselves for the coming mission.

In fact, only 16 aircraft are scheduled to take part in the raid but, so as to minimise the possibility of success being compromised by aborts, four additional F-111s will launch and accompany the primary strike aircraft to the commit point, one "spare" being provided for each cell of four "Aardvarks". If the spares are not needed, they will then deposit their ordnance on a target of opportunity in the vicinity of the front line.

Magdeburg is the target, this having been identified by NATO intelligence as a major staging point and resupply area for Soviet ground armies active to the west. This afternoon's raid is, in fact, merely one of several scheduled for this day so as to cause maximum disruption to the enemy offensive, the disruption taking a variety of forms.

Bombing is by far the most visible and im- . . and the widespread destruction is . . beginning to exact its toll, hastily . . d repair gangs being hard at work at a . . key points in and around the city. . . equally disruptive is the delivery of . . .ction devices, for it is first necessary . . . hese before repair work can resume in . .ty. Finally, the all-too-frequent air raid alerts cause problems by taking people away from far more important functions until the all clear sounds.

Dutch and Belgian F-16s and German Phantoms began that day's work soon after dawn and the impact of the first raid is still being felt by bomb disposal teams who are in danger of being overwhelmed by calls for assistance. A repeat visit by Luftwaffe Phantoms in mid-morning adds to the difficulties and even as the 20th TFW aircrews ready themselves for action in England, six RAF Tornados strike at three previously untouched targets. Each Tornado carries two JP233 munitions dispensers and between them they deposit 360 cratering devices, causing massive damage to two truck parks and a railway yard. As if that isn't bad enough, the task of clearing up is made immeasurably more difficult by the presence of no fewer than 2,580 air-delivered delayed action mines.

Targets for the Americans comprise two railway marshalling yards, a vehicle park and a barrack block which is evidently being used to house ground troops as they pass through to the battle area. Four F-111Es are to hit each target simultaneously with a mixture of Mk.82 500lb and Mk.84 2,000lb bombs as well as CBU-58 cluster bomb units. Ingress and egress routings are carefully planned to cut down the risk of collision and also to limit exposure to

Above: *Preparation for an EF-111A Raven mission is inevitably a lengthy process, pilots looking after such details as route and orbit areas while the Electronic Warfare Officers study intelligence data pertaining to the enemy's electronic order of battle in the area concerned.*

Right: *Before proceeding from the squadron's hardened operations complex to their aircraft, the aircrew visit the life support section where they will don specialised flight kit. Part of the preparation process includes verifying that oxygen masks work correctly.*

enemy gun and missile threats, for Magdeburg's defences have already destroyed three NATO aircraft that day. If executed correctly, all 16 aircraft will pass through the lethal threat envelope in little more than a minute, compression of this order being planned to saturate the defences which will also have to contend with the attacking force's chaff, flares and jamming pods.

Even more importantly, though, it is hoped

Left: *While the aircrew are otherwise engaged in planning for the upcoming mission, ground support technicians are no less busy, readying their charges for flight. Here, a member of ground crew busies himself in the Raven's cockpit, ensuring that all is ready.*

directed at those radars which are deemed to pose the greatest "threat" to the strike force.

In practice, of course, the extensive use of automation significantly eases the work-load, for the ALQ-99E package may be pre-programmed to detect, identify, locate and initiate electronic jamming entirely independently of the EWO, and much of the mission pre-planning is inevitably concerned with setting up "the system". Free of the need individually to counter known "threats", the EWO can instead divert his attention to looking for and dealing with previously unidentified radars.

 1135 hours

Mission briefing is, inevitably, a long and almost tortuously complex business. In addition to more conventional matters such as routing, weather, radio call-signs and timings, much time is spent on discussing such aspects as electronic "threats", operational tactics, orbit areas and evasion procedures in the event of enemy fighters attempting to interfere.

The latter is, in fact, difficult to resolve since there is an understandable reluctance to put such complex and valuable assets at risk. Clearly, the easiest solution to a threat posed by enemy fighters is for the EF-111s to "bug out" (remove themselves from the threat area), but that will mean they have failed in their objective and will increase the degree of danger faced by friendly strike elements.

Recent deployment of the "Compass Call" EC-130H ComJam (Communications Jamming) platform has, however, tilted the odds a shade more in favour of the Ravens. The presence of this bizarre-looking variation on the Hercules theme means that Soviet GCI (Ground Controlled Interception) networks are almost certainly going to be severely impaired and it is not beyond the realms of possibility that Soviet fighter control could break down completely. In conjunction with escorting fighters (ideally the F-15, although the F-16 could be used), this seems to offer the best means of furnishing protection to the EF-111A Ravens.

 1205 hours

With briefing now over, the next port of call is the survival section, where the crews complete the job of dressing for flight go on, helmets are collected and sid gathered up in little more than m before the crews return to the op room to await transportation to the shelters and their respective aircraft.

 1210 hours

"Transport's arrived, guys," shouts a member of the operations staff, adding, almost as an

that the attack will come as a complete surprise and it is for this reason that three other aircraft are being prepared for action at Upper Heyford. Also hidden from view inside hardened shelter accommodation, three of the 42nd Electronic Combat Squadron's fleet of 13 General Dynamics/Grumman EF-111A Ravens are being readied for flight. The trio comprises two mission aircraft and a spare. In this case, though, the process is far less visible,

for they will go into action unarmed, save for a couple of AIM-9 Sidewinder heat-seeking air-to-air missiles which will bestow a modicum of defensive capability in the event of their being engaged by enemy fighters.

Beneath the surface, however, it is a rather different story. Technicians "tweak" the sophisticated suite of avionics that constitute the AN/ALQ-99E Tactical Jamming System (TJS). Utilising jamming signals emanating from antennae buried in the ventral canoe radome, the Raven will "blind" enemy early warning radars and in so doing accomplish its task of protecting the strike-dedicated elements which should then be able to penetrate to the target area undetected by electronic means.

 1055 hours

While their aircraft are being checked out, the three Raven crews are busy elsewhere, planning for the upcoming tasking. As is ever the case, the pilots are mainly concerned with matters aeronautical, such as routings, orbit areas and altitude. Eventually, they agree on an orbit pattern that will position the Ravens some 20 to 30 miles (32-48km) from the forward edge of the battle area (FEBA) on the friendly side of the line, one to fly its racetrack pattern to the north of the ingress route with the other operating to the south. There, they will be sufficiently far from the high threat zone to limit the risk to themselves, while still being able to degrade the capability of the enemy radar system.

1100 hours

As they consider these matters, their respective Electronic Warfare Officers or "EWOs", who will monitor the EW environment from the right-hand seat, devote their attention to data concerning the enemy's electronic order of battle so as to ensure that jamming power is afterthought, "Have a nice day." Encumbered with personal kit, charts and other impedimenta, the crews move towards the exit.

1250 hours

With pre-flight inspection complete and with both TF30 engines now running sweetly, the pilot of the leading Raven snaps off a smart salute to the crew chief before gently nudging the throttle levers forward. The noise level inside the shelter increases in intensity as the EF-111A begins to move.

Before it clears the shelter, the pilot nudges the brakes, causing the nose to dip smartly, before, satisfied that all appears to be in order, he manipulates the throttles yet again, squinting momentarily as the aircraft emerges into bright sunlight. Alongside him, intent on his scopes and displays, the EWO stays "head-down", adjusting the brightness controls to compensate for the sudden glare that floods into the cockpit.

1253 hours

Turning left out of the dispersal area, Raven lead heads for the active runway, taxiing quite fast so as to minimise time spent on the ground. As the aircraft moves briskly along, flaps are lowered ready for take-off and the pilot runs through yet another check-list. He pauses momentarily to remind his EWO to lower his visor as a precaution against a bird-strike when they depart.

Two more EF-111As emerge, falling neatly into trail as they too make for the runway, the pilot of the second aircraft taking a few moments out to look about him as they trundle along. Heyford is clearly "jumping" today as preparations for the mass launch near their climax. All over the airfield, TAB-V shelters are open and, as he rolls by one of them, the pilot can see ground crew going about their well-rehearsed pre-departure routines. Beneath the wings of the F-111E inside the shelter, munitions specialists run one final check on fuse settings and remove the last "safing" devices. Others stand by to "eyeball" the flight control surfaces which are brought into play in quick succession — in the fleeting glimpse he gets before the shelter and its occupants are lost from view, he faintly discerns the fully-variable horizontal tailplanes swivel about their axis.

Ahead of him as he swings around towards the runway, he sees his flight leader depart, amidst a blast of vapour and flame as two TF30 turbofans working at full bore propel the Raven aloft. Barely 20 seconds later, he begins his own take-off roll, the aircraft accelerating smoothly down the runway to break ground at around the 3,500ft (1,060m) mark. As the nose lifts, so the third EF-111A begins its noisy journey down the concrete strip.

1356 hours

Transit to the designated working area is accomplished at medium altitude and speed but even though they are not exactly hurrying, it takes less than an hour to reach their orbit point, which lies on the Allied side of the

FEBA, in the relative security offered by "friendly" territory. Now, there are just two Ravens, the spare having turned back and returned to home base when it became clear that the primary mission aircraft were in good shape and fit for the task ahead.

At 22,000ft (6,663m), they are well above the cloud layer and make an inviting target for any enemy aircraft bold enough to try for an interception. They also appear to be alone in the sky but that is not in fact the case, since pairs of F-15s from the Soesterberg-based 32nd Tactical Fighter Squadron are performing escort CAP duty. These are on a high "perch", almost directly above, ready to pounce in the event of the EF-111As being threatened.

1400 hours

Both Ravens have begun to fly their orbit patterns and are monitoring the ether although they have yet to commence jamming. Defensive ECM equipment is active, though, the display linked to the passive AN/ALR-62 terminal threat warning sub-system (TTWS) occasionally indicating the presence of a missile

A: Tracks flown by a pair of orbiting EF-111A Ravens from the 42nd Electronic Combat Squadron at RAF Upper Heyford. Initially, they operate in "passive" mode, utilising electronic kit to detect, locate and classify any "threats" that exist within their area of responsibility. Only at the appointed time will they begin to emit high-powered jamming signals aimed at disrupting the enemy's radar network and preventing them from detecting the inbound strike package of F-111Es.
B: Flight path taken by F-111Es as they run in to attack.

control radar. Such strobes are weak, however, and confirm that there is no immediate danger to their continued well-being. At the same time, the ALQ-137 multi-band deception jammer is receiving hostile radar signals which are "painting" the aircraft, delaying and then regenerating them in an effort to mislead the enemy as to the whereabouts of the two Ravens.

In both cases, a "racetrack" pattern is employed, one being positioned to the north of the ingress route and one to the south, and the task of station-keeping is immeasurably aided by the inertial navigation system which has been programmed with details relating to turn points. Autopilot is also engaged by both aircraft and the aircraft are essentially flying themselves, permitting the pilots to devote most of their attention to keeping a look-out for hostile fighters while the EWOs concentrate on the electronic "battle".

On the main digital display indicator which dominates the instrument panel in front of each EWO, there is evidence of considerable electronic activity across the border. Enemy long-range early warning radars are on the alert for intruders, as are height-finding and target acquisition systems. The computer associated with the Raven's ALQ-99E package analyses signals picked up by the fin-mounted antennae farm and presents it to the EWO in a more readily understood format. Data available includes information on enemy radar types and frequencies as well as a line-of-sight indication to each emitter.

Studying the screen, the EWO quickly selects the radars he wishes to jam, before using the control panel located on the right console to tune some of the ten high-powered jamming transmitters to the desired frequencies. As he works, the directional aerials associated with each transmitter are trained on the radars against which they will operate when the time comes to begin emitting.

That time is now fast approaching, for the strike-dedicated F-111s are well on their way to the target area. Staying low as they speed across Western Germany, they have thus far remained unseen but their chances of escaping detection decline as they penetrate further into the radar "thicket".

 1405 hours

At precisely the moment called for in the battle plan, both EWOs activate their respective systems. Below, invisible but high-powered jamming signals radiate from the transmitters situated in the ventral canoe, reaching out towards the hostile radars which constitute their "targets".

On the ground to the east of the FEBA, enemy radar operators — who have been observing the two orbiting Ravens intently — look on almost bemusedly as their radar displays are instantaneously covered with hundreds and possibly thousands of spurious returns, rendering them electronically "blind". Different radars, working on different frequencies, are brought into play and for a few moments the picture clears....

 1407 hours

In the EF-111As, the EWOs have been anticipating such a move and quickly observe the appearance of this new radar "threat". Seconds later, they act, calling spare transmitter capacity into play to counter the enemy ploy — within moments, overwhelmed by a new wave of jamming on a different frequency, the Russian controllers are again effectively reduced to the status of a blind man looking for a black cat in a dark room.

And so it goes on, Russian move being countermanded by American move in an electronic equivalent of "cat and mouse". Meanwhile, far below, the strike package splits up as it closes on the target. Thus far, it has escaped detection by electronic means but ground-based observers using nothing more sophisticated than a good pair of binoculars

(Zeiss, naturally) in conjunction with the "Mk.1 eyeball" have reported their passage by land-line. An astute local commander guesses that they are heading for Magdeburg and alerts elements of the ground defences to the probability of yet another air raid. In and around the city, the sirens begin to wail for the sixth time that day....

 1421 hours

Far from the scene of the action, the two Ravens continue to orbit, erecting an electronic screen to cover the strike force as it withdraws. Most of the 16 F-111Es have come through safely but Magdeburg's defences have exacted some penalty, one aircraft being downed by accurate anti-aircraft artillery (AAA) just seconds before bomb release. Another is limping clear on one engine, one of its TF30 turbofans having had to be shut down following a near miss from a shoulder-fired heat-seeking missile.

By and large, though, the Heyford-based bombers have achieved their objectives, with the enemy truck park being hardest hit, since the raid coincided with the presence of a large quantity of fuel and ammunition en route to the front. Now, a large pall of smoke hangs over that part of the city and secondary explosions continue to rock nearby buildings, many of which show signs of considerable blast and shrapnel damage.

 1423 hours

Elsewhere, the electronic battle continues. On

Below: *Having reached their selected working area, which lies well on the Allied side of the front line, the pair of Ravens begin to orbit. Initially, they will study the electronic environment, selecting those enemy radars which pose the greatest "threat" to the strike force.*

this occasion, the Ravens appear to have won the day. Soviet controllers have been perpetually frustrated in the face of sustained jamming directed against their radar network and their communications systems, a "Compass Call" EC-130H also being in action from a point of safety far to the rear of the front line. In the 20 minutes or so that have elapsed since the Ravens began radiating, ground-based radars have been unable to present a clear picture for more than a few seconds at a time and the few Soviet fighters that were airborne were unable to achieve anything in the absence of effective control.

 1424 hours

By chance, two of the Soviet fighters begin to move westwards and for a few moments it looks as though they might well present a threat to the southerly EF-111A. Alert to the possibility of determined counter-action, two of the escort CAP Eagles react quickly, moving east to position themselves along the line of approach that the Soviet fighters will most likely take if they continue coming. In the event, the two "bogeys" soon reverse their track and head back towards the relative security of eastern European skies and home base in East Germany.

 1425 hours

Less than a minute later, with the damaged "Aardvark" now back on the Allied side of the front line and heading for a nearby divert field, the two Ravens abandon their orbit and turn

for home, ceasing emitting as they too withdraw. Behind them, Soviet radar displays magically clear, revealing a handful of returns which recede and eventually disappear as the EF-111s and their escorting Eagles retire.

Although their task is now essentially complete, the Raven crews still face the prospect of a one-hour transit flight back to Upper Heyford, followed by a lengthy debriefing involving discussion of the mission itself. In addition, they will also be called upon to submit a fairly detailed intelligence analysis which will go towards updating the ever-evolving picture of the enemy's electronic order of battle. At least they will not be forced to rely on memory for they will have the mission tapes to help them.

Below: Following tradition, the pilot occupies the left seat but it is to his right, where the Electronic Warfare Officer sits, that the Raven's mission is accomplished. Dominating the EWO's work station is the digital display indicator screen and its associated control panel.

Above: On return to base, Raven crews gather up mission tapes and turn them over to intelligence specialists for analysis. In addition, they also undergo a detailed debriefing session which examines not only the conduct of the mission but also the intelligence gathered.

Top: With flaps and leading edge slats deployed and with the undercarriage down, an EF-111A returns to Upper Heyford at the end of another mission. Clearly visible behind the nosewheel is the long ventral canoe through which jamming signals are transmitted at enemy radars.

The 'Wild Weasel' Mission

OF ALL the many and varied aspects of air-to-ground warfare, the job of defence suppression is potentially the most hazardous for it almost inevitably requires a "Wild Weasel" crew to expose itself to enemy missile control radars before it can contemplate engaging them with anti-radiation missiles such as the AGM-45 Shrike and AGM-88 HARM. Of course, it is by no means essential to actually destroy an enemy surface-to-air missile site in order to acheive the objective of suppressing the

defences and there are indeed many instances on record where enemy radars simply went off the air once they had been alerted to the presence of the "Wild Weasels". In the operation described here, elements of Spangdahlem's 52nd Tactical Fighter Wing take on surface-to-air threats situated close to a petroleum, oil and lubricants storage facility that will shortly become the target for a strike mission to be conducted by General Dynamics F-16A Fighting Falcons of the Belgian Air Force.

1430 hours

For three members of the Spangdahlem-based 52nd Tactical Fighter Wing — USAFE's only in-theatre "Wild Weasel" assets — the day's first mission looks like being a relatively low-key affair. The target comprises a small POL (petrol, oil and lubricant) storage facility situated just a few miles to the east of the FEBA (forward edge of battle area). Defences are adjudged to be light, consisting mostly of low calibre AAA and small arms but at least two mobile SA-8 "Gecko" surface-to-air missile launchers have been reported, giving credence to the briefing officer's comment that the facility is a particularly low-value target.

Even though it is less effective than later Soviet SAMs, "Gecko" still poses a definite threat and is not a weapon to be taken lightly, especially since it looks as though a considerable amount of thought has been given to the disposition of these units. They lie on high ground to the north and south of the target, along the approach path which will most probably be taken by any attacking force. Reconnaissance pictures taken a few hours earlier show the location quite clearly, but, while it offers the "Land Roll" missile control radar an excellent field of view, it also has the disadvantage of rendering them particularly vulnerable to the attentions of the "Weasel".

The NATO strike force which will be operating against this target will comprise half-a-dozen Belgian F-16A Fighting Falcons from No.349 Squadron at Beauvechain, and the attack is timed to coincide with a far larger — and well escorted — strike against a key military target some way to the north. That, it is hoped, will divert Soviet air defences away from the modest resources that are being committed in the south and it is for that reason that no MiG-CAP is being provided. Those responsible for preparing the "Frag" order have specified that all aircraft carry a couple of AIM-9 Sidewinders to provide some self-defence

Above: *The AGM-88A HARM anti-radiation missile is now the primary tool used by "Wild Weasel" configured F-4G Phantoms engaged in defence suppression although the older AGM-45 Shrike still features in the operational inventory. Both types of missile are carried by this 52nd TFW Phantom.*

capability in the event of their being "bounced" by enemy fighters.

As far as the Belgians are concerned, their game plan is to try to overwhelm the defences by putting all six aircraft through the lethal threat envelope in no more than 30 seconds. The first two will undoubtedly be most at risk, since their attack profile calls for them to fly near-reciprocal courses along the valley line to deliver Mk.20 Rockeye cluster bomb munitions. Fused for low-altitude air burst, these will, if everything goes according to plan, puncture the various storage containers and cause their valuable contents to escape.

Moments later, the remaining four aircraft will perform a co-ordinated high-speed attack from various compass points, each depositing a dozen Mk.82 "Snakeye" 500lb (227kg) retarded general-purpose bombs which ought to result in a healthy conflagration.

At Spangdahlem, hidden from view in two of the many TAB-V hardened aircraft shelters that dominate the skyline, ground crew have been working almost round-the-clock for the

past three days, preparing the "Wild Weasel"-configured F-4G Phantoms and the marginally less "magic" F-16C Fighting Falcons to meet the 52nd TFW's impressively heavy upcoming work-load.

With several hundred combat sorties already completed, the aircrew are also beginning to show signs of fatigue but the arrival of more personnel — mostly instructors pulled in haste from the 37th TFW's "Weasel College" at George AFB, California — means that some can take a brief but no less welcome respite.

Indeed, the F-4G crew for this afternoon's strike are fresh arrivals, but they do at least have the advantage of being familiar with the

Above: *A relatively new addition to the "Wild Weasel" team, the F-16C Fighting Falcon can use radar-homing missiles but will most probably operate with cluster bomb units and conventional "iron" bombs. Here, a 52nd TFW F-16C Fighting Falcon departs on another mission.*

Below: *The numerous antennae associated with the F-4G Phantom's sophisticated AN/APR-38 Radar Homing and Warning System are clearly visible on this "lizard"-camouflaged example. Beneath the wing can be seen a single AGM-88A HARM "fire-and-forget" anti-radar missile.*

European environment, having completed tours of duty with the 52nd TFW before being reassigned to the USA to serve as instructors. The pilot of the F-16C which will operate as part of the two-ship team is now viewed as an "old hand" in that he already has four combat sorties under his belt.

Even as they undergo pre-strike briefing, their aircraft are being prepared for action. In the case of the F-4G, this is most definitely a complex operation, involving fuelling and arming — AGM-88A HARM missiles are the primary armament — as well as checking out and programming the computer which forms part of the sophisticated AN/APR-38 Radar Homing and Warning System (RHAWS). Readying the F-16C is slightly less demanding but munitions experts are kept quite busy muscling a mix of conventional Mk. 82 Bombs and Rockeye CBUs into place, as well as ensuring that the integral Vulcan M61A1 20mm cannon has a full magazine.

Both aircraft also carry AN/ALQ-131 noise/deception jamming pods for defensive pur-

poses against ground threats, as well as AIM-9 Sidewinders for use against airborne threats even though "Weasel" doctrine is fundamentally predicated upon avoiding "mixing it" in aerial combat, discretion most emphatically being the better part of valour. On this occasion, however, the three airmen do not expect to run into enemy fighters, but it is as well to be prepared for that eventuality.

For the pairing, the operational plan is to reach the target area some four or five minutes before the Belgian force. This margin is adjudged sufficient to probe the enemy's defences in order to locate major threats and, if the opportunity presents itself, to utilise either missiles or bombs to negate those threats. Approach to the combat zone will be at low level in standard tactical line abreast formation with about 5,000 to 7,000ft (1,5000 to 2,100m) separation, a measure of mutual protection being provided by "continuous fluid manoeuvring" (frequent co-ordinated crossovers) which will permit each crew periodically to check the other's six o'clock position.

During the ingress phase, both aircraft could well prove vulnerable to marauding enemy fighters since both feature basically grey camouflage. The Weasel crew grimace when they learn that their machine is one of the freshly repainted examples rather than one that retains the less aesthetically pleasing but far less visible "European One" camouflage finish which offers superior protection when viewed against the heavily wooded terrain over which they will fly. Sustained combat operations during the previous couple of days have clearly revealed this to be an unwelcome hazard, and some of the 52nd's aircraft have received a hastily-applied coat of darker-coloured paint — unfortunately, neither of the two machines being used today is among this batch.

Once in the working area, the F-4G will be at greater risk, since, if it is to do its job correctly it must periodically "unmask" so as to allow the AN/APR-38 RHAWS a clear look at the electronic threats. This, in turn, allows enemy missile control and guidance radars a sight of the "Weasel" itself — the trick is judging just how long is safe and when to head back down to the security of surrounding terrain.

 1500 hours

With the briefing over, the three aircrew turn their attention to planning their mission, perusing maps to establish the best path to pursue in order to reach the target area. While it is most desirable to proceed direct from Spangdahlem, today's intense allied aerial activity means that this is not possible and the routing they eventually settle on is something of a compromise, offering reasonably good protection in that they will be able to utilise the cover of rolling terrain to disguise their approach while at the same time avoiding known hazards. It also features a couple of highly visible waypoints along the planned line of flight so there is little risk of them becoming lost.

 1520 hours

The next stop is the locker room, where, in company with half-a-dozen other crews, they waste little time in donning their kit and collecting helmets and side-arms, the Weasel's "Bear" (Electronic Warfare Officer) remembering to transfer a packet of chewing gum from one of his hip pockets to a breast pocket before putting on his G-suit.

A few hundred yards away, in the 480th's shelter complex, ground crew put the final touches to their aircraft, polishing cockpit canopies and gathering up the red "remove before flight" streamers from various points on the respective airframes. Elsewhere in the shelters, munitions specialists stand by, ready to perform the few actions that are necessary to transform the ordnance from an inert to a fully-armed state.

 1530 hours

Back at operations, the two pilots and the EWO gather up their belongings and head out to the bus that will ferry them to dispersal.

FIGHTER MISSIONS

Apart from a security police vehicle and one or two figures visible in the tower they see nobody, but the apparent lack of activity is misleading, since primary and back-up aircraft are being readied for flight in at least a dozen hardened shelters.

1534 hours

The Weasel crew disembark first and quickly scuttle into the security of the concrete cavern which houses their F-4G. Once inside, the pilot quickly button-holes the crew chief and sets about completing the few items of paper-work that are necessary to make it "his" air-craft. Log books are perused, revealing no snags and he then turns his attention to the air-craft itself. The brief pre-flight inspection is lit-

tle more than a formality although he does take a very close look at the weapons rails and their cargo of missiles. In the background, a generator bursts into life, providing power to permit the "Bear" — who has already taken up station in the rear cockpit — to bring his com-plex array of electronic wizardry to life.

1539 hours

Moments later, he is joined by the pilot, who quickly runs through the routine pre-start checks, conferring briefly with the EWO to confirm that the intercom system is fully operable. Then, exchanging hand signals with the crew chief, the pilot initiates engine start procedure. The generator note deepens as it feeds air to spin up the turbine blades of one of the J79 turbojets. With that engine running, bleed air is diverted to start the second engine.

At the same moment, the massive doors of a dozen shelters begin to rumble open, clearing the way for their occupants to depart for the active runway, an action which is preceded by the armourers removing the last inhibiting devices on the various weapons loads and by the activation of ejector seats.

1548 hours

"Dixie 29" (F-4G) and "Dixie 30" (F-16C) are last to vacate their shelters, taking their place at the end of the queue of aircraft converging on the active runway, which still bears visible evidence of an attack by WarPac fighter-bombers two days earlier. Even as they brake to a halt, the first F-4G winds up to full power and begins to accelerate down the runway.

Seconds later, it is followed by an F-16, alter-nating pairs thereafter departing in quick suc-cession during the next minute or so and disappearing northward at low level.

1552 hours

With no aborts so far, it is beginning to look as if the spare F-4G and F-16 will be out of luck, but they continue to wait while "Dixie 29" and "Dixie 30" move into position. Holding for a few seconds to allow "Dixie 30" to come alongside, the pilot of "Dixie 29" smartly ad-

vances the throttle levers and monitors his instruments as the twin J79s rapidly wind up to full dry power. Satisfied that everything is working as advertised, he releases the brakes and advances the throttles through the gate, initiating afterburner.

1553 hours

"Dixie 29" begins to roll, sluggishly at first but rapidly gathering speed under the impetus of a pair of J79s working at full bore. Within seconds, the pilot senses that the rudder is

A: Active enemy missile control and air defence radars. **B:** F-4G Phantom "Dixie 29" unmasks from protection of nearby terrain and pulls up for attack on SA-8 control radar. **C:** F-4G launches single AGM-88A HARM anti-radar missile. **D:** AGM-88A HARM strikes SA-8 radar, resulting in its destruction. SA-8 "Gecko" missile fired moments earlier goes ballistic as a result of being starved of electronic guidance. **E:** F-4G "Dixie 29" dives back towards the security offered by terrain masking. **F:** Belgian F-16s attack POL dump.

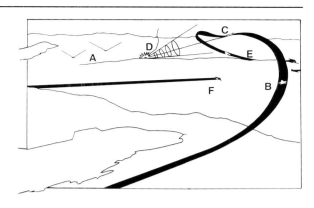

beginning to "bite" and he eases back on the stick causing the Phantom's nose to rise. Behind him, the exhaust flame vaporises a puddle on the rain-slick runway and then the F-4G is airborne, wallowing slightly as it passes through the disturbed air left by the aircraft which preceded it.

Five seconds later, "Dixie 30" leaves the runway, both pilots quickly cleaning up their aircraft before swinging around on to the south-easterly course that will take them to the first waypoint which consists of a ruined mediaeval schloss (castle) just to the west of Worms and about 80 miles (129km) from Spangdahlem AFB.

1608 hours

Even though they are only cruising at a modest 400mph (644km/h) at 500ft (150m), it doesn't take long for the two aircraft to complete the first sector and the Weasel's "Bear" looks down into the courtyard of the now-deserted castle as they pass directly overhead in a smart 4g turn.

Seconds earlier, the F-16 had also passed directly above the ruin, and its pilot now also reefs into a 4g turn, the change of course being planned to include a cross-over manoeuvre which results in the Weasel ending up on the left of the formation. Now, they pursue a more easterly track which, by coincidence, results in them skirting the southern environs of Wurzburg, a town that gave its name to German radar in World War II.

1621 hours

Dropping even lower, to little more than 100ft (30m), just after passing Wurzburg, they very quickly pick up the second waypoint — a river crossing from left to right — and swing around to the north, confirming they are on time and track when they pass to the east of Schweinfurt just a couple of minutes later.

Even at the modest speed of 400mph (644km/h), they cover close to seven miles (11km) every minute and both pilots are constantly alert for obstructions such as power lines. In the Phantom, the "Bear" is no longer content merely to observe the scene below, for he has now gone "head down" and is devoting all of his attention to monitoring his display screens. This task is rendered more difficult by moderate turbulence which causes the F-4G to buck and sway as it bores its way northwards, and by the cross-overs which are being made ever more frequently now that "Dixie 29" and "Dixie 30" are in an area of increased threat.

1625 hours

Thus far, virtually all of the radars which have been detected by the AN/APR-38 system are friendly. It is during this final sector that they begin to receive intimations of the presence of enemy forces via the visual displays in the rear cockpit, their aircraft being "painted" momentarily as they occasionally rise above the security offered by the undulating terrain. It is clear that quite a few enemy radars are active and it almost certainly follows that War-

Pac forces are aware of their presence, if not their objective. However, the fleeting contacts are so brief as to deny any possibility of a missile site achieving a firing solution, and the major threat at this time almost certainly lies with small arms fire.

In the event, apart from the evidence presented by electronic means, they see nothing to confirm or deny the presence of an enemy until they reach their operating area a few minutes later, immediately establishing an electronic order of battle "racetrack" orbit on the periphery of the lethal threat zone. For the time being, the F-16 stays low, hiding behind the terrain, while the F-4G "unmasks" (rises above the horizon) so as to permit the multitude of antennae associated with the AN/APR-38 package to begin gathering data pertaining to electronic "threats" in the immediate vicinity of the target.

1629 hours

On the first pass, at least four radars acknowledge their presence, visual confirmation of these being presented on the 10inch (25.4cm) plan position indicator scope in the rear cockpit, along with details of radar type, bearing and range. Two of the much-feared ZSU-23-4 mobile anti-aircraft artillery guns are noted, as is one of the two SA-8 sites, but in each case the low pulse repetition frequency rate confirms that they are active only in a routine search mode and are not necessarily expecting trouble.

1631 hours

If the situation was relatively quiet on the first pass, that is most certainly not true when the F-4G next unmasks. At least four more ZSU-23-4 radars are active but the most alarming indication stems from the SA-8 site, which goes to high PRF almost instantaneously, indicating that it is looking straight at the Weasel and close to "locking on".

Hastily diving down to the protective cover of the terrain, the F-4G's "Bear" is in full agreement with the computerised system that the SA-8 site poses the greatest threat. Breaking radio silence for a few moments, the F-4G pilot calls his colleague in the F-16 which is still orbiting nearby.

"Dixie Lead to Dixie 30. Let's go for plan bravo", this cryptic message alluding to one of several alternative attack scenarios that had been discussed prior to departure from Spangdahlem.

"Rog, that's bravo," is the response "Give me 30 seconds to set up."

1633 hours

Flying an identical path to that taken by the F-4G on its previous two passes, the F-16 stays low initially as it nears the lethal threat zone,

Right: *With its task successfully accomplished, a "Weasel" F-4G Phantom cruises serenely at medium altitude as it heads back to the relative security of home base. Once there, it will be hastily refuelled and rearmed so as to return to combat action in the shortest possible time.*

Below: *Streaming its braking parachute behind it, an F-4G decelerates following a safe return to Spangdahlem. Suspended from the forward fuselage beneath the air intake can be seen an AN/ALQ-131 noise and deception jamming pod, this item being carried for self-defence purposes.*

Above: Once well clear of the battle area, the F-4G and F-16C "Weasel" pair rejoin shortly before recovering at Spangdahlem where they will quickly be housed in hardened shelters. For the crews, the mission will still not be over, since they will have to face an extensive debriefing.

before popping up above the terrain in an attempt to mislead the defences. At the same moment, the F-4G initiates a 20-degree pull-up, its APR-38 now in fully-automatic mode. With line-of-sight to the radar threats restored, the associated computer instantly recognises the SA-8 control radar as the major threat and instigates countermeasures. The two crew members feel a slight jolt as an AGM-88A HARM missile leaves the rail, its integral radiation seeker head already locked on to its target as a result of data fed to it via the APR-38 RHAWS Wild Weasel set.

 1633:30 hours

Accelerating rapidly to a speed in excess of Mach 2, the single HARM noses over and begins its terminal dive, homing unerringly on the radar which is its target. Even as it closes, the "Bear" calls "missile launch" but the F-4G is already diving down towards the security of nearby terrain, its pilot having seen the SA-8 leave its site amidst a gout of white smoke and orange flame.

Two seconds later, the HARM's high explosive warhead reduces the control radar to little more than scrap metal. Evidence of its demise is provided by its sudden disappearance from the plan position indicator display in the F-4G.

As for the SA-8, now starved of its electronic guidance, it goes "ballistic", disappearing into the distance before falling more or less harmlessly to earth about 15 miles (24km) away, but not before it causes a few anxious moments for elements of the approaching Belgian F-16 strike force.

 1634:30 hours

On this occasion, the attack plan is executed almost perfectly, the orbiting F-4G crew catching a brief glimpse of the leading pair of F-16s as they make their weapons delivery runs, utilising jamming pods, flares and chaff in an attempt to confuse the defences further and draw off any radar-directed artillery or infra-red homing missiles which might be aimed in their direction. This is evidently successful, for, despite moderately heavy ground fire, all of the Belgian machines escape unscathed.

 1635 hours

While the attack is in progress, the "Bear" continues to monitor his threat display screen for indications that the second SAM site is preparing to enter the action, but it stays quiet, indicating that it is either "down" for maintenance or has moved to another area, a distinct possibility since the reconnaissance material they had perused earlier was by no means fresh.

"Can we take a fast swing by the target area, Mac?" he says, over the intercom. "I'd like to check out that other Gecko site while we're here."

"That's a negative, Dave. Those ZSUs are a bit too active for my liking," replies the pilot. "And anyway, one of the Belgians went right over the top of it. His strike camera should have got some good pictures if it's still there."

"OK, you're driving this thing...."

 1636 hours

"Holy cow, will you look at that!" In the front cockpit, the pilot is enjoying an impressive display of pyrotechnics. The CBUs delivered by the first pair of F-16s have achieved their desired objective of causing massive spillages, vast quantities of fuel and oil being ignited by the heavier metal which falls from the second wave of aircraft.

Now, even from ten miles (16km) away, pilot and "Bear" can see that the whole complex is blanketed in thick black smoke, occasionally shot through with vivid flames as petrol and oil tankers "cook off" and explode in the intense heat.

 1637 hours

Almost reluctantly, the pilot thumbs the radio switch and speaks, "Dixie lead. OK, let's go home." Swinging around to a westerly track, their route takes them just to the south of Fulda and directly overhead Koblenz, culminating in an on-time arrival at Spangdahlem. Both aircraft stop in front of the shelters from which they had departed, little more than an hour earlier.

 1706 hours

Once shut down, they remain in their respective cockpits, only disembarking after their aircraft have been winched back into their shelters, the massive doors have been secured and the ejection seat and ordnance "safing" pins have been restored.

 1713 hours

Pausing only long enough to complete the small amount of paperwork that is necessary, the three crew members next head for the hardened Wing operations block where intelligence specialists can be seen talking to several crews who have only recently returned from operations.

1719 hours

Although debriefing can, on occasion, last more than an hour, for the crews of "Dixie 29" and "Dixie 30" it is completed fairly swiftly, their verbal report on the action and assessment of the threats being temporarily preserved on a portable tape recorder. Since their routing to and from the combat area had not taken them close to any enemy concentrations, little in the way of hard intelligence results from the verbal debrief, but the IO in charge does make a note to contact Beauvechain for a copy of the Belgian strike film so as to clarify the position with regard to the second SAM site. Subsequent analysis of the mission tapes will perhaps provide more in the way of useful data but for pilots and "Bear" that is of little interest since they are convinced that a return to today's target is unlikely to be necessary immediately.

THE
ANTI-TANK
MISSION

Evolution of the Mission

ALTHOUGH the tank made its combat debut in British hands during the latter half of the Great War of 1914-18, it exerted only minimal influence on the outcome of that conflict. Traditional concepts relating to the employment of infantry and cavalry tended to hold sway, and the battlefield remained to a large extent stagnant, with rigid adherence to trench warfare. Certainly, from the British point of view, little consideration seems to have been given to exploiting the tank's unparalleled mobility. Those officers who were quick to recognise the promise offered by this revolutionary new weapon found that their arguments almost invariably fell upon deaf ears.

Perhaps even more remarkable, though, was the fact that operational doctrine changed only slightly during World War II, when British Army tank resources concentrated on two main types. These were the heavily armoured but generally slow and often unwieldy "infantry" tanks and the rather more mobile but inadequately armed and poorly protected "cavalry" tanks. With hindsight, it would have been better to look for a vehicle with the best features of both types — good performance, adequate defensive armour and a powerful gun.

Birth of Blitzkrieg

If those responsible for determining British Army operational policy failed to grasp the true significance of the tank, the same mistake was most certainly not made by the Germans. They listened carefully to the tactical doctrine propounded by Maj. Gen. J.F.C. Fuller and Capt. B.H. Liddell Hart both, ironically, officers of the British Army. Broadly based on the use of speed and shock to overwhelm an opponent and destroy his will and ability to continue fighting, their ideas were put into practice with devastating effect during the early stages of World War II as the so-called "Blitzkreig" or "Lightning War". Under this battle-winning concept, air and ground power operated in a co-ordinated fashion, Poland being the first victim to feel the full weight of Nazi military might.

Despite the best efforts of the Polish Air Force, the Luftwaffe soon gained virtual air supremacy. Junkers Ju 87 Stuka dive bombers worked with deadly effect to clear a path for ground forces while heavier bombers such as the Heinkel He 111 and Dornier Do 17 hit targets far behind the front line. Even as the Stukas unleashed their deadly cargo, fast-moving and powerfully-armed tank formations of the Wehrmacht punched their way

through the front line. Motorised infantry followed close behind and consolidated on the gains made by the "big guns" of the tank divisions before the subsequent Soviet attack from the East heralded Poland's demise as an independent nation. Five weeks after the invasion, the last Polish resistance was crushed.

Norway and Denmark came next. Then in

the spring of 1940, Allied problems were compounded when Hitler's forces launched what was perhaps their most ambitious venture with the invasion of the Low Countries and France on 10 May 1940. Once again, speed and surprise was a keynote of "Fall Gelb" (Plan Yellow). The ensuing campaign represented a high point in Germany's war for

Above: *Many German aircraft, including this Bf 109G-6/R2, were fitted with pairs of Wfr.Gr.21 rocket tubes, which launched massive 210mm rockets. They were not used against tanks, however, but to break up the massed formations of Allied bombers which were pounding Germany.*

Below: *One of the first Republic P-47B Thunderbolts on test in 1942. More than two years later P-47s used bombs and rockets against German armour, notably (when the weather permitted) in trying to stem the advancing Panzers in The Battle of the Bulge, in December 1944.*

Most countries were amazingly slow to recognise that the tank meant a revolution in the art of land warfare. Only Germany and the Soviet Union developed effective tanks, specially designed anti-tank aircraft and methods for using both. Today both aeroplanes and helicopters are serving in the dedicated anti-armour role, while multirole interdiction aircraft can carry dedicated anti-armour weapons.

it was carried through with quite remarkable rapidity, Holland capitulating on 14 May, Belgium continuing to resist until 28 May and France finally agreeing to an humiliating armistice at Compiègne on 22 June. By then, the British had gone from mainland Europe, evacuated at Dunkirk and were now beginning to absorb the bitter lessons of little more than two weeks of intense warfare in which armoured vehicles had again been permitted to play a vital role.

Admittedly, Germany's stunning success had not been achieved without cost, some 1,254 aircraft being destroyed but the cost to the Allies was, if anything, even more serious, RAF aircraft losses alone totalling 944 while the hurried departure from Dunkirk had resulted in huge amounts of military equipment being left behind.

Effective weaponry

However, this first encounter with the enemy resulted in a clearer appreciation of just what was needed if Germany was ultimately to be defeated. One of the most obvious and immediate requirements was for fighter aircraft to counter the expected aerial assault on the British Isles but in the longer term, so too would efficient anti-armour weaponry be a high priority if Nazi military might was to be engaged in combat on anything approaching equal terms.

For the most part, standard cannon and rocket-armed fighter-bombers such as the British Hawker Typhoon and Tempest and the American P-47 Thunderbolt and P-51 Mustang met this requirement but some specialised "tank killers" were also developed, notable among these being the Hawker Hurricane IID.

Used extensively in the Western Desert, this aircraft embodied a particularly powerful punch in the shape of a pair of 40mm anti-tank guns, but it did possess a couple of fairly major drawbacks. Initial production examples utilised the Rolls-Royce B.F. gun which was eventually supplanted by the Vickers Type S weapon, but since the associated magazines could carry only 12 or 15 projectiles respectively, it was frequently necessary to return to base to rearm and refuel. Perhaps more serious from the point of view of the pilot was the fact that the Hurricane IID was not exactly ideal as a gun platform. Recoil associated with firing the weapon caused a nose-down pitching moment of some five degrees. This undesirable characteristic naturally prohibited sustained bursts of fire, for it was always necessary to bring the nose back up and take fresh aim before firing again. But, following its

Above: The Il-2 was no easy prey even for Luftwaffe fighters. The original Il-2 was armed with two 20mm shVAK and two 7.62mm fixed guns, underwing racks for eight 82mm rockets and four 220lb bombs. These are rear-gunned models in 1944.

Below: Head-on view of a Bell UH-1 "Huey" armed with launchers for 2.75in rockets. The UH-1 led directly to the AH-1 gunship which has as one of its primary missions the destruction of enemy armoured vehicles. As a consequence, the AH-1 is heavily armed and armoured.

entry into service in the summer of 1942, the Hurricane IID did play a key part in the eventual defeat of Rommel's Afrika Korps, accounting for many enemy tanks and other vehicles in the lead-up to the decisive second battle of El Alamein.

The opposing Axis forces also made extensive use of "big guns", developing and deploying a variety of high-calibre weapons during the latter stages of World War II. Almost inevitably, the Luftwaffe was the principal exponent, fitting 30mm cannon to the Bf.109G-6 and 37mm cannon to the Ju.87 Stuka, but its heaviest weapon seems to have been the BK5 50mm cannon that was installed on both the Ju.188S-1 and the Me.410.

The Soviet tank destroyer

Another combatant which devoted a considerable amount of attention to the development of anti-armour capability was the Soviet Union. The Ilyushin Il-2 "Shturmovik" was the principal ground attack type and featured a pair of 20mm cannon as well as up to eight 56lb (25.4kg) rocket projectiles. This combination was used to good effect in attacks on trains and concentrations of Wehrmacht armour. In addition, both the Lavochkin La-5 and La-7 were fitted with extremely useful 20mm gun armament.

In the 20 or so years which followed the ter-

mination of hostilities, little effort was directed towards developing anti-armour capability, virtually all air arms allocating the task of destroying tanks to the so-called fighter-bomber aircraft. Guns and unguided rockets remained the primary armament and while some progress was made in this area it probably did not keep pace with tank development. New "lightweight" tank armour was combined with new engine technology to produce a generation of more mobile and less vulnerable main battle tanks.

Mobility versus weight

At the same time, changing philosophy with regard to the conduct of ground warfare resulted in the introduction of many new classes of armoured vehicle, personnel carriers and mobile anti-aircraft artillery pieces being just two examples. The advent of these and other systems and the increasingly accepted doctrine of battlefield mobility to some extent sounded the death knell for anti-tank artillery, since the ever-"harder" targets required greater penetrative capability. That, in turn, tended to dictate size and weight, with the result that anti-tank artillery became larger, heavier and more unwieldy, factors that were eminently undesirable in the context of modern warfare.

Clearly, what was needed was a new system

Above: The Sikorsky S-55, seen here in its US Army H-19C Chickasaw version in 1952, was the first helicopter to have the capability of doing a useful job with weapons. Small numbers were used in experiments with various guns and rocket launchers in the early 1950s.

possessing the ability to move swiftly around and over a battlefield in order to engage enemy forces. Conventional aircraft obviously met the mobility requirement in that they could very quickly bring weapons to bear across a wide front. However, their very speed was arguably their greatest drawback for they were perhaps too mobile. The term "fast mover" was by no means inappropriate in that modern jet fighters were (and, to some extent, still are) less than ideal in a fluid battlefield situation where the "Mk.1 eyeball" still remains perhaps the best sensor of all.

The advent of the helicopter

The helicopter, on the other hand, did seem to offer considerable promise, marrying the ability to move "fast" when the situation demanded it with the potential either to hover or land in the battlefield area and await developments. In the early to mid-1950s, though, the piston-powered helicopters that existed possessed a number of shortcomings, payload and en-

Above: *Normally the Boeing Vertol CH-47 Chinook is used strictly as an unarmed transport helicopter, but this example was one of four ACH-47As evaluated in Vietnam with weapons. Dubbed Go-Go-Birds, they had various guns and also 2.75in rocket launchers, here being loaded.*

Below: *The Bell AH-1Q HueyCobra was an interim version of this famed gunship helicopter, modified to fire and guide the TOW anti-tank missile (here being launched). Subsequently the US Army acquired numerous improved AH-1S TOWCobras.*

durance characteristics being far from ideal. At the same time, of course, suitable helicopter-mounted anti-armour weaponry just did not exist and it was to be some years before the armed and armoured helicopter became a familiar sight above the battlefield, arguably the greatest spur for development being the Vietnam War.

In the meantime, the advent of efficient turbine engines quite literally revolutionised this form of flight. This was perhaps the single most important factor in permitting the helicopter to make the transition from being a mere personnel and cargo carrier to a deadly weapon of warfare in its own right. Bell's UH-1 Iroquois led the way, the much-loved and much-feared ''Huey'' being one of the abiding images of the Southeast Asia conflict, operating with great success throughout virtually the entire period of US involvement.

It was in fact the US Army which initially deployed the UH-1 as an armed helicopter but this was by no means the first ''gunship'' to appear in Army insignia. Development testing of armed helicopters predated massive US combat involvement in Vietnam by several years. Initial trials were undertaken by a somewhat maverick unit at Fort Rucker, Alabama, where a leading light of the Army Aviation School's Combat Development Office, Colonel Jay D. Vanderpool, began work in June 1956 with a small team made up of two officers and two enlisted men. One of his first actions was to form the so-called "Sky-Cav" platoon, subsequently redesignated the Aerial Combat Reconnaissance Platoon by the summer of 1957 and eventually providing the basis for the 7292nd Aerial Combat Reconnaissance Company (Provisional).

Like most pioneers, their initial efforts were accomplished in the face of considerable opposition, and lack of finance meant that they were sometimes forced to resort to near-clandestine methods of obtaining equipment with which to conduct their experiments. These examined not only the the fitment of armament to helicopters but also the development of tactics which could be employed in performing aerial reconnaissance by fire.

By 1957, Vanderpool and his cohorts had somehow managed to acquire a fleet of four helicopters — made up of one H-19 Chickasaw, two H-21 Shawnees and one H-25 Army Mule. They armed these with a weird and wonderful array of weaponry and, in the process, proved beyond all doubt that helicopters and weapons were by no means mutually exclusive.

Helos in Vietnam

The next few years saw only modest progress, terminating with deployment of the first two helicopter companies to Vietnam. These arrived in-country aboard the USS *Card* on 11 December 1961 and brought with them 32 examples of the Vertol H-21 Shawnee. More Shawnees followed in January 1962 and the early part of that year also witnessed deployment of the first Hueys, these being assigned to a Medical Detachment (Helicopter Ambulance) and used in the "Dust-Off" casualty evacuation role.

Early experience of combat revealed that the Viet Cong were by no means averse to taking on the Shawnee helicopters (or, for that matter, the H-34s of the US Marine Corps) with small arms fire and it very quickly became apparent that these large and slow moving machines made attractive and vulnerable targets. Attempts at arming the H-21 were confined to installing a light machine gun at the door but this was soon revealed to be largely ineffective, especially when the troop-carrying helicopters came under intense ground fire from a variety of sources.

As far as the Army was concerned, it moved fairly quickly to provide increased protection for its troop-carrying "slicks", despatching the Utility Tactical Transport Helicopter Company (UTTHC) to Vietnam in September 1962. The initial element was made up of 15 UH-1A Iroquois armed with two .30 calibre machine guns and two eight-tube 2.75in rocket launchers, this armament package being fabricated locally. Subsequently, in November, 11 copies of the slightly more powerful UH-1B arrived, each carrying four factory-fitted M-60 machine guns and two locally-installed eight-tube rocket launchers.

The UTTHC's primary task was that of suppressing enemy defences prior to and during a helicopter assault. At the same time, it also served as a kind of "guinea pig", experience gained in the course of 1,779 combat support flying hours between 16 October 1962 and 15 March 1963 forming the basis of an Army Concept Team in Vietnam (ACTIV) report which analysed the role and effectiveness of the armed helicopter in a combat theatre. Between the dates mentioned, the armed Hueys were credited with an estimated 246 Viet Cong casualties and there were also 11 instances of these early gunships being hit by enemy fire although this did not result in any being shot down. In view of that, the ACTIV report concluded that "the vulnerability of armed helicopters was well within the acceptable risk limits".

Following this, heavily-armed "Hog" variants of the Iroquois played an increasingly important part in the US Army's airmobility doctrine. In doing so, they paved the way for other armed helicopters such as the Hughes OH-6A Cayuse and the Bell AH-1G HueyCobra while even the massive Boeing-Vertol CH-47 Chinook served as a weapons delivery system.

The initial combat application of this large helicopter was as a "bomber" in 1967, riot agents such as tear gas being simply rolled out

Below: As this book goes to press the ultimate expression of the armed helicopter, in the West at least, is the AH-64A Apache. Combining effective firepower with night and bad-weather capability, this impressive machine has been built at a sufficient rate to be priced at some $6 million.

of the rear of the CH-47 with fusing accomplished by means of a static line. During the same period, some Chinooks also used an identical method to deliver napalm. A single CH-47 possessed the ability to deposit up to two-and-a-half tons with great accuracy, although such activities were confined to use against targets where, for various reasons, more conventional forms of tactical air power could not be employed.

The Go-Go Birds

Perhaps the ultimate armed Chinook was the celebrated "Go-Go Bird", an appellation which referred to the four CH-47As that were fitted with an impressive array of weapons including two fixed forward-firing M-24A1 20mm Gatling-type rotary cannons, two 19-tube XM-159 2.75in rocket pods, a nose-mounted turret housing an M-5 40mm grenade launcher and no fewer than five .50 calibre machine guns. Combat testing was accomplished by the 53rd Aviation Detachment and the 1st Aviation Detachment in conjunction with ACTIV personnel in 1966-67. However, severe maintenance requirements, an overriding need for heavy lift capability and the loss of three aircraft ultimately prevented

wide-scale adoption, even though ACTIV's final report was generally favourable. Incidentally, one of the quartet managed to achieve the rare feat of shooting itself down when a mounting pin on one of the M-24A cannons failed during a firing run, causing the gun to shift upwards and discharge through the forward rotor blade arc, with tragic consequences for all on board.

The first gunships

As the "Go-Go Bird" was being put through its paces, the AH-1G HueyCobra was nearing its combat debut. This radical variation on the Iroquois theme was the first purpose-built example of the gunship genre. Building on experience gained with the private-venture OH-13X Sioux Scout, the HueyCobra reached South Vietnam at the beginning of September 1967, initial deliveries to the war zone being assigned to the Vung Tau-based New Equipment Training Team (NETT). This unusual unit acted in a largely supervisory capacity and was basically responsible for overseeing the initial training of those who would ultimately fly and service the new helicopter.

Armed with a mixture of rockets, guns and grenades, the HueyCobra soon demonstrated that it was a force to be reckoned with but Army and Marine Corps combat experience ultimately revealed that it lacked sufficient "clout" to deal with armoured fighting vehicles. In Vietnam, that wasn't too much of a problem since enemy armour was pretty thin on the ground. In Europe, however, an entirely different situation prevailed and it was for that reason that the HueyCobra eventually acquired more sophisticated armament in the

Above: *Though in late 1988 it was thought to be in development difficulties, the Soviet Union's Kamov gunship known to NATO as "Hokum" is said to possess "an air-combat capability missing from Western helicopters". Its speed is estimated at 350km/h (217mph).*

Below: *France is one of the countries which uses the nimble Gazelle as an interim anti-armour helicopter, seen here firing a HOT missile. Though relatively cheap, helicopters in this class lack the vital ability to operate in bad weather, which is when they are likely to be needed.*

shape of the Hughes BGM-71 TOW (Tube-launched, Optically-tracked, Wire-guided) anti-armour missile during the early 1970s.

Helicopter-launched anti-tank missiles had, of course, been around for quite a while but prior to the advent of the HueyCobra the job of dealing with enemy armour was still largely perceived as being pretty much a task for the humble foot-soldier and his colleagues in the artillery. In consequence, most of the so-called anti-tank helicopters then in use were basically modifications of existing utility types, such as the French Alouette and the British Scout. Lacking armour protection, it is doubtful if they would have lasted longer on a modern battlefield, such as would certainly be the case in any major European war.

The HueyCobra/TOW pairing represented a very real breakthrough and can be said to have been a pioneering combination. Certainly, modernisation of the basic AH-1G via the AH-1Q/R into its current AH-1S form (and concurrent updating of the USMC 'Cobra from AH-1J via the AH-1T to today's AH-1W) paved the way for succeeding generations of armed and armoured helicopters. Typifying this new breed are the Soviet Union's Mil Mi-24 "Hind" and Mi-28 "Havoc", as well as Italy's Agusta A129 Mangusta.

Modern gunships

In the USA, further helicopter gunship development first explored the blind alley that culminated in the ill-fated Lockheed AH-56 Cheyenne before settling on the rather more fortunate McDonnell Douglas AH-64A Apache which is now in quantity production for the US Army and which will eventually become that service's principal rotary-winged anti-armour vehicle. Comparison of these types soon reveals that they can all lay claim to having their roots in Bell's original concept, for they all feature a tandem two-seat cockpit layout, a complex array of sensors and a generous weapons payload.

In reality, of course, virtually any modern small helicopter can be adapted as a "tank-buster". All that is basically needed is a mounting point for the missile launch tubes plus space to accommodate a sighting system and a certain amount of associated electronic and avionic equipment. Hence the proliferation of

dedicated anti-tank variants of the Lynx, Gazelle, Bolkow Bo.105 and Hughes 500.

A considerable amount of effort has also been directed towards the development of ever more potent weaponry. Existing missiles like the Hughes TOW and the Euromissile HOT were progressively updated in terms of warhead capability, guidance systems and the like. At the same time, they have been joined by new missiles such as the Rockwell AGM-114A Hellfire and the Soviet AT-6 "Spiral". The former uses semi-active laser-homing, incorporating a seeker head which searches for and then follows reflected laser energy to the target. Since the laser designator may be nothing more than a hand-held device operated by a foot soldier, Hellfire does permit the launch vehicle to employ "fire and forget" techniques. In addition, though, it is in fact rather more than just an anti-armour weapon since it may be used against all types of "hard" land targets. "Spiral" was also at one time believed to employ laser-homing but it now appears that it actually relies on radio command guidance, albeit with increased resistance to electronic counter-counter-measures for greater lethality.

New tactics

Improved armament and equipment has gone more or less hand in hand with the development of new tactics, for today's battle-field is potentially an exceedingly deadly place. Long established threats such as small arms fire have been joined by newer hazards, high among them being radar-guided anti-aircraft artillery, extremely accurate surface-to-air missiles and other helicopters or fixed-wing aircraft with powerful weapons.

Fast-movers have historically relied on speed for protection but that is a luxury which is denied to the helicopter. In consequence, stealth is now the name of the game, the use of ultra low level nap-of-earth flying techniques being one way of enhancing the likelihood of survival, and helicopter crews now regularly train to perfect such methods, making maximum use of existing cover to approach, observe and engage targets.

Technical improvements have had quite a marked impact on the physical appearance of the modern battlefield helicopter. For in-

Above: *Here seen coming in to land, the Sukhoi Su-25 (NATO name "Frogfoot") was thought at first to be a Soviet copy of the losing USAF AX contender, the Northrop YA-9A. It saw extensive service in Afghanistan, where it was used in conjunction with helicopters to combat the well-armed but elusive guerrilla forces that were active in many areas.*

Below: *A small selection from the vast wealth of armoured vehicles that are now active with and deployed by Soviet ground forces. From top to bottom, they comprise the T-64 and T-80 main battle tanks, the deadly ZSU-23-4 flak vehicles with radar guided 23mm guns with water-cooled barrels, the SA-13 SAM vehicle and the BMP-2 APC.*

Soviet Armour

T-64

T-80

ZSU-23-4

SA-13 Gopher

BMP-2

A-10A Armament

Above: *Here seen firing its devastating 30mm gun, which has depleted-uranium projectiles, the USAF's A-10A does everything it can to survive over the battlefield. Apart from the canopy most parts are designed to withstand 23mm hits, but not the warheads of SAMs.*

Right: *The most important weapons carried by the A-10A.* **1:** *Snakeye retarded bomb.* **2:** *Rockeye cluster bomblet dispenser.* **3:** *Paveway laser-guided bomb.* **4:** *Maverick precision-guided missile (various versions).* **5:** *GAU-8/A 30mm gun, with its ammunition drum.* **6:** *2,000lb "slick" GP bomb.*

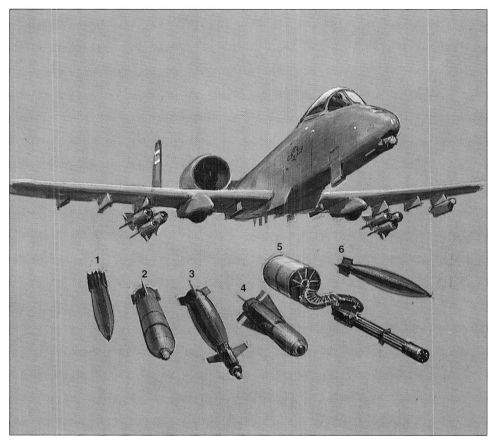

stance, "black hole" exhaust nozzles cut down infra-red "signature" and make it less vulnerable to heat-seeking missiles, while chaff and flare dispensers are now standard equipment as, indeed, are radar warning receivers. Development of night vision equipment is also helping the helicopter to make the transition from being purely a day attack system to one that possesses genuine all-weather capability. These improvements, in concert with constantly refined tactics, should help it to remain a viable and effective weapon of war for the foreseeable future.

The fixed-wing answer

At about the same time as the HueyCobra was undergoing the metamorphosis described earlier, so too was another rather different strand of anti-armour aerial warfare being explored. This time, however, the impetus behind the project lay with the US Air Force which was becoming increasingly anxious to acquire a weapon system capable of taking on the ever growing threat posed by Soviet armour on rather more equal terms. It led directly to the A-X (Attack-Experimental) concept, competing design proposals being the Fairchild-Republic YA-10A and the Northrop YA-9A, both with twin turbofan engines.

After a competitive fly-off during late 1972 and early 1973, the YA-10A was selected as being worthy of further evaluation, and Fairchild-Republic was awarded a contract for

FIGHTER MISSIONS

a handful of development airframes. Yet another fly-off, this time against the Vought A-7D Corsair II, took place in the spring of 1974 before Congress finally put its weight behind the new close air support specialist, the A-10 Thunderbolt II.

Following further testing, initial deliveries of production-standard aircraft to the USAF began in November 1975, although it was not until March 1976 that the 355th Tactical Fighter Training Wing received its first aircraft at Davis-Monthan AFB, Arizona. Even then, well over a year elapsed before the first fully-operational squadron (the 356th TFS) attained combat ready status at Myrtle Beach AFB, South Carolina as part of the 354th TFW. Subsequent production permitted one other fully-fledged Tactical Air Command wing to be equipped, while examples of the A-10 also joined front-line elements of Alaskan Air Com-

mand, the Pacific Air Forces and the United States Air Force Europe organisations as well as second-line echelons of the Air National Guard and the Air Force Reserve.

The A-10's weapons

A relatively unsophisticated but immensely tough aircraft, the A-10 possesses considerable payload capability, no fewer than 11 external stores stations being provided. Maximum payload is about 16,000lb (4,877kg), although this figure can be achieved only by sacrificing fuel capacity and, in turn, combat radius. Weapons options range from conventional "iron" bombs through Maverick air-to-surface missiles to "smarter" devices such as the Hobos TV-guided 2,000lb (907kg) bomb, but perhaps the most remarkable item is the

massive General Electric GAU-8/A Avenger 30mm cannon. Its associated ammunition drum may carry a maximum of 1,350 rounds of either high explosive or armour piercing shells and it is possible to select two rates of fire — 2,100 or 4,200 rounds per minute. In practice, of course, such a rate of fire can be sustained only momentarily and it is usual for live firing exercises to feature bursts of just two seconds duration with at least a one-minute cooling interval between each.

Like the armed helicopter, the A-10 cannot rely on sheer speed for survival above the battlefield. Indeed, if it is to do its job correctly, it will repeatedly have to expose itself to possible ground fire.

Here again, specially formulated tactics will help to increase the probability of survival, for the A-10 is designed to fly and fight at extremely low level, making use of topography and

	A-10A Thunderbolt II	Su-25	AH-54A Apache
Maximum speed: Obviously the aeroplanes are in a different class from the helicopters, but high speed makes it harder to hide behind cover; and the helicopters attack whilst hovering.	0 kt — 600 kt		
Combat radius: Again the fixed-wing aircraft are in a class of their own, though the actual figures depend crucially on such variables as cruising altitude and use of external fuel.	0 nm — 600 nm		
Weapons: Attention is drawn to the importance of "+" or "or", especially in the case of the helicopters which have fewer weapon-mounting points than the aeroplanes.	16,000lb (7,258kg) AIM-9, 30mm gun, Maverick ASMs, cluster dispensers	9,920lb (4,500kg) AA-8 Aphid, 30mm gun 1,102lb bombs, ASMs, rockets or cluster dispensers	1,700lb (771kg) 30mm gun, Hellfire ASMs, rocket launchers
Terrain masking: Though they make full use of undulations in the ground it is not feasible for fast jets to hide behind trees, barns or similar small obstructions.			
All-weather capability: Here there is big variation, the Mi-24 and Apache having pioneered this essential capability for helicopters. The A-10 was not designed for European weather.	1988 / 1990		

This diagram omits some of the parameters used to compare fighter-type aircraft, but adds one peculiar to the anti-tank mission. The ability to hide behind natural cover, known as terrain-masking, obviously can make the difference between surviving or being blasted from the sky. Amazingly, even the carefully planned AH-64A Apache has to expose itself throughout the process of sighting on targets and guiding its missiles. The answer is obviously to use a mast-mounted sight and, if possible, a self-homing missile with infra-red guidance. NATO is trying to equal the Soviet Union with Trigat 3-LR, which will make such guidance available in about 1998. All of the types examined here share the attribute of being highly manoeuvrable and agile.

◀ **Su-25**

Power plant: Two Tumanskii R-13-300 (9,340lb/41.5kN)
Span: 46ft 11in (14.3m)
Length: 50ft 6.75in (15.4m)
Max TO weight: 42,330lb (19,200kg)
Crew: 1

◀ **A-10 Thunderbolt II**

Power plant: Two General Electric TF34-100 (9,065lb/40.3kN)
Span: 57ft 6in (17.53m)
Length: 53ft 4in (16.26m)
Max TO weight: 50,000lb (22,680kg)
Crew: 1

◀ **AH-64A Apache**

Power plant: Two General Electric T700-701 (1,696shp/1,265kW)
Main rotor diameter: 48ft 0in (14.63m)
Length overall: 58ft 3in (17.76m)
Max TO weight: 17,343lb (7,867kg)
Crew: 2

available cover to limit periods of exposure to enemy fire. What it lacks in speed is, to some extent, compensated for by quite outstanding manoeuvrability and in any aerial combat an opponent is likely to find it extremely frustrating trying to position his gunsight "pipper" on an A-10 for long enough to get off a burst of gunfire or an air-to-air missile. Such manoeuvrability is also likely to cause problems for ground-based anti-aircraft systems, always assuming that the A-10 comes close enough to be within the lethal threat envelope. The aircraft's theoretical ability to absorb severe structural damage and yet remain airworthy should also stand it in good stead. In addition, of course, a measure of air defence capability is provided in the shape of at least two AIM-9 Sidewinder heat-seeking missiles and these, in conjunction with the fearsome GAU-8/A gun, ought to persuade any

would-be aggressor to think twice before taking on a "Wart Hog". Other defensive equipment includes externally carried AN/ALQ-131 ECM pods and integrated chaff and flare dispensers to confuse hostile missiles.

The Soviet Union has also conceived its own "slow mover" in the shape of the Sukhoi Su-25 "Frogfoot". This is also a relatively unsophisticated machine and it shares many features in common with the A-10, marrying the ability to tote a substantial ordnance load with great durability and outstanding manoeuvrability. Compatible weaponry includes laser-guided and conventional bombs, AT-6 "Spiral" anti-armour missiles, unguided rocket pods and cluster bomb units. It also features integral gun armament but this cannot yet be assessed in detail. Knowing the full performance of the GAU-8/A it is very unlikely the Soviet designers would settle for anything in-

ferior, but all that is known is that the Su-25 gun has twin barrels of 30mm calibre.

What cannot be denied is that "Frogfoot" is indeed a powerful weapon system in its own right and it does possess one quite valuable advantage over its American counterpart in that it is now a battle-hardened type. Although apparently not in widespread service with the Soviet military machine, modest numbers have been exposed to the rigours of combat in Afghanistan. Here, they have combined with the Mi-24 "Hind" helicopter to pose the greatest threat to the continued well-being of Mujahideen guerrilla forces. Quite how well the "Frogfoot" — and the A-10A — would fare in the event of a war in central Europe, against sophisticated opposition on the ground and in the air, must remain a matter of conjecture, but it seems reasonable to expect that both types would prove very effective.

Lynx Mk 7　　　　**Mi-24 and 25**　　　　**A129 Mangusta**　　　　**AH-1S Huey Cobra**

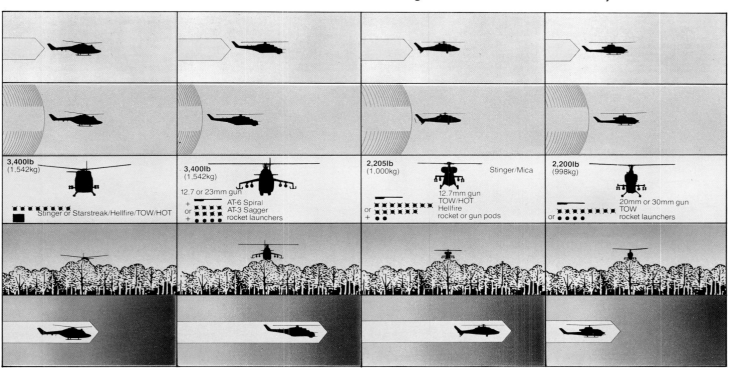

◄ Lynx Mk 7

Power plant: Two RR Gem 60 (1,115-1,346shp/832-1,004kW)
Main rotor diameter: 42ft 0in (12.8m)
Length overall: 50ft 9in (15.47m)
Max TO weight: 13,000lb (5,896kg)
Crew: 2

◄ Mi-24 and 25

Power plant: Two Isotov TV3-117 (2,200shp/1,640kW)
Main rotor diameter: 55ft 9in (17.0m)
Length overall: 70ft 6.5in (21.5m)
Max TO weight: 28,660lb (13,000kg)
Crew: 2

◄ A129 Mangusta

Power plant: Two RR 1004D (1,018shp/7594kW)
Main rotor diameter: 39ft 0.5in (11.9m)
Length overall: 46ft 10.5in (14.29m)
Max TO weight: 9,039lb (4,100kg)
Crew: 2

◄ AH-1S HueyCobra

Power plant: One Textron Lycoming (1,800shp/1,342kW)
Main rotor diameter: 44ft 0in (13.41m)
Length overall: 53ft 1in (13.41m)
Max TO weight: 10,000lb (4,536kg)
Crew: 2

The Thunderbolt Mission

I N THE highly specialised anti-armour role, it is probably fair to say that the distinctly unattractive Fairchild-Republic A-10A Thunderbolt II ("Wart Hog") has few peers. What it lacks in sheer out-and-out speed, it more than compensates for in manoeuvrability, making optimum use of terrain masking for survival when flying and fighting at ultra low level. The Thunderbolt II clearly has a key part to play in the anti-armour mission and must surely figure highly in NATO's plans to defeat the Warsaw Pact's numerically superior armoured forces. Current operational doctrine calls for many of USAFE's 100 or so "Wart Hogs" to deploy from air bases in Britain to four forward operating locations (FOLs) situated in West Germany so as to be within easy reach of the main area of combat action, namely the so-called "Fulda Gap". It is from one of these FOLs that four Thunderbolt IIs of the 81st Tactical Fighter Wing's "Mandrake Flight" will shortly move into action in order to engage an enemy armoured column.

 1315 hours

Orbiting at an altitude of 500feet (150m) some 30 miles (48km) behind the battlefront, the four 510th Tactical Fighter Squadron A-10 pilots all feel decidedly aggrieved at the apparent lack of action. They have now been circling for some 10 minutes, during which time "Mandrake lead" has regularly called the Command Reporting Post ("Blue Jay") to enquire if their services are needed yet. Each call meets with the same response, a terse "Negative, Mandrake formation. We'll keep you informed".

Two of the aircraft carry pairs of TV-guided AGM-65B Maverick anti-armour missiles while the other two are unarmed save for the integral Avenger 30mm cannon. All are equipped with wing-mounted AN/ALQ-131 jamming pods. These, in conjunction with chaff and infra-red flares, comprise their primary means of defence.

When they took-off from Norvenich, in North Germany, all four pilots had been eager to get into battle, following the hasty move from home base at Bentwaters, England, on the morning of that same day. Since they had all been recalled from leave, it wasn't too surprising that they found the apparent inactivity particularly galling, their sense of frustration being heightened by the hurried pre-departure briefing. Then, the IO (Intelligence Officer) had assured them that they would very quickly be committed to action, an assurance which they now felt to have been manifestly untrue.

They had in fact transferred from Bentwaters as part of a reinforcement effort aimed at boosting the 2nd Allied Tactical Air Force's anti-armour capability in order to counter a major armoured thrust that was anticipated. Intelligence sources had observed a significant build-up of Soviet AFVs (armoured fighting vehicles) to the rear of the main battle area and confidently predicted that an attempt at a break-out would soon follow.

All four pilots had attended the "mass brief"

Above: For the pilots who formed part of "Mandrake" flight, mission preparation had begun at Norvenich following a hasty move from Bentwaters. However, with their latest target still to be confirmed, planning and briefing was inevitably of a rather general nature.

at Norvenich, which covered items of "common interest". Safe transit corridors, FAC procedures, penetration aids, chaff/flare dispenser settings, aerial threats and potential hazards in the immediate vicinity of the base from which they were operating were all covered in little more than ten minutes.

After that, individual taskings were assigned, Mandrake flight having been directed to get airborne as soon as possible and proceed to a contact point where they were to hold pending further instructions from base. Since they were unclear as to their target, the specific briefing that followed was, of necessity, very general in nature.

Communications frequencies — the A-10 carries three radios, one being set to the frequency of the general command communications net, one to a frequency on which all four elements of the flight can converse, and the last to a setting which permits lead and wingman pairs to communicate only with each other — were jotted down as was the routing that they would take to the contact point and the formation that they would adopt. Much, however, is standard operating procedure, instilled into each pilot through hours of peacetime training over the very area that they now fly. A few moments were also devoted to the consideration of tactics before the briefing was wrapped up by a quick dissertation from the IO on the area in which they were likely to be called upon to operate in any dispense ordnance.

Charts were gathered up and stowed in the pockets of the "saddlebag" — a handy device which serves two primary purposes. Sitting astride the cockpit coaming, it ensures that maps are within easy reach at all times while it also holds them securely, the often violent manoeuvres of the A-10 inevitably permitting anything that is not firmly fixed to float around the cockpit with potentially hazardous consequences.

Video tape cassettes were also distributed for stowage in a compartment beneath the aft fuselage. These will record any combat that takes place for post-mission analysis of tactics and for intelligence purposes. With these details attended to, they headed out to the shelters which housed their aircraft, getting airborne barely 40 minutes later, en route to the contact point at "Delta".

 **1317 hours**

"Mandrake three to lead. You sure there's a

Left: *Although they still required firm details of their target, the remaining preparatory actions were familiar from peacetime flying activity. These included the donning of flight kit and gathering up of maps and charts prior to moving out to their aircraft.*

Above: *Even as "Mandrake" flight made ready to go to war, so were the ground support troops preparing their aircraft, a task which included loading the huge magazine of the A-10A's GAU-8/A Avenger 30mm cannon with lethal armour-piercing incendiary shells.*

Right: *Having arrived at their aircraft, pilots performed a brief external walk around inspection before climbing up the access stairs and settling down in their cockpits. Within moments, each was busy running through a much practised sequence of pre-start drills.*

war on?"

"Well, the IO says there is and you know those guys are always right," comes the response.

"Goddamn wing weenies. What do they know?" chips in the pilot of Mandrake four.

 **1320 hours**

"Mandrake lead. Blue Jay. Confirm your position."

"'yo, Blue Jay. We're holding at point Delta as requested. Got anything for us yet?"

"Ah, yeah we have, Mandrake. We just got word from ASOC (Air Support Operations Center). Proceed direct to point Juliet and contact the FAC (Forward Air Controller) on button five. That's 'Kingfisher' by the way."

"Rog," says Mandrake lead. "Direct Juliet, call Kingfisher, button five. Authenticate AB."

 1321 hours

Consulting his map, Mandrake lead quickly determines that point Juliet lies almost due east of their present position and then thumbs his microphone switch. "I guess you guys heard that. Let's go and take a look see...."

The four A-10s hold battle formation as they set off eastwards, Mandrake lead and his wingman flying more or less parallel to each other, some 5,000ft (1,500m) apart. Roughly 7,000ft (2,133m) behind and slightly offset to starboard, the second element of Mandrake

flight maintains a similar amount of lateral separation. As they move east, they descend further, levelling out at little more than 100ft (30m) above the heavily forested terrain.

 1323 hours

"'lo Kingfisher. Mandrake flight inbound point Juliet."

"Hallo Mandrake, Kingfisher. What's your ETA (estimated time of arrival) at Juliet?"

"'bout four minutes, I reckon. Where are you and what've you got for us, Kingfisher?"

"We're four clicks (kilometres) north-east of Juliet, little village just this side of the river bridge. Have you pinpointed that, Mandrake?"

"Er, that's affirmative Kingfisher. What's the problem?"

"Tanks. 'Bout a dozen T-72s, I'd say. They're in the trees on the ridge line and they're giving us a real hard time. Haven't seen any infantry but there's a pair of Shilkas (ZSU-23-4 mobile AAA) out on the flanks so you'd better keep your heads down."

"Thanks 'fisher. You got a designator with you?"

"Affirmative Mandrake."

"'kay. Can you mark the Shilkas for us. I'd like to deal with them first."

 1327 hours

From a vantage point in the upper floor of a

partially ruined house overlooking the bridge, the FAC confers briefly with an Army 2nd Lieutenant and requests him to aim the laser designator at the left-hand ZSU-23-4, positioning the cross-hairs of the device centrally on the target. Although undetectable by the human eye, to the "Pave Penny" laser spot seeker device which hangs from the forward right-hand side of the A-10 the invisible beam marks the artillery piece as effectively as a can of bright yellow paint.

 1329 hours

Running in low from different compass points so as to confuse the enemy forces, Mandrake lead and Mandrake two emerge from cover at a distance of about four miles (6km) from their first target, the spot tracker on Mandrake two immediately detecting the reflected laser energy. Utilising target location information projected on the head-up display, within a matter of seconds the pilot has locked on the missile's TV-seeker head, confirmed by means of a TV display screen that the weapon is targeted correctly, and hit a switch on the control column to initiate launch.

 1330 hours

Boosted by a Thiokol TX-481 solid-fuel rocket motor, the Maverick leaves its rail and immediately begins to climb so as to get a clearer view of the target, the TV-seeker device in the nose swivelling downwards as the missile rises. With the weapon safely on its way, the pilot of Mandrake two wastes no time in vacating the area, a gut-wrenching turn to the left being followed by an immediate dive for cover. Similar violent manoeuvres are performed by Mandrake lead who is "running interference" to complicate matters for the Soviet ground forces by providing multiple choice of targets.

 1331 hours

Even as they disappear behind the tree-line, the Maverick noses over and begins its terminal dive. Cruciform control surfaces at the rear of the missile make several minute adjustments so as to keep the target image securely centred. Seconds later, it impacts squarely on the Shilka, the 130lb (59kg) hollow-charge warhead channelling a jet of vaporised metal and gas into the interior with deadly consequences for the occupants.

 1333 hours

Barely a minute later, the second Shilka meets an equally fiery end when it falls victim to another Maverick, Mandrake three and Mandrake four using identical tactics in executing

Right: Unlike many modern combat aircraft the cockpit of the A-10A Thunderbolt II is fundamentally very basic although it contains all that is needed if a pilot is to perform his designated mission of destroying enemy armour in an efficient and effective way.

their attack. Now, in the absence of effective anti-aircraft artillery, the way is clear for Mandrake flight to employ the Avenger cannon against the Soviet tanks which have continued to bombard the US troops even as the A-10s take on the ZSU-23s.

 1335 hours

Since the tanks are hidden from plain view by the screen of trees, Mandrake lead thumbs his radio switch.

"Kingfisher, Mandrake lead. I think we could use some help here."

"Rog, Mandrake. What's the problem?"

"Ahhh, we can't see the tanks too well from up here. Why don't you mark 'em with the laser to give us an aiming point?"

"That's affirmative, Mandrake."

 1336 hours

Switching channels, Mandrake lead speaks to his colleagues. "Right, guys. Kingfisher's gonna' laser mark for us. We'll stay in pairs, lead engaging the designated target with the wingman looking for muzzle flashes. Call in and out, OK?"

 1337 hours

"Lead's in." Running in fast and low from behind the village, Mandrake lead rises above the cover of the terrain, the laser spot seeker immediately picking up the reflected laser energy and providing a visual reference to the first target's exact location on the head-up display screen.

Above: With both engines running sweetly and with all instruments "in the black", the pilot of Mandrake Lead adds just a touch of power and steers his machine clear of the hardened aircraft shelter in which it has been standing, armed and ready, while awaiting the call to action.

Kicking right rudder, Mandrake lead feels his aircraft skid round to the right and waits for the gunsight "pipper" to coincide with the laser indication before squeezing the trigger at a range of about 4,000ft (1,200m). Below and ahead of him, the massive Avenger cannon briefly erupts into life, driven by one of the two hydraulic motors. In barely half-a-second, 30-odd armour-piercing incendiary rounds leave the weapon's seven barrels before the pilot pushes the control column hard over to the left, initiating a knife-edge turn through 90 degrees. Straightening up, he jinks away down the valley and is lost from view in less than three seconds, calling "Lead's out" as he leaves the area.

 1338 hours

As he manoeuvres, the shells begin to impact on the tree line, the first few to arrive causing terminal damage to part of the forest and clearing a path for succeeding rounds. A fraction of a second later, four rounds score direct hits, the depleted uranium penetrator of each punching a hole through the tank's exterior and simultaneously igniting, directing a jet of flame into the interior.

Secondary explosions follow almost instantaneously, as the tank's fuel and ammunition erupt, pressure inside blasting the main access hatch free from its restraints. A few yards away, another T-72 dies in similar spectacular fashion after a well-aimed burst from Mandrake two.

1340 hours

"Three's in...." Approaching from an entirely different compass point, the second element of Mandrake flight begins its attack and again the reflected laser energy betrays the presence of a Soviet tank which fires even as Mandrake three's gun erupts into action. Moments later, this tank reels under multiple hits that reduce it to little more than scrap iron.

Meanwhile, intent on engaging another target, the pilot of Mandrake four fails to see the tell-tale smoke trail left by an SA-7 "Grail" infra-red homing surface-to-air missile that suddenly bursts forth from the right-hand edge of the tree line.

 1341 hours

Breaking hard to the left after loosing off a burst of gunfire that fails to find a target, Mandrake four unwittingly exposes the tailpipes of his turbofan engines to the heat-seeker, which rapidly overhauls his aircraft and detonates alongside the starboard rear fuselage. Fragments of the warhead penetrate the engine cowling and wreck the low-pressure turbine of the TF34 contained within. Further damage is sustained in the vicinity of the aft fuselage which is literally peppered with shrapnel — most is of a fairly minor nature but two of the rudder hinges are destroyed, this component momentarily flapping free before it is torn away by slipstream effect.

Sensing the jolt which accompanies missile detonation, the pilot of Mandrake four, heart thumping and perspiring, is well aware that he has been hit. He quickly scans the cockpit instrument displays, noting with dismay that the starboard engine readings are indicative of a serious problem. RPM (revolutions per minute) and oil pressure counters unwind rapidly while temperature indicators rise.

Below: Once on the active taxiway, the four A-10A Thunderbolt IIs move quickly towards the runway. Speed on the ground is essential if they are to avoid running the risk of being destroyed before they can take to the air. Once aloft, however, they are all much safer.

Then, a fire warning light on the cockpit coaming illuminates. The pilot abandons engine shut-down procedures for a moment or two in order to pull the lever which will activate the fire extinguisher bottle adjacent to the engine. Seconds later, starved of oxygen following the use of fire-retarding inert gases, the light flickers on and off momentarily before going out.

 1342 hours

Even as all that is going on, he stays low, relying on terrain-masking for protection, for he is reluctant to subject his battle-damaged aircraft to violent manoeuvring until he learns more about the extent of the damage. Activating the radio, he calls, "Mandrake four to lead. I've taken a hit."

"Rog', four. What's the damage?"

"Ah, not too sure, lead. Starboard engine's shut down right now. Controls feel kind of weird but she's still flying OK."

"Can you make base?"

"Yeah, think so."

"Er, lead to three. You better bug out too. See he gets home safe."

"'kay, boss. See you later."

 1344 hours

"'lo Kingfisher, Mandrake lead. Looks like we got a problem with SAMs. Did you eyeball the launch?"

"Affirmative, Mandrake. Right end of the tree line."

"Roger, 'fisher. A couple of our guys are bugging out but we'll stick around for a while. Keep marking the tanks and we'll do our best to nail 'em for you."

"Thanks Mandrake."

 1344:30 hours

Changing channels, Mandrake lead pauses for a moment to contemplate tactics before activating his radio again.

"Lead to two. Kingfisher's gonna' carry on marking. Give me a few seconds start on the

next run. I wanna' try and tempt that SAM into going for a shot."

"Rog, lead."

 1346 hours

"Lead's in." In a reprise of the flight path taken by Mandrake four, the A-10 pilot quickly finds his designated target and fires a half-second burst before racking his aircraft round in a right-hand 90 degree turn. As he moves the control column to the right, he commands the ejection of a number of infra-red flares which

continue to pursue the original flight path taken by the Thunderbolt for a few seconds before gravity takes over and they begin to fall towards the ground.

Behind him, another SA-7 missile lifts skywards, the tell-tale smoke cloud which betrays the fact of its launch being spotted by Mandrake two who is running in to attack at roughly 90 degrees to his leader's flight path.

On this occasion, the violently manoeuvring A-10 succeeds in breaking missile lock and the Grail's seeker head turns its attention to one of the decoy flares, detonating harmlessly just a few moments later. Three seconds after

Above: Moving swiftly along the taxiway, Mandrake Lead is soon joined by other Thunderbolt IIs as he passes the shelters that have housed them. Within moments, he and his wingman will begin their take-off roll, to be followed seconds later by the other two A-10As.

A: "Mandrake" flight A-10A emerges from cover to initiate attack with GAU-8/A Avenger 30mm cannon. **B:** A-10A opens fire with Avenger gun as it dives towards its target. **C:** Target is being "marked" by laser designator hidden in ruined house and operated by Army 2nd Lieutenant. **D:** WarPac T-72 main battle tank explodes after being hit by armour-piercing shells from the A-10A. **E:** A-10A takes violent evasive action and uses terrain masking to escape. **F:** Second A-10A begins attack from different quarter.

that, rounds from Mandrake two's 30mm gun begin bursting around the launch site, that section of the tree line being quickly engulfed in smoke and flames when two unused missiles are hit detonate.

1348 hours

"Mandrake, ah, Kingfisher here. Looks like you won't be troubled by SAM again."

"Thanks Kingfisher. Keep designating."

Two further passes by the remaining pair of A-10s have resulted in the destruction of three more tanks while a fourth has been badly damaged by a single hit.

"Mandrake, Mandrake. Kingfisher. They're pulling out."

"OK, Kingfisher. Want us to stick around for a few minutes?"

"Er, negative Mandrake. We're gonna' be moving out ourselves real soon. Thanks for your help though, and sure hope your buddy makes it home OK."

"It's a pleasure Kingfisher. Have a nice day."

1354 hours

Swinging around to a more westerly course, Mandrake lead studies his instruments and notes ruefully that he possesses sufficient fuel for only about another 15 minutes of orbiting at point Delta before it will be necessary to return to base to refuel and rearm. He flicks the radio switch. "Lead to two, let's head back to Delta. What's your fuel state?"

"It's getting marginal, skipper."

"I've got about 15 minutes orbit time. Can you match that?"

"Ah, negative boss. Ten at most."

"Roger, two. I'll contact Blue Jay, see if they'll let us go on home."

"Sounds good to me, skip."

1355 hours

"Blue Jay, Blue Jay. Mandrake flight just passing point Juliet, outbound to Delta."

"Thank you Mandrake. Any news for us?"

"Roger, Blue Jay. Two Shilkas, an SA-7 site and about half-a-dozen T-72s dead for sure. Rest have withdrawn. Four took a missile hit and bugged out early with three. Me and my wingman are getting low on fuel so unless you've got an immediate I'd kinda like to go home too."

"OK Mandrake. That's no problem. Pintail and Heron flights are inbound point Delta right now. You better proceed direct base."

"Return to base for Mandrake one and two. Er, Blue Jay, have you any news of three and four?"

"Stand by one, Mandrake."

1357 hours

Staying low as they left the forward edge of battle area, the pair of A-10s gradually swing around on to a westerly course that will take them direct to the forward operating location at Norvenich. As they withdraw, Mandrake lead's headphones crackle. "Mandrake formation. Blue Jay."

"Blue Jay, Mandrake, go..."

"Thought you'd like to know Mandrake four made it to the divert field safely. Three went straight back to the nest."

"That's good news, Blue Jay. Guess we'll see you later. Mandrake out."

1420 hours

After an uneventful return flight, Mandrake lead taxis fast towards Detachment Four's TAB-V complex at Norvenich. Swinging his aircraft round, he waits outside the shelter, shutting down the engines while the ground crew prepare to return the A-10 to the security of the reinforced concrete structure.

1424 hours

Once inside, he quickly runs through the integrated combat turn (ICT) procedures, the APU whining softly as it spools up. Ahead of him, a rapidly narrowing chink of daylight confirms that the shelter doors are being secured against the risk of a surprise enemy air attack. Below, ground crew move in to service the aircraft, one going to the rear to remove the video cassette and slot in a replacement while another moves to the port undercarriage fairing, opening an access panel to reveal the single-point pressure refuelling connection and quickly coupling up the hose through which fuel will flow.

Elsewhere, munitions specialists move in to replenish the gun's magazine, others manipulating Maverick missiles into place on the racks beneath the A-10A's wings. Above, still securely strapped in but with the canopy now open, the pilot confers with an intelligence officer via the intercom, furnishing details of the recent combat and receiving the next mission tasking.

As he talks, another ground crewman clambers up the access ladder and hands him a box which contains the only lunch he will get today, as well as a "piddle-pack" in case he needs to answer a call of nature.

The expected Soviet thrust has come and for the "Wart Hog" pilots cockpit readiness will be the routine for the remainder of this day. In less than an hour, having completed pre-departure briefing while still in the cockpit, the pilot of Mandrake lead will be on the move again....

Above: Manoeuvring hard at low level, the A-10A flown by Mandrake Leader manages to avoid running into trouble even though he is compounding the defender's options by providing a multiple choice of targets as Mandrake Two engages a ZSU-23-4 with a TV-guided Maverick missile.

Below: Despite the fact that one A-10A Thunderbolt suffered battle damage, all four pilots make safe landings at Allied air bases. Within a very short time, three of them will be back in action, as NATO forces try to slow the progress of the advancing Warsaw Pact forces.

The Lynx Mission

ALTHOUGH there are still some dedicated tank-busting aircraft like the Fairchild-Republic A-10A Thunderbolt II and the Sukhoi Su-25 "Frogfoot" in service with each of the two superpowers, this increasingly important mission is for the most part now entrusted to helicopters which possess several unique advantages when it comes to operating at low level over the battlefield. Some, like the US Army's AH-1 HueyCobra and AH-64 Apache, are designed to withstand a considerable amount of battle damage before they are forced to withdraw from the fight while others, such as the Lynx and Gazelle, are rather more vulnerable. In the mission that is recounted here, Westland Lynx AH.1 anti-tank helicopters of the Army Air Corps' 656 Squadron have hastily deployed from their home airfield at Netheravon to the Continent. Now, operating from a forward base in West Germany, they are about to take on a WarPac armoured column that is moving westward in the face of stiff opposition from the NATO alliance.

0515 hours

Since the enemy's main armoured thrust began some three days earlier, life has been particularly hectic for the air and ground crews assigned to No. 656 Squadron, Army Air Corps. Normally, they reside at the British Army airfield at Netheravon in England, from where they routinely operate in support of the United Kingdom Mobile Force (UKMF), a command whose primary operational role is to reinforce either North Germany or Denmark in the event of a major Warsaw Pact (WarPac) attack.

Such an attack took place several days earlier and 656's fleet of Lynx and Gazelle helicopters is now well established at a number of sites in Northern Germany while aircrew are fast acquiring combat veteran status, having been in the thick of the action on a number of occasions. Five TOW-armed Lynx and a couple of Gazelles are to be found

Above: Almost unrecognisable beneath a shroud of anti infra-red camouflage, one of the Lynx AH.1 helicopters assigned to No. 656 Squadron, Army Air Corps awaits the call to battle. Armed with the anti-tank TOW missile, it can be airborne within 30 minutes or so.

at the squadron's main Helicopter Landing Site (HLS), situated roughly 19 miles (30km) from the FEBA (forward edge of battle area) — it is from here that virtually all combat missions are flown against WarPac forces.

Even further back from the front line is the squadron's rear echelon, which is primarily concerned with performing functions such as "heavy" maintenance — although necessary if the unit is to maintain an efficient combat posture, such work is best undertaken at a, relatively, safe distance from the battle zone. Today, one Lynx and one Gazelle are receiving treatment, the Lynx having sustained damage to one engine when it ingested several

birds on take-off.

Finally, much closer to the scene of the battle, are a brace of Gazelles — operating from a small landing facility co-located with the Headquarters of the 13/18th Royal Hussars. These perform a variety of tasks, of which the most significant are reconnaissance for the HELARM assets, forward air control and artillery fire co-ordiantion/direction.

At the main HLS, the night has witnessed fairly intense activity on the part of technicians and ground crew so as to ensure that the helicopters are ready to return to battle. Routine maintenance, refuelling and rearming are three of the more important tasks and are invariably accomplished first, before the helicopters are "tucked up" for the night, draped in anti infra-red camouflage netting to reduce the chance of detection.

Tented accommodation is available for crew rest at night but many aircrew prefer to remain with their Lynx helicopters, choosing to bed down in the main cabin. This has the virtue of providing rather more protection from the elements than a canvas tent, since the weather is pretty awful, rain having fallen almost continuously for the past three days and nights. Now, with first light, the unit is again preparing for action and has just come to normal daylight RTM (ready to move) state. This is RTM30 in which aircraft remain camouflaged, with aircrew ready for tasking and able to depart the HLS within 30 minutes from receiving the order to move out.

0520 hours

Around the HLS, the indistinct shapes of five Lynx and two Gazelles are faintly discernible in the slowly strengthening light of dawn. Although all are still draped in camouflage, ground crew are beginning to ready their charges for flight — within an hour, they will be gone, leaving the support team to catch up on some much needed sleep and wait for them to return.

0530 hours

Thirty yards away (27m), secure from chance sighting in the adjacent woods, a faint wisp of smoke emanating from a larger tent betrays the presence of a field kitchen. For the aircrews, breakfast is usually taken on the run, the fare that is available being quite wholesome and, to an outsider, surprisingly appetising, given the difficulties that catering staff invariably face when supporting forces in the field. Nevertheless, there are still those who complain, but such complaints are more of a good humoured leg pull than anything else and the kitchen staff certainly give as good as they get, perhaps tacitly acknowledging that such banter is one way in which aircrew alleviate the stresses and strains that are inherent in combat.

Reminders of the fact that they are in combat are never far from mind. A few yards away, the upwind NBC (nuclear, biological, chemical) sentry stands in full protective kit. His job is to alert the rest of the personnel in the event of a sudden NBC attack, when every second is vital — indeed, just five seconds are allowed for the remaining members of the squadron to don their respirators when the word is passed. Longer than that and they are unlikely to play any further part in this or any other war.

NBC is not the only threat, of course, and this was brought home in spectacularly stark fashion just yesterday when a Gazelle on a reconnaissance task was shot down by ground fire while working with the screen force. The ensuing crash and fire claimed the lives of both crew members, these being the first casualties to be sustained by 656 although there had been a few "near misses", one Lynx taking a couple of hits from ground-based small arms fire. These passed harmlessly through the tailboom and were hastily patched by battle damage repair specialists improvising with a thin sheet of metal taken from a Coke can of all things.

0555 hours

In anticipation of being called to action, word is passed to bring the squadron to a heightened alert state with effect from 0600 when they will move to RTM15. A shouted message notifies support personnel who begin to remove some of the camouflage cover from the nearby helicopters. At the same time, Aircraft Commanders (who, incidentally, are responsible for operating the TOW sight and firing the missiles) move to the Command Post (CP) in anticipation of briefing.

During the night, intelligence assessments of enemy positions and intentions have been passed by the Squadron Second-in-Command, who is located at Brigade Headquarters, as the Aviation Liaison Officer to the command post. This information is marked on a large map covering 656's area of responsibility. Further information is also filtering in from the pair of forward-deployed Gazelles which are now reconnoitering the forward battle area in conjunction with the Royal Hussars. It is fast becoming clear that a major enemy build-up has occurred during the night and that a breakout in force will soon be attempted.

Above: *The Aircraft Commander occupies the left-hand seat in the Lynx cockpit and it is from here that the BGM-71 TOW missile is controlled. Sighting and tracking is accomplished via the roof-mounted sight, with steering commands being issued via a pressure stick operated by the right hand.*

Below: *Here two members of the Army Air Corps drag a fuel line to the starboard side of a Lynx to top up its tanks prior to the start of the mission. Refuelling in the field is a relatively uncomplicated matter, as is the loading of the BGM-71 TOW missile into the launch tubes.*

Some study the map, which shows friendly force dispositions as well as the latest information on enemy concentrations of troops and armoured fighting vehicles, the rate of advance of the opposing forces having slowed significantly in the face of determined opposition from West German troops and armour. Superimposed on this is the Squadron's HELARM overlay, a transparent sheet on which are marked previously reconnoitered HELARM engagement areas as well as the FARP (forward arming and refuelling point), air defence assets such as Rapier surface-to-air missile sites, routes and selected rendezvous points, the latter essentially being "waypoints" to aid navigation and facilitate regrouping and command and control in the event of the helicopters being "bumped"

Above: *With engines running and rotors turning, a trio of Lynx AH.1 anti-tank helicopters of 656 Squadron, Army Air Corps prepare to depart on yet another HELARM mission. Once airborne, they will rendezvous with a Gazelle helicopter which will guide them to their firing positions.*

(engaged by enemy air power such as the Mil Mi-24 "Hind").

HELARM engagement areas have been selected to meet a number of criteria. Cover is naturally a key consideration, since it is obviously desirable to engage enemy forces from a position of relative security, where the attacking helicopters are unlikely to be seen before they open fire. For that reason, rising ground — preferably on the flank of the estimated line of advance — is favoured, since this will provide a measure of terrain-masking. At the same time, it also has the merit of offering a good field of view when the time comes to attack, for, despite the sophistication inherent in such weapons as TOW, it is still necessary to detect a target visually with the sight before one can engage it.

 0557 hours

Other pilots and gunners prefer to wait until after the briefing to study the map and they indulge in idle conversation to while away a few minutes.

"They tell me the 13/18th have challenged our lads to a game of football when this lot's over. You interested in turning out?"

"Yeah, why not. Could be a laugh, I s'pose. Count me in."

"Okay, I'll put you down as goalkeeper, all right."

"Oh, now hang on a moment. I'd be no good in goal."

"I think you'd be just about ideal and we're not playing at Wembley, you know."

"You reckon?"

"Hmm, definitely. After all, you've certainly got big enough hands for it."

"OK. Mind you, I'll know who to blame if I can't play the piano again afterwards."

 0600 hours

"OK, gentlemen, can I have your attention please?" says the Officer Commanding, 656 Squadron. "HELARM orders. Situation as per Sitrep and today looks as though it could be pretty hectic. WarPac forces are expected to attempt a break-out along a fairly broad front. Our mission is to destroy enemy in engagement area Hotel Delta 021 and sizeable concentrations of enemy armour have been noted here . . . here . . . and here," he added, indicating the various locations on the map with the aid of a pointer.

"OK, to continue. Execution. A recce pair of Gazelles are already working with the screen and have been observing a build-up of armour since first light. Timings . . . can't be too specific right now since we await final confirmation but I expect to get orders to move at any moment. Route is via RVs (rendezvous) 7, 5, 4 and 9 to FRV (final rendezvous) 6. Firing order on count-down by Lynx Flight Commander.

"Right, Service Support. FARP is at grid uniform bravo 376438 and it's six missiles per aircraft. Command and Signals — I'm HELARM Commander, alternate is Lynx Flight Commander. There's no change to the present locstat board and frequencies and call-signs are as per the sheet which you should all have a copy of. Any questions so far?"

"Er, I presume you'll want us to maintain radio silence as much as possible, Sir?"

"Yes, radio silence unless you hit a problem. Only call I expect to hear is that you have acquired a target at the fire position. OK, normal tactical bounds prevail, so you're free to

manoeuvre but don't bunch up in close country. No more than two shots for this engagement before you withdraw as we don't want to lose anyone if we can help it.

"Return to FRV post attack. We'll regroup there and move on to the next engagement area to re-engage if necessary. If you encounter problems, try and hold on till we get to the rendezvous — then flash your landing light and we'll talk about it.

"Weather's a bit iffy, as you've probably noticed. If you get bumped, split up and return independently to main HLS. Our people know we're going to be working the area and we've cleared the air defence safe lanes but they might be a bit trigger-happy so I'd advise you to stick to the RV route as given. We'd like to avoid any own goals, you understand gentlemen."

"I think that just about wraps it up unless you've any more questions? No. Good. Right, time check . . . 0603 in 15 seconds. Wait . . . 0603 now."

 0603 hours

Even as the Officer Commanding is bringing his briefing to a conclusion, word is passed via the command communications network to bring 656 Squadron to RTM5, the sergeant on command post duty notifying support personnel by the simple expedient of shouting the news. Within moments, the final camouflage protection is being removed, while the Second Pilots, who have remained with the Lynx throughout, buckle down to completing final preparations for flight.

 0604 hours

Barely 60 seconds later, another message orders 656 Squadron into action, last minute cups of tea and egg banjos being left behind as the Aircraft Commanders run to their charges where the second pilots, alerted over the radio, are initiating engine start procedures.

 0609 hours

Easing back on the collective and pulling pitch, the pilot of the third Lynx lifts his helicopter clear of the ground amidst a miniature dust storm generated by the whirling rotor blades. Stabilising momentarily and checking that instrument readings are satisfactory, he continues to ascend, rising vertically until clear of the tree-tops before moving ahead to the edge of the forest where he brings the craft back to the hover.

Through the windscreen ahead of him, he can see two more Lynx, their basically dark shapes standing out starkly against the field of corn over which they hover as they wait to move out. A flash of movement off to his right alerts him to the presence of yet another Lynx which moves smartly into position and, in a nose low attitude, begins to accelerate away. At the same moment, he begins the transition to forward flight, speed rising as the Lynx takes up its designated slot in the formation.

Initially, the formation of helicopters moves fairly fast, confident that they are unlikely to encounter enemy opposition this far behind the front line. Skimming over the fields at about 50 feet (15m), they make use of whatever cover is available, skirting woodland and following valleys as they move east above the gently rolling countryside.

0612 hours

Occasional squalls of rain limit visibility and call for intense concentration on the part of the pilot who maintains a constant look-out for obstructions which could pose a threat to their continued well-being. As usual, he is aided by the aircraft commander and the intercom is seldom quiet for more than a few seconds, flight at low level being very much a team effort.

"Power lines at two o'clock," says the Aircraft Commander.

"Rog, I see them," is the response, the helicopter sliding beneath the wires at a fast hover taxi.

"Two radio masts dead ahead, 'bout a mile."

"Seen."

"Aircraft in our ten o'clock, 'bout 200 feet, crossing left to right . . ."

"Oh damn. What is it?"

"s'OK, it's a Tornado."

"Thank God for that."

0616 hours

Now close to the battle zone, they begin to move with even greater caution, dropping down to no more than 10 feet (3m) above the ground and slowing their rate of forward progress to just a few miles an hour. To their left, little more than 30 feet (9m) away, a ridge line provides protection from prying eyes and they move ahead steadily, secure in the knowledge that they are unlikely to be seen just yet.

Ahead, a large expanse of open ground seems to offer little chance of concealment and it is with relief that they drop down into a railway cutting, the tips of the main rotor being little more than five feet (1.5m) from the embankment on either side.

"I hope the boss consulted a timetable before we set out," says the second pilot, adding, "we'll look a bit silly if we hit a train."

"Oh, I dunno. Adds a whole new meaning to the phrase 'on the waggon'," comments the Aircraft Commander.

"I suppose I asked for that," is the response.

0620 hours

The five Lynx maintain a hover at the final rendezvous while the Gazelle Commander indicates by means of a board the grid reference and bearing to the target, Aircraft Commanders aboard each Lynx employing the TOW sighting device to read off the figures before entering them into TANS (Tactical Air Navigation System), setting a "bug" on the compass and checking the map. They are now no more than a couple of miles (3.2km) from the Fire Position (FP) and while they wait for the call to action, the respective Aircraft Commanders take a few moments to check again that the sighting devices are working satisfactorily and perform a functional check of the TOW system.

The other Gazelle, meanwhile, has moved out ahead to scout for the approaching column of armoured fighting vehicles, always a hazardous task since it is obviously desirable to find the enemy without betraying one's own presence, something that is by no means easy to achieve on a fluid battlefield.

0622 hours

Confident that the targets have entered the engagement area, the Aircraft Commander of the Gazelle briefly activates his radio and

speaks, "Move now." Within seconds, the five Lynx transition from the hover to forward flight, heading towards the firing position just a couple of miles away. As they approach the firing position, they fan out into a broad line abreast formation which will bring them to their respective firing slots, the leader occupying the centre of the line with Nos. two and four to his left and three and five to his right. Meanwhile, the Gazelle drifts off towards the left flank, where it will maintain a watching brief on the attack formation's vulnerable six o'clock position while they engage the enemy armoured column.

A: Westland Lynx AH.1 helicopters move into firing positions which offer a clear view of the engagement area while at the same time providing good cover so as to reduce the risk of being observed. **B:** Having selected a target, an Aircraft Commander initiates launch of a BGM-71 TOW missile. Whenever possible, launch takes place after a short count-down in order to obtain maximum shock effect. **C:** TOW missiles impact on WarPac armoured fighting vehicles almost simultaneously.

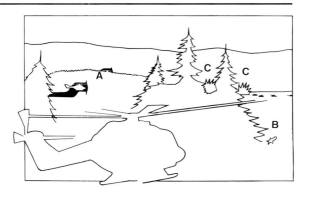

0626 hours

The Lynx hover as they await the coming action, each occupying a position which offers a good view of the selected engagement area. Aboard each machine, the Commanders have already swung the eyepiece for the M65 Telescopic Sighting Unit (TSU) down from its stowed position and they now utilise the sight's low magnification setting (x2) to scan the area through which their targets are expected to pass. This setting has the advantage of offering a wide field-of-view — for engagement, a higher magnification factor (x13) will be selected so as to permit the TOW missile to be accurately guided to its target.

Holding the Lynx in hover with only the rotor and TOW sight protruding above the tree line, the second pilot concentrates on maintaining position, frequently checking the reference points he has selected to assist in station-keeping.

 0627 hours

Ahead of them, beyond the copse which provides cover, a fairly large clearing is visible, numerous tree stumps and a few large piles of logs indicating that it is, to some extent, man made. It is about a mile long (1.6km) and three-quarters of a mile (1.2km) wide, breaks in the serried ranks of trees revealing the presence of numerous tracks which criss-cross almost haphazardly through the forest. It is down some of these tracks that the WarPac armoured column is expected to come and while they wait the Aircraft Commander devotes a few seconds to preparing the TOW missiles for firing, hitting various switches on the control panel to programme the system for automatic missile selection so as to enable him to devote all his attention to acquiring and tracking targets.

He has only just finished when his attention is caught by a clearly visible puff of smoke above the trees, about 200 yards (183m) into the forest from where the clearing begins. Although the risk of being overheard is non-existent, the anticipation of combat and the desire to remain undetected causes his voice to rise barely above a whisper as he speaks softly to his pilot over the intercom.

"I think they're coming now. Just saw what looked like exhaust smoke above the trees in our two o'clock."

"Rog," comes the reply, the second pilot responding in a normal tone of voice. For a brief moment, the Aircraft Commander is tempted to tell his colleague to keep his voice down, but he quickly realises that he is possibly over-reacting to the tension of the moment and he remains silent while he waits for the next development.

Through the TOW sight, he detects evidence of movement at the mouth of one of the tracks but, as yet, he is unable to identify the type of vehicle, which remains tantalisingly screened by the forest edge.

"I think they smell a rat," he remarks.

"No, they're just being cautious," is the reply, "that clearing must look about five miles across."

"Hmm, he's backing off. Wonder if they know we're here?"

"Doubt it, an' even if they shut down to listen, I doubt that they'll hear us 'cos the wind's in the wrong quarter."

 0629 hours

"It's too quiet. What on earth are they doing in there?"

"P'raps they've stopped for breakfast."

"Either that or they're calling in an air strike . . ."

"You reckon?"

"No, they're just a bit cagey, that's all. You'll see . . ."

A sudden eruption of smoke above the tree-line is the first indication of the break-out, which begins simultaneously at three tracks, small fast-moving light AFVs bursting forth from the depths of the forest and steering haphazard courses as they lay down a smoke-screen for the bulkier main battle tanks. Within seconds, the clearing is virtually enveloped in smoke which effectively renders the Lynx gunners blind as it drifts slowly towards the waiting helicopters.

 0630 hours

Aboard the lead Lynx, the Aircraft Commander's frustration is evident when he speaks. "Clever devils — they're using smoke."

"What can you see?"

"Nothing but smoke."

"Any chance of a clear shot . . ."

"No way. Can't see a thing. I only wish we had thermal imaging fitted now."

"'kay, let's head for the rendezvous and try again."

Even as he reaches that conclusion, the Lynx Flight Commander speaks, the clipped transmission lasting no more than two seconds, "RV four, go." He receives no acknowledgement of this rather cryptic message.

 0643 hours

They have spent just a few minutes at the rendezvous point before moving on again, in company with one of the two Gazelles, the commander of which had been keeping track of the enemy column and also been in contact with the Brigade Liaison Officer so as to remain fully informed of developments more or less as they occurred. Now, after a short transit, they are lying in wait at the next engagement area, the rolling countryside offering little cover for the enemy armour as it continues to advance westwards.

"Wonder if they'll pull that smoke stunt again?" muses the Aircraft Commander.

"Shouldn't think so," is the reply. "It's not really a bottleneck here, not like the last spot. I reckon they'll just blast through as fast as they can go."

 0644:15 hours

Within a minute, his conjecture is proved accurate. From their right, half-a-dozen T-72 main battle tanks suddenly emerge from the far side of a clump of trees and, with blue smoke pouring from their exhausts as the throttles are opened, proceed to move across the open expanse at high speed, fanning out to advance on a broad front.

Seconds later, more tanks appear, amongst which can be seen a few examples of the 2S3 mobile howitzer and several BRDM-2 missile-

Below: Having reached a suitable firing position and acquired a target, the Aircraft Commander depresses the firing trigger at the end of a short count-down. Less than two seconds later, the TOW missile leaves its launch tube at the start of its brief but deadly flight to the target.

armed tank destroyers, these too fanning out as they accelerate towards the distant cover.

In the five Lynx, Aircraft Commanders are now actively tracking targets, awaiting the order to fire. Through his telescopic sighting device, one commander can clearly see a T-72 as it moves from right to left through his field of view. The fore-finger of his right hand rests against the pressure stick that controls movement of the roof-mounted sight and it takes just a few seconds to steer the cross-hairs into position over the bulky Soviet tank which lies some 3,500 yards (3,200m) away, comfortably within the TOW missile's maximum range, of 4,100 yards (3,750m).

0644:55 hours

Now that he is tracking the tank satisfactorily, he allows the cross-hairs to slide down until they rest over the target's tracks and wheels. A hit in that area will almost certainly immobilise the tank even if it fails to destroy it. In his left hand, he holds the grip that contains the trigger which will command launch of a missile. Satisfied, he activates the VHF AM radio and speaks, "Three ready."

In the centre of the line, the Lynx Flight Commander waits until all have indicated that

Above: *Moving at low level as it stalks the enemy armoured column, the Gazelle is mainly used to reconnoitre firing positions and to guide the TOW-armed Lynx to these locations. Although unarmed, it does feature a roof-mounted sight which is a useful tool in the reconnaissance task.*

they are tracking targets and ready to fire, so as to maximise shock effect by the near-simultaneous detonations that will occur when the missiles strike home.

Aboard the third Lynx, time seems to stretch as the commander continues tracking his chosen target, the wait for the order to fire seeming almost interminable. Over the intercom, his pilot can hear the commander mutter. "Come on. Come on. What're you waiting for." Such remarks are now a familiar aspect of each and every engagement but post-attack chat reveals that the commander has no recollection of giving voice at all.

0645:06 hours

"Three . . ."

The commander stiffens momentarily, for, although expected, the start of the countdown always succeeds in startling him.

"Two . . ."

He quickly adjusts his grip on the trigger, applying gentle pressure with his left forefinger as he prepares to fire.

"One . . ."

A last quick check confirms that he is still tracking the target satisfactorily.'

"Fire . . .!"

His finger completes the action of depressing the trigger and, as usual, he holds it in place for a couple of seconds during which unseen electrical impulses initiate the launch procedure. Below and behind him, batteries and gyro are activated, feeding power to the launcher and synchronising the electronic kit associated with guidance.

Ignition of the solid-propellant launch motor takes place, the 0.04-second burn providing just enough power to boost the TOW missile clear of its launch unit, which it leaves at an initial velocity of 220ft/sec (67m/sec), precisely 1.57 seconds after the trigger is fully depressed by the commander.

Now clear of the launch tube, the weapon's stub wings and control surfaces deploy and an infra-red light source in the missile is also switched on. This is an integral part of the steering system since it is tracked by an optical sensor in the sighting device as the missile flies towards its target.

Flight motor ignition occurs, this second-stage solid-fuel booster accelerating TOW to a maximum speed which exceeds 621mph (1,000km/hr). Arming of the warhead also occurs during the brief powered flight, for the booster engine's fuel supply is exhausted after just 1.5 seconds. The weapon thereafter coasts to its target, its speed declining to about 292mph (470km/h) at maximum range of 4,100 yards (3,750m) when control is lost as a result of automatic wire-cut.

0645:15 hours

As the missile moves towards its target, the commander continues to hold the cross-hairs firmly on the tank's flank, this being vital if the TOW is to home accurately. Control commands are relayed to the missile via a pair of extremely fine copper wires which are paid out from a dispenser in the rear of the launch tube. These activate an air bottle contained within the missile itself, providing power to

drive the control surfaces which initially cycle some 25 times per second during the acquisition phase of flight — later, this falls to around 12 times per second as the weapon stabilises for the terminal homing phase.

0645:28 hours

On the ground, as yet unaware that they are under attack, the armoured column continues to move westwards. Three of the leading wave of T-72s, a ZSU-23-4 mobile anti-aircraft artillery piece and a BTR60PB command vehicle lurch to an abrupt halt when, within the space of just two seconds, five TOW missiles strike home. The rapidly-blossoming clouds of flame and smoke quickly dispel their commander's belief that they have managed to penetrate this far unobserved.

Each of the warheads impacts more or less right on target, one being deflected slightly by additional defensive armour which succeeds in saving the crew but fails to prevent their vehicle from being immobilised. The other crews are less fortunate, secondary explosions following almost instantaneously as their stock of ammunition "cooks off" in the intense heat with catastrophic consequences.

Elsewhere, alerted to the threat, smoke-generating equipment is brought into action but the freshening breeze and a certain amount of understandable confusion renders this almost worthless. Indeed, it is actually counter-productive, a T-72 in the second wave colliding with an armoured command vehicle as it swerves to avoid one of the damaged tanks which has been shrouded by thick smoke.

In the meantime, the Lynx Commanders waste no time in seeking fresh targets after their initial success, each launching a second missile within the space of five seconds. These, too, home unerringly, accounting for two more T-72s (one of which is possibly a command vehicle, judging by the additional antennal), a couple of 2S3 howitzers and a BRDM-2, the latter being almost torn apart by a series of spectacular detonations as its clutch of six AT-3 Sagger anti-tank missiles explodes barely a minute later.

By then, the Lynx are gone, staying low as they withdraw to the FARP to top up fuel tanks, replenish missiles and be ready to return to combat within 15 minutes.

0702 hours

While that necessary work is performed, the Lynx flight commander takes advantage of a lull in activity to pass a post-HELARM report via radio to the Liaison Officer back at Brigade Headquarters. This includes details of the HELARM number, engagement area, time of engagement, identity and strength of the engaging unit, missiles expended and an assessment of targets destroyed, the latter being further broken down by type of vehicle.

Even as he speaks, the accompanying Gazelles are still shadowing the now badly shaken enemy column, which continues to move slowly westwards. Maintaining contact in this way is imperative if 656 Squadron, Army Air Corps is to re-engage the enemy-armour and inflict further damage.

THE MARITIME MISSION

Evolution of the Mission

O F ALL THE many and diverse areas of contemporary military aviation, there can be few that are more spectacular than operations from the flight deck of one of the US Navy's massive nuclear-powered aircraft carriers. Displacing in excess of 90,000 tons when fully laden, the latest Nimitz-class vessels represent perhaps the ultimate expression of sea-borne air power, and the USA has seldom been reluctant to employ its carrier fleet to project American military might and protect American interests around the world.

Today's generation of so-called "supercarriers" — epitomised by vessels like *Nimitz*, *Dwight D. Eisenhower* and *Carl Vinson* — are able to accommodate a Carrier Air Wing (CVW) which typically exercises control over nine subordinate squadrons with close to 90 aircraft and helicopters between them. The force mix may, of course, be altered to meet a specific set of circumstances or military requirements but the usual peacetime complement will consist of two fighter (VF) squadrons, two light attack (VA) or two fighter-attack (VFA) squadrons, one medium attack (VA) squadron, one airborne early warning (VAW) squadron, one tactical electronic warfare (VAQ) squadron, one fixed-wing anti-submarine warfare (VS) squadron and one rotary-wing anti-submarine warfare (HS) squadron. Squadron strength vary.

Following the adoption of the multi-purpose "CV" concept in the early to mid-1970s, for well over a decade this mix of resources was felt to be the most satisfactory compromise in that it theoretically enabled a carrier to meet most contingencies. In more recent times, however, the Navy has been experimenting with CVW structure, one instance of this involving replacement of the pair of A-7E Corsair-equipped light attack squadrons by a second A-6E Intruder-equipped medium attack squadron with CVW-3 aboard the USS - *John F. Kennedy* (CV-67).

Defending the Fleet

Returning to the more usual peacetime mix, each of the two VF squadrons will typically possess a dozen Grumman F-14 Tomcats, one squadron including three reconnaissance-dedicated machines with the Tactical Air Reconnaissance Pod System (TARPS) in its complement. Leaving aside the reconnaissance mission — which is only a near to mid-term requirement pending acquisition of the RF-18 Hornet — the traditional role of fleet defence is still perceived as being the primary concern of Navy fighter squadrons. This is mainly accomplished by three variations on

Above: *Grumman has long been a major supplier of combat aircraft to the US Navy. Here a KA-6D tanker is topping up the tanks of one of a pair of F-14A Tomcats of VF-41 "Ace of Spades" squadron. For 16 years one of the world's most capable fighters, the Tomcat is now upgraded as the F-14D.*

Below: *Now replaced aboard US Navy carriers by the F/A-18 Hornet, the Vought A-7E Corsair II set a new high standard in the delivery accuracy of free-fall weapons. The Lockheed S-3 Viking (background) transformed carrier-based ASW capability, and now carries Harpoon anti-ship missiles.*

the combat air patrol (CAP) theme, specifically BARCAP, FORCAP and TARCAP.

The first two of these acronyms relate to the protection of fleet assets, FORCAP signifying provision of interceptor air cover for the task force while BARCAP involves barrier defence in which a fighter "screen" is established some considerable distance from the carrier in order to negate the possibility of retaliatory or pre-emptive air attacks. Finally, there is TARCAP or target cover for attack aircraft operating in enemy airspace. Tomcats engaged in this duty escort friendly strike forces to and from the

target area and intervene to prevent enemy fighters from interfering with successful execution of the attack.

Light VA or VFA squadrons respectively operate the Vought A-7E Corsair II or the McDonnell Douglas F/A-18A Hornet and, once again, each will deploy with a dozen aircraft. VA squadrons are predominantly attack orientated but may, on occasion, be called upon to fulfil some CAP work, the trusty AIM-9 Sidewinder missile being employed for this mission and to bestow a modicum of defensive capability when operating in the pure

What the US Navy calls organic seagoing airpower is unique to that Navy (though to a small degree it is a capability possessed by Britain, France, Argentina, India and the Soviet Union). By, in effect, using airfields that can move anywhere there is deep water, airpower can be projected to any point on the planet. The fact that the airfields are mobile also makes them relatively invulnerable, though with carrier positions continuously monitored by hostile satellites even this is changing.

Above: *Here seen about to be catapulted from USS* Saratoga, *the Grumman E-2C Hawkeye multiplies the effectiveness of every aircraft in the Air Wing. Powered by two Allison turboprops, it can do most things a Boeing AWACS can do, at a small fraction of the cost.*

Below: *Grumman's A-6E Intruder, seen here flying with VA-52 from Kitty Hawk, is a standard US Navy medium attack aircraft. It was a big blow to Grumman when the A-6F was cancelled and the A-12A Advanced Tactical Aircraft (the next generation) awarded to McDonnell Douglas and GD.*

ventional iron bombs, "smart" weapons, air-to-surface anti-shipping missiles and even nuclear bombs. Sidewinder is also usually carried for defensive purposes. KA-6Ds are less flexible but do retain limited day attack capability, albeit of an impaired nature due to structural limitations imposed on the airframe.

Other elements, while perhaps less glamorous, are no less valuable although their numerical contribution to overall strength does not necessarily reflect their true worth. VAW units are now wholly equipped with the Grumman E-2C Hawkeye, embarked strength being modest, at just four aircraft per squadron. Although mostly associated with the role of fleet defence, in which it works closely with the F-14 Tomcat to identify and counter the threat posed by enemy fighter and attack aircraft, the E-2C may operate as a mini-AWACS, exercising control over offensive and defensive elements of the CVW. In this capacity, data link equipment is used to direct strike forces to the target, returning aircraft then being vectored straight back to the parent carrier or, if they require additional fuel, to an Intruder tanker. Air traffic control is yet another function, most notably in bad weather, when the E-2C's crew supervises the recovery procedure while it can also relay radar data to the carrier, thus extending the area covered by that vessel's line-of-sight radar system.

VAQ squadrons operate yet another Grumman product in the shape of the EA-6B Prowler, four being the normal complement when deployed. Missions vary from ECM escort of a strike force through stand-off jamming to acquisition of electronic intelligence.

The vital ASW battle

Finally, there are the ASW resources. VS squadrons usually deploy with 10 Lockheed S-3 Vikings for long-range tasks, patrolling far from the parent carrier so as to set up a sub-surface screen in much the same way as BARCAP-dedicated Tomcats counter aerial threats. The HS squadron satisfies close-in ASW needs with half-a-dozen Sikorsky SH-3H Sea Kings which also perform the search and rescue (SAR) "plane-guard" function during launch and recovery, as well as undertaking a limited amount of resupply work during underway replenishment operations.

In addition, forward-deployed carriers assigned to either the Mediterranean (6th Fleet) or the Western Pacific (7th Fleet) may regularly host one or two examples of the Douglas EA-3B Skywarrior, these somewhat nomadic veterans being employed in conjunction with

strike/CAS roles. Experience has shown the A-7E Corsair to be almost equally at home in long-range strike or close air support duties as it demonstrated so effectively in Vietnam.

VFA units may effectively be described as "swing-fighters", the Hornet being able to switch from attack to fleet defence and back again, as and when the need arises, apparently with no loss of effectiveness. However, on those carriers which number the F-14 in their complement, the Hornet will mainly be expected to fulfil attack functions.

The two older carriers of the Midway class

employ a somewhat different CVW structure since they are unable to support Tomcat. In consequence, they both feature four VFA squadrons, each with a dozen Hornets, and these share responsibility for fulfilling fleet defence and attack taskings.

Medium VA units are universally equipped with the Grumman Intruder, 10 or 11 purely attack-dedicated A-6Es being accompanied by a quartet of KA-6D in-flight refuelling tankers. Long-range all-weather strike is the metier of the Intruder and it may operate with a multiplicity of ordnance, encompassing con-

Lockheed EP-3B/E Orions to gather data pertaining to a potential enemy's "electronic order of battle". VQ-1 fulfils this mission from Agana, Guam, on behalf of the Pacific Fleet — its Atlantic Fleet counterpart is VQ-2 at Rota, on the south coast of Spain.

With no fewer than 15 aircraft carriers now in commission and with two more Nimitz-class vessels due to join the fleet in the early 1990s, the United States is clearly firmly committed to sea-borne air power as a means of both projecting national strength and protecting national interests. Eight other nations also operate aircraft carriers but few of these possess genuine multi-mission capability and most of the ten or so that are presently active are what might be described as task-orientated, for national needs.

For instance, France's two Clemenceau-class vessels are mainly concerned with attack missions, each embarking an air group which is dominated by the Super Etendard strike fighter, although it also includes some examples of the F-8 Crusader for fleet defence, as well as a handful of Alizés and Super Frelon helicopters to to fly ASW and friendly missile-submarine support missions.

Carriers around the world

The Super Etendard and, to a lesser extent, the A-4 Skyhawk provide Argentina's *25 de Mayo* with a not inconsiderable punch, although in the light of Royal Navy activity in the Falklands War it seems doubtful if Argentina's solitary carrier would be committed to action in anything but an overwhelmingly favourable tactical situation. *25 de Mayo* is also able to fulfil ASW duties with a mixture of S-2 Trackers and SH-3 Sea Kings.

Brazil's *Minas Gerais* and Italy's *Giuseppi Garibaldi* are fundamentally ASW-dedicated, as indeed are the three members of Britain's Invincible class, although these may embark additional Sea Harriers in order to provide a greater measure of offensive capability to the fleet. India's naval air arm has two carriers, the long-serving INS *Vikrant* having recently acquired a "ski-jump" to facilitate operation of the Sea Harrier. The same type will also serve with the second carrier's air group, HMS *Hermes* having been purchased from the UK in 1986. Now known as the INS *Viraat*, the latter vessel is expected to form the core of a battle group of frigates and destroyers.

A close relative of the Sea Harrier, the EAV-8B Harrier II will form the primary equipment to be embarked aboard Spain's *Principe de Asturias,* although, once again, ASW capability is a key feature, the principal tool being the Sikorsky SH-3H Sea King.

Finally, there is the Soviet Union, which, after shunning sea-borne air power for many years, is fast becoming an ardent convert. Beginning tentatively with the ASW helicopter cruisers *Moskva* and *Leningrad* in the late 1960s, the USSR took a major step forward in

Right: The "Wright Flyer" of the jet-lift STOVL era, the BAe AV-8A Harrier was nevertheless found so useful by the US Marines that they are building up a large force of the much more effective AV-8B Harrier II. These are the original version, seen recovering on deck.

the middle of the next decade with the *Kiev*. The lead ship of a class of four — the others are the *Minsk, Novorossiysk* and *Baku* — *Kiev* was also quite clearly optimised for ASW, about 16 to 20 examples of the Kamov Ka-25 Hormone helicopters normally being embarked. In addition, though, *Kiev* and her sister ships routinely carry about a dozen Yakovlev Yak-38 Forger V/STOL fighters, bestowing a strike capability, though far removed from that possessed by US Navy carriers.

Above: A production Lockheed S-3A Viking on carrier trials from USS Enterprise, *before the latter's island was rebuilt. Designed as an ASW platform, the Viking can also fly anti-ship roles, and has been evaluated as a tanker and COD transport. Perhaps the total of 184 was too few but most are to be updated and improved to S-3B standard.*

Even more interesting developments are in prospect for the future, work on the first of an entirely new class of nuclear-powered carriers having begun at the massive Nikolayev yard during 1983. Possibly known as the Kremlin class, construction of the first example was accomplished at a quite remarkable rate, with the "super-carrier" being launched in December 1985. The next couple of years were spent in fitting-out but sea trials were confidently predicted to begin in 1988

Below: Seen about to be launched, the Super Etendard would have little capability were it not for the fact that it can carry the AM39 Exocet anti-ship missile, which has been used in action by Argentina and Iraq. Here the load comprises merely drop tanks and two rocket pods. Today, Super Etendards serve with France and Argentina.

although it remains to be seen as to what equipment will be assigned to the embarked air group. Some sources mention a new development of the Yak-38 Forger but the provision of catapult and arrester gear tends to confirm the belief that a new naval fighter has been under development. However, this may well transpire to be a navalised variation of an existing warplane such as the MiG-29 or Su-27.

Regardless of equipment, when the new Soviet carrier eventually leaves port for her maiden cruise in the early 1990s it will almost certainly herald the end of an era in which the US Navy has reigned virtually unchallenged in exercising control of the skies above the world's oceans.

All of this is, of course, a far cry from the rather tentative beginnings of naval air power. The early pioneers would surely be thunderstruck by the progress which has been made since their initial experiments. Since it is today the principal exponent of sea-borne aviation, it is particularly fitting that the US Navy played an instrumental part in bringing about the successful marriage of air and sea power, the service first expressing interest in the potential of flying machines in March 1898, more than five years before the Wright brothers recorded the first powered flight at Kitty Hawk, North Carolina.

Relatively little was done, however, until 1910 when a civilian pilot by the name of Eugene Ely performed the very first take-off from a ship. The vessel concerned was the light cruiser USS *Birmingham* and Ely's runway consisted of a wooden platform which had been built up above the foredeck while the ship lay at anchor in Hampton Roads. Flying a Curtiss Model D biplane, Ely successfully "launched" on 14 November but almost came to grief when he nosed over to gain additional speed after clearing the deck. Although the wheels and the propeller both struck the water, Ely was able to remain airborne but wisely elected to head for the nearest land, touching down safely at a place called Willoughby Spit, some two-and-a-half miles (4km) from his point of departure.

The first "landing on"

Just over two months later, on 18 January 1911, Ely continued his pioneering work when he recorded the first ever ship "trap" (landing) although on this occasion the scene of the action had shifted to the US west coast. Flying from Presidio Field, adjacent to San Francisco Bay, Ely touched down upon a 120ft (36m) long "flight deck" aboard the cruiser USS *Pennsylvania*. Grapnel hooks attached to the landing gear of the Curtiss DIV biplane engaged the "arrester gear" which consisted of nothing more ambitious than a series of 22 transverse ropes to which were tied 50lb (22.6kg) sand bags, one at each end.

It could by no means have been described as a "perfect trap" for Ely's aircraft missed the first 11 ropes, snagging the 12th and succeeding lines and coming to a halt with 50-ft of deck to spare. Less than an hour later, he took-off again, in the process confirming beyond doubt that aircraft could operate from ships at sea with a reasonable margin of safety.

In view of the success of these early tests, it is perhaps surprising that the US Navy had to

Above: *Another type bought in inadequate numbers was the Douglas A-3 Skywarrior. Originally nuclear bombers, the 280 built were converted for many other roles. This pressurised-fuselage EA-3B ECM platform is seen serving with VQ-1 World Watchers based at NAS Agana, Guam.*

Left: *The very first take-off from a ship, by Curtiss demo pilot Eugene Ely from USS Birmingham on 14 November 1910. It was a rather tricky operation, like a lot of carrier flying since that time. As the photograph confirms, the cruiser was lying at anchor at the time.*

Above: *The very first landing on a ship, on 18 January 1911. The pilot was again Ely, and he landed on a wooden platform built on the armoured cruiser Pennsylvania on which were numerous transverse cables with heavy sacks at each end. Later that day he took off again.*

wait until March 1922 to acquire its first true aircraft carrier. In the meantime, it had been the British who had taken developments several stages further, accomplishing the first take-off from a ship under way on 4 May 1912 and successfully operating aircraft from a variety of converted ships during World War I. The Royal Navy crowned that achievement with the completion of the first true aircraft carrier in September 1918, just a few weeks before that conflict ended. The vessel concerned — actually a conversion of an unfinished Italian liner — was the HMS *Argus* and it began operations with the Sopwith Cuckoo torpedo bomber shortly before the end of

1918 although it was to exert no influence on the outcome of World War I.

Throughout this early period, however, most of those in authority still viewed the battleship as the prime naval weapon, refusing to believe that air power could achieve much apart from performing visual reconnaissance for the fleet and observing fall of shot during artillery bombardments. The conflict which had so recently ended had provided evidence that air power was potentially rather more versatile but with such firmly entrenched beliefs in high places, it was hardly surprising that there was a considerable amount of reluctance to divert money and other scarce resources to what they felt to be largely a waste of time. As a consequence, in the immediate post-war era carrier development more or less ground to a halt and it was not until the early 1920s that real headway again began to be made, with Britain, Japan and the United States leading the way, albeit with meagre funding.

Between then and World War II, all three nations channelled a considerable amount of effort towards transforming the fledgling aircraft carrier into a potentially effective weapon of war. Early British efforts in this field were mainly conducted with converted vessels. For instance, HMS *Courageous*, HMS *Furious* and HMS *Glorious* were all modified cruisers but some purpose-built carriers had joined the Royal Navy by 1939 and several more were then under construction.

The USA's first true aircraft carrier was the USS *Langley*, a converted collier which entered service in 1922 and which spent the first three years of its naval career on an extensive series of trials. She was subsequently joined by the USS *Lexington* and the USS *Saratoga* which had both been laid down as battle cruisers.

They were followed by the USS *Ranger* which was built from the keel up as an aircraft carrier and which possessed the ability to carry

no fewer than 75 aircraft. Commissioned in June 1934 and with a displacement of just 14,500 tons, the *Ranger* was a "one-off" unlike the next American carrier which was placed in service at the end of September 1937. This, the USS *Yorktown*, proved to be the forerunner of a class of three much larger ships, the others being the USS *Enterprise* and the USS *Hornet*, respectively commissioned in May 1938 and October 1941. Each displaced some 27,100 tons and could carry as many as 100 aircraft.

The Rising Sun

Japan, like Britain an island nation and therefore heavily dependent on the sea, adopted a slightly different approach in that its first and subsequent carriers were all built as such, the *Shoho* leading the way. By 1939 it had been joined in Imperial Japanese Navy service by five more, making it second only to Britain in terms of available carrier resources.

Improvements in carrier technology were to some extent matched by progress in the aeronautical field, Japan perhaps having achieved most in this area by the autumn of 1939. However, it is probably fair to say that naval aircraft were generally inferior to their land-based counterparts throughout the interwar years, slow and lumbering biplanes still being very much the rule rather than the exception. Nevertheless, by 1939, carrier aviation had made a number of important strides, and sea-based aircraft could now perform such missions as fighter, torpedo and dive bomb-

ing, fleet reconnaissance and gunfire direction.

The impetus provided by World War II changed carrier aviation irrevocably and out of all recognition. Outdated equipment was one of the casualties, Britain and the USA conceiving, developing and deploying ever more capable warplanes as the conflict progressed. Japan, which had perhaps made the greatest progress at the time of its entry into the war, as the devastating attack on the key US naval base at Pearl Harbor in December 1941 showed, didn't lag behind as far as aircraft development was concerned.

For Japan, however, their misfortune in not finding any of the US Navy's three Pacific Fleet carriers at home in Pearl Harbor was to cost them dear. Four of the six carriers which took part in the Pearl Harbor mission — the *Akagi*, *Hiryu*, *Kaga* and *Soryu* — were sunk during the Battle of Midway in June 1942. They were by no means the first losses to US air power, the light carrier *Shoho* having been sunk in the Battle of the Coral Sea just one month earlier, while another veteran of the Pearl Harbor attack (the *Shokaku*) sustained serious damage in this encounter with the US Navy and was forced to withdraw for repairs.

Yet another heavy blow followed soon after, in late August, when the *Ryujo* went to the bottom during the Battle of the Eastern Solomons. In the space of just three months of intense activity, no fewer than seven Japanese aircraft carriers had been sunk, the loss of these capital ships being a blow from which it was near impossible to recover and it was hardly surprising that Japanese carrier-borne naval air power played little further part in the

Left: USS Langley *was converted from a fleet collier in 1922 to become the US Navy's first aircraft carrier. This photograph was probably taken in the late 1920s, when her aircraft included Curtiss Hawks and Vought Corsairs. Her funnels are being folded horizontal.*

Below: *The* Akagi, *one of the great fleet of carriers built by the Imperial Japanese Navy between the wars, is seen here in Sukomo Bay in April 1939. She displaced 42,650 tons, after a rebuild in 1938, and could accomodate 91 aircraft. She played a major role at Pearl Harbor.*

Above: *The world's first giant aircraft carrier was HMS Furious, converted from a battle cruiser and seen here with Sopwith 2F.1 Camels on her "flying off deck" in 1918. Amazingly, she fought all through World War II, seeing many prolonged actions, and was scrapped in 1945.*

Above: *HMS Illustrious flying off Fairey Albacore torpedo bombers, probably in 1942, with Grumman Martlets (Wildcats) on deck. Intended to replace the Fairey Swordfish ("Stringbag"), the Albacore was in fact outlived by the older type, which was produced in much greater numbers.*

Below: *A remarkable photograph, taken from one of her own aircraft, of the shattered and burning Hiryu at the Battle of Midway, 6 June 1942. This series of battles destroyed Japanese naval air power and marked the turning point, for US military power, in the war in the Pacific.*

conduct of the war in the Pacific.

The lessons learned by the Americans in that theatre and by the British elsewhere in the world were instrumental in bringing about a change in perception as to the role and value of the aircraft carrier. This henceforth took over the position of being the prime naval weapon, in the process relegating the large and heavily-armed battleship to the second division of capital ships.

Although the battleship was able to project awesome power in World War II, it was somewhat restricted in that it possessed a fairly limited radius of action and was thus unable to exert direct influence on events that were taking place several hundred miles away. On the other hand skilful use of air power could do just that and it was precisely for that reason, if no other, that the aircraft carrier inherited the battleship's mantle.

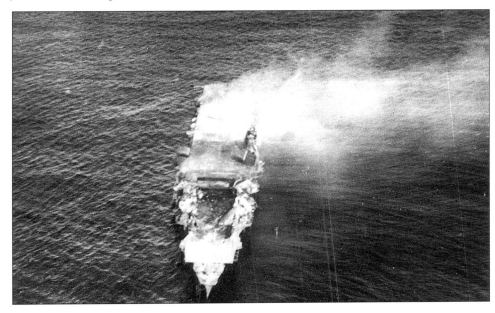

The Post-war era

By the end of World War II an entirely new generation of carrier-compatible warplanes had appeared, as sea-borne air power grew to maturity. These were epitomised by the classic Vought F4U Corsair and the Grumman TBM Avenger which served with distinction with both the US Navy and Britain's Fleet Air Arm. Equally impressive new types were in prospect, the Grumman F8F Bearcat and Douglas AD Skyraider being two of the most outstanding of the types that entered service with the US Navy in the immediate post-war era, while Hawker's elegant Sea Fury soon became the Royal Navy's Fleet Air Arm's principal fighter.

By that time, of course, post-war retrenchment had bitten deep into naval resources on both sides of the Atlantic Ocean and the number of active aircraft carriers had been all but decimated. US Navy carrier strength falling from 98 in July 1945 to just 15 in July 1950. It wasn't all gloom and doom, though, for these savage cuts were, to some extent, compen-

sated for by the advent of increasingly capable equipment, the five-year period in question witnessing deployment of the first turbojet-powered combat aircraft as well as a number of other interesting developments.

Amongs the more exciting projects was the successful launch of a captured German V-2 rocket from the flight deck of the USS *Midway* on 6 September 1947. Although marred by the erratic post-launch behaviour of the missile, this test proved that aircraft carriers could be employed as launch platforms for long-range bombardment missiles.

Perhaps of greater significance in the light of the Navy's desire to develop the capability to deliver nuclear weapons was a test which took place on 27 April 1948. On that date, a pair of Lockheed P2V-2 Neptunes utilised the aid of JATO (jet-assisted take-off) bottles to launch from the USS *Coral Sea* which was cruising in the Atlantic Ocean off Norfolk, Virginia. Further trials with the P2V-3C variant of the Nep-

tune in 1948-49 confirmed that it could operate effectively from the larger carriers of the Midway class, and the Navy eventually went on to establish a small number of squadrons with the ability to deliver the Mk.IV device which was the first true "production" atomic or "fission" bomb to enter the US strategic arsenal.

Jets go to sea

US Navy trials with jet aircraft effectively began with the P-80A Shooting Star in the summer of 1945 but one notable type that did see limited use between 1945 and 1947 was the Ryan FR-1 Fireball. This unique hybrid employed a novel mixture of propeller and turbine power, although it soon became apparent that the Fireball possessed most of the drawbacks associated with the former means of propulsion and few of the advantages of-

Above: The F9F-5 was one of the most important members of the Grumman Panther/Cougar family, which ran to well over 3,000 examples. Made possible by the British RR Nene turbojet, these aircraft saw much action in the Korean war, in both air combat and ground attack.

Above: This McDonnell F2H-2 is typical of the family of Banshee fighter and photo-reconnaissance aircraft that partnered the F9Fs in Korea. Powered by two slim Westinghouse engines, the F2H series included radar-equipped night fighters armed with four 20mm cannon.

Above: The Royal Navy's de Havilland Sea Venom FAW.21 was a two-seat night fighter with the same Westinghouse radar as some Banshees. This example, painted in the black and yellow stripes for the war against Egypt in 1956, is making a belly landing on the flight deck.

fered by the latter. It was therefore doomed to disappear very quickly from the contemporary scene.

Even while the Ryan type was enjoying its brief operational career, the US Navy was aggressively pursuing plans for the switch to pure jets, a P-80A providing conclusive proof that this still relatively new type of warplane could operate from ships at sea when it completed a brief series of trials aboard the USS *Franklin D. Roosevelt* in November 1946. By then, work on the McDonnell FH-1 Phantom and the North American FJ-1 Fury had begun to make very real headway. Both types duly began to enter service with elements of the Fleet in 1947, VF-17A of the Atlantic Fleet receiving Phantoms while VF-5A of the Pacific Fleet got the Fury. In the event, VF-17A secured the distinction of being the first jet-equipped squadron to become carrier-qualified in three fairly hectic days aboard the USS *Saipan* in May 1948.

These primitive jets were, however, destined to be little more than a "stepping stone" and both had been eliminated from the operational inventory by the summer of 1950. Their replacements fared rather better. McDonnell's F2H-1 Banshee entered service as a direct replacement for the FH-1 in March 1949, and on-going development resulted in the appearance of specialist night-fighter and reconnaissance-dedicated variants. Some 894 examples of all sub-types had been completed for Navy service when production terminated in August 1953.

The great F9F family

Grumman's straight-winged F9F Panther proved even more successful, almost 1,400 having been completed by December 1952. Production then switched entirely to the swept-wing Cougar, the initial F9F-6 variant making its maiden flight in September 1951 with deliveries getting under way in November 1952. Between then and acceptance of the last F9F-8T trainer in December 1959, no fewer than 1,985 Cougars emerged from Grumman's Bethpage factory.

In the normal course of events, production

Above: The Vought F4U-1 Corsair was one of the greatest fighter aircraft of World War II. It is most unfortunate that the first three years of its life (1940-42) were spent mainly on tests and modifications. When it finally got fully into action it proved outstandingly capable.

of the Banshee and Panther/Cougar would probably not have resulted in such large quantities being built for service with the Navy and Marine Corps. War was once again the catalyst, the USA making a major contribution to the United Nations forces which intervened following the invasion of South Korea by North Korean troops on 25 June 1950.

Almost inevitably, naval air power was called into action. Carrier-borne aircraft of the Navy's Pacific Fleet wasted no time in entering combat when they joined aircraft of the Fleet Air Arm in a series of strikes on targets in the vicinity of Pyongyang on 3 July. For the Panther and the Skyraider, that day witnessed their first exposure to the rigours of combat. The Panther acquitted itself particularly well in that two aircraft of VF-51 accounted for a pair of Yakovlev Yak-9s during the very first strike mission. Later they met MiG-15s.

In Britain, post-war development proceeded at a rather more leisurely pace but in view of the fact that rationing was still a fact of everyday life and with vast sums of money being directed towards rebuilding cities which had previously been the subject of intense bombing by the Luftwaffe, that was hardly surprising. Nevertheless, serious consideration was being given to the deployment of jet-powered aircraft aboard aircraft carriers.

The rubber-deck fiasco

One of the most bizarre experiments of the late 1940s involved the "flexdeck" concept. Essentially, flexdeck was a system whereby fighter aircraft could be stripped of conventional landing gear, the space thus made available being given over to additional fuel, this in turn extending range and endurance quite considerably. Launch could be effected from a special dolly or catapult device, while recovery would take place on an inflatable rubber landing mat. Friction and an arrester hook combined to bring the aircraft safely to a halt. At least that was the theory...

In order to test flexdeck, two Vampire F.3s were modified but the trials programme started inauspiciously when one of these was destroyed on the first attempt to land on a mat which had been installed at Farnborough, happily without injury to the pilot, Cdr Eric "Winkle" Brown. Undeterred, the trials continued and the first successful landing was accomplished on 29 December 1947. Subsequent developments witnessed the conversion of half-a-dozen Sea Vampires for a series of sea trials which took place between November 1948 and May 1949 aboard HMS *Warrior*. Thereafter, the flexdeck concept died a lingering death in Britain, only to be resurrected by the US Navy which conducted a number of tests at Patuxent River, Maryland, in the mid-1950s before it too abandoned the concept in March 1956.

Although flexdeck was ultimately doomed to failure, the Fleet Air Arm did succeed in deploying jet-powered aircraft of a rather more conventional format, beginning with the Supermarine Attacker which achieved operational status in the spring of 1952 when No.800 Squadron embarked aboard HMS *Eagle*. Like the American Fury and Phantom I, the Attacker met with only limited success, barely 100 being built. Despite that, there can be no doubt that it did make a significant contribution to the history of British naval aviation for it provided valuable expertise in the techniques necessary for the successful operation of jets at sea. In doing so, it paved the way for succeeding generations of rather more effective types, spearheaded by the Hawker Sea Hawk day fighter which joined the fleet in 1953 and the de Havilland Sea Venom all-weather fighter which entered service in 1954.

Although the British lagged behind the Americans when it came to the deployment of jets at sea, they were by no means so tardy with regard to improving the parent vessel itself. Indeed, all three of the major developments of the 1950s originated with the British, less successful projects like flexdeck being matched by more solid and enduring achievements of which the angled deck was perhaps the most valuable.

The angled deck

Like the later "ski jump" concept, it was almost brilliant in its simplicity and it eliminated at a stroke several of the more worrying aspects of carrier operations. For a start, the somewhat higher approach and landing speeds required by jets were of less concern in that any aircraft which failed to hook a wire could perform a "bolter" (go round again) without fear of crashing into the forward deck parking area. At the same time, it also permitted the arrester gear to be simplified for it was

Left: The Hawker Sea Fury FB.11 was one of the greatest of all piston-engined fighters. This example served aboard HMS Theseus off Korea with Royal Navy No 807 Sqn, which flew over 800 combat missions in one six-month period (from November 1950 to April 1951).

no longer imperative to achieve a successful "trap" (landing) on each pass. Thus, carriers could effectively operate with fewer cross-deck pendants (arrester wires), modern warships of this type having only four compared with at least a dozen often required on the old straight-deck vessels. In addition, this development theoretically permitted simultaneous launch and recovery operations.

The second important British development was the steam catapult which was soon recognised as being far superior to the hydraulic devices used thus far in terms of both power and reliability. The mirror landing system also did much to improve the at times abysmally poor safety record. This was essentially a mirror landing sight consisting of a stabilised light-projector which showed the pilot whether he was on, above or below the correct flight path.

Between them, these three developments ensured the survival of the aircraft carrier, but it was to be the USA which would in future do most to maximise this type of warship's potential. Apart from the USSR, which was not then a devotee of sea-borne air power, it was the only nation with sufficient financial "clout" to bear the vast expenditures involved. Britain, France and a number of other countries did, however, continue to operate aircraft carriers with which to protect national interests but they were no longer to occupy positions in the big league (which had dwindled to one).

The US Navy, although bitter over the cancellation of the first "supercarrier" — the USS *United States* which was axed in 1948 — purchased a new carrier class in the 1950s. Leading the way when it commissioned on 1 October 1955, the 76,000-ton USS *Forrestal* was indeed a "super-carrier". By 1959, it had been joined by three sister ships but investment in a new fleet didn't end there, three Kitty Hawk-class vessels being delivered between 1961 and 1965, as well as the nuclear-powered USS *Enterprise* (still dimensionally the world's largest warship) in 1961 and the fossil-fuelled USS *John F. Kennedy* in 1968.

The ASW mission

The advent of these new carriers was by no means the only exciting development of the 1950s, for several of the older and smaller Essex-class ships were converted to serve in the anti-submarine warfare role. Capability in this increasingly important mission was initially only marginal but the advent of the purpose-built Grumman S2F Tracker and the Sikorsky HSS-1 Seabat measurably increased sub-hunting and -killing potential. As a result, the ASW-dedicated carrier and its associated Air Group (CVSG) remained an important element of the fleet until the mid-1970s, when Navy ASW doctrine underwent a fundamental and far-reaching change.

Above: In 1945 many thought the Douglas Skyraider was already obsolete. Over 20 years later the US Navy realised 3,180 (finishing in 1957) was not nearly enough! This example is launching on a Vietnam mission in 1966 from the USS Intrepid *(today a floating museum off Manhattan).*

Below: A formal right-side view by the Douglas El Segundo plant photographer of a production A3D-1 Skywarrior on 14 April 1956. Weighing 82,000lb, they were among the biggest carrier aircraft ever. Later all were converted for other duties, as for example on P.187 (top).

FIGHTER MISSIONS

Although many Essex-class carriers were reconfigured for the ASW task, quite a few remained active as pure attack carriers for some considerable time, albeit in diminishing numbers as more examples of the Forrestal and later classes became available. Nevertheless, both the USS *Hancock* and the USS *Oriskany* remained purely attack-orientated right up until the time that they were withdrawn in the mid-1970s.

Other attack carriers comprised the three members of the Midway class, extensive refits accomplished in the 1950s and 1960s permitting these to remain effective for rather longer than originally anticipated. Indeed, two of them — the USS *Midway* itself and the USS

Coral Sea — still form an important part of today's Navy. The third member, the USS *Franklin D. Roosevelt,* was withdrawn from use in 1977 but its final cruise to the Mediterranean was quite innovative in that it witnessed the first occasion on which V/STOL aircraft operated as an integral part of a carrier air wing, with Marine Corps AV-8A Harriers of VMA-231 serving alongside the F-4N Phantoms and A-7B Corsairs of CVW-19.

The 1950s and 1960s were also notable for the appearance of a bewildering succession of new warplanes. Some, like the Chance Vought F7U Cutlass and Grumman F11F Tiger, were to prove relatively short-lived and of only questionable value. Others, such as the

Douglas A3D Skywarrior, Douglas A4D Skyhawk, Chance Vought F8U Crusader, McDonnell F4H Phantom II and the Grumman A2F Intruder, were infinitely more durable and successful.

Indeed, it is fair to say that they enabled the Navy to project American military might more or less anywhere in the world at very short notice. Demonstrations of such resolve occurred on several occasions in the 1950s, most notably in conjunction with the Lebanon and Taiwan crises of 1958, and again in the blockade of Cuba during the missile crisis of October-November 1962.

On those occasions, US military might was evidently backed up by political strength of purpose, something which was sadly lacking when Naval air power was next used in support of American desires and objectives. That was in Southeast Asia, where carrier-based air power was in action within hours of the second attack being staged by North Vietnamese motor torpedo boats in early August 1964. In a series of attacks on five locations along North Vietnam's coast, aircraft from the USS *Ticonderoga* and the USS *Constellation* put some 25 MTBs out of action as well as inflicting serious damage to fuel storage and other associated facilities.

Between then and mid-August 1973, carrier aircraft played a major part in the air war against North Vietnam but that was by no means the only target, parts of overrun South Vietnam also feeling the weight of US Navy-delivered bombs, rockets and gunfire, as did Laos and Cambodia. Ultimately, it was all to prove fruitless, for despite the skill and tenacity of Navy and Marine Corps aviators (and of their Air Force counterparts), political considerations outweighed purely tactical matters and resulted in the available air power being somewhat emasculated. Indeed, it was only in the final days of US involvement that air power was given free rein, the unfettered use of the B-52 in December 1972's sustained "Linebacker II" campaign against Hanoi and Haiphong enabling President Nixon to claim "peace with honour".

Above: In the 1970s the British Government of the day cancelled a big new carrier and announced that the Fleet Air Arm would henceforth fly only helicopters. The Buccaneers and Phantoms seen here aboard Ark Royal were handed to the RAF and the ship paid off in 1978.

Below: Two McDonnell F2H Banshees drop their hooks before landing on USS Essex after bombing North Korea in September 1951. At that time this famous ship class was very important; today only one is active, because at 42,000 tons they are too small for modern US airpower.

Changed ASW deployment

The closing stages of the war in Southeast Asia coincided with a fundamental shift in US Navy thinking with regard to the conduct of anti-submarine warfare. In part prompted by a decline in the numbers of available ASW-dedicated Essex-class carriers — down from ten at the end of 1960 to just three at the end of 1970 — and in part by the desire to retire the fifties-vintage Grumman S-2 Tracker in favour of the up-to-date Lockheed S-3A Viking, this resulted in a shift to the current multi-purpose CV concept in which fixed-wing aircraft and helicopters routinely operate alongside fighter and attack types aboard the Navy's present fleet of large-deck carriers.

Trial basing of ASW assets on attack carriers actually predated the changeover. One early test involved the deployment of VS-28's S-2Es and HS-7's SH-3Ds aboard the USS *Saratoga* for that vessel's Mediterranean cruise in the latter half of 1971. *Saratoga* in fact became the first carrier to adopt the new CV designation on 30 June 1972. It was followed by a second Atlantic Fleet carrier (the USS *Independence*) at

the end of February 1973, and the Pacific Fleet gained its first multi-mission ship on 29 April 1973 when the USS *Kitty Hawk* was officially redesignated as the third CV.

One other Atlantic Fleet vessel was redesignated at the beginning of December 1974, this being the USS *John F. Kennedy* and 30 June 1975 marked the end of an era when no fewer than 11 more carriers adopted the new title. In some cases, redesignation was little more than a token gesture; vessels such as the *Hancock, Oriskany, Midway, Coral Sea* and *Franklin D. Roosevelt* were multi-mission CVs in name only for they lacked both the space and the specialised equipment necessary to support all the aircraft.

Even as the CV era opened, so too had the US Navy begun to receive a new class of aircraft carrier, the first for almost seven years. USS *Nimitz* was the lead vessel and it was formally commissioned on 3 May 1975. Initially classified as a nuclear-powered attack aircraft carrier (CVAN), and in terms of displacement the world's largest warship, it was redesignated a CVN in line with the new concept just under two months later. At that time, though, it lacked the specialised mission-related equipment and its first couple of deployments were made without the benefit of organic ASW assets.

Above: *With TF30-414A engines in full afterburner, this F-14A Tomcat is about to be catapulted from USS* Saratoga. *Apart from the USA only France and the Soviet Union are seeking to continue to deploy this kind of fixed-wing airpower. France's need is not obvious.*

Below: *Seen here during the Falklands campaign, HMS* Hermes *played a valuable role acting as a base for Sea Harriers (which used the ski ramp seen in the background) and Sea Kings. Today she is the* Viraat *of the Indian Navy, still operating Sea Harriers and Sea Kings.*

More US giants

Three more members of the Nimitz class are now in service, the USS *Dwight D. Eisenhower* (commissioned in October 1977), the USS *Carl Vinson* (March 1982) and the USS *Theodore Roosevelt* (October 1986). Present plans call for another two to join the Navy in the early 1990s. Two more former Presidents will be honoured by these vessels, the USS *Abraham Lincoln* being set to commission in 1990 with the USS *George Washington* following in 1991.

As far as other navies are concerned, the post-Korea period has essentially been one of unremitting attrition. Dwindling defence budgets are partly responsible, while the decline of colonial powers has also been an influential factor. Several nations — including Australia, Canada and the Netherlands — have abandoned carrier-borne air power completely. Others, of which Britain is perhaps the prime example, have forsaken the classic aircraft carrier format in favour of the "Harrier carrier", itself a formidable package but one which lacks the sheer offensive muscle of the American approach.

In the right hands, of course, even the relatively modest "Harrier carrier" can inflict a considerable amount of damage, as British experience in the 1982 battle for the Falkland Islands showed. However, the Royal Navy was perhaps fortunate in still having HMS *Hermes* available for combat operations. Had Argentina waited another year or so, the outcome could have been very different.

Maritime Attack

O F ALL the many impressive sights to be seen in the world of contemporary military aviation, that of a large United States Navy aircraft carrier such as the USS *Nimitz* or the USS *Enterprise* at work is arguably the most spectacular and probably the most dangerous. With a carefully balanced mix of tactical assets able to effectively perform a complex spectrum of missions ranging from long-range nuclear or conventional strike through anti-submarine warfare and airborne early warning to air superiority, the

modern Carrier Air Wing is indeed a powerful force in its own right and one that actually exceeds the size of many of the world's smaller air forces. Most of the missions that may be undertaken by sea-based air power, American-style, are examined in some detail in the accompanying scenario which looks first at preparations before moving on to describe an anti-shipping missile and bombing attack on a small convoy that is engaged in carrying a load of urgently required military supplies to a belligerent African state.

2300 hours

In the communications centre aboard the USS *Theodore Roosevelt*, a rating yawns, stretches and reaches for a cup of coffee. Draining the remaining few ounces of the by now tepid liquid, he remarks to nobody in particular, "Six days we bust our guts to get here and for what? We've been here three days, goin' round and round in circles and what's happened? I'll tell you what's happened. Nothing. And I'll tell you something else, I don't think it's likely to either and that's for sure."

"Oh, can it, McGraw," says a voice from the corner, "We've got better things to do than listen to you bellyache all night."

What passes for silence settles briefly on the room, the ever present hum of machinery preventing total quiet while the handful of men on duty can sense rather than hear the distant roar of a J52 turbojet being put through its paces on the engine test cell at the rear of the ship. From the passageway outside, they hear the sound of someone stumble, followed quickly by the anguished remark, "Goddamn knee-knockers!"

McGraw yawns again, idly scratches himself and then opens his mouth to speak, just as a teleprinter clatters into action. The sudden noise jerks everyone to a state of wakefulness.

"Now what can CinCLant (Commander-in-Chief, Atlantic Fleet) have to tell us at this time of night?" says McGraw.

"Perhaps it's a recall to Norfolk," someone mutters.

"No chance," remarks someone else, "We're here to rot."

Putting down the code book, McGraw whistles softly, rises and heads for the passageway...

2310 hours

In his cabin, the Captain absorbs the import of the short message, which instructs him to take those actions that are necessary to "prepare to implement Operation Sunflower". At the same time, it advises him that additional intelligence data will follow over secure communications channels in due course.

One of a number of contingency plans drawn up while in transit to their present

operating station, "Sunflower" is in broad terms a shipping strike aimed at disrupting the flow of fuel, munitions, and other urgently needed war materiel.

At this precise moment, in the absence of hard data relating to the size of the convoy to be attacked, it is impossible to anticipate just what will be needed in the way of Air Wing resources. However, since it is clear that additional messages could well be filtering into the *Roosevelt*'s communications centre even now, he sets events in chain with the first of many orders to follow by directing the ship's Executive Officer and the respective heads of the Air Department (the "Air Boss"), the Operations Department and the assigned Carrier Air Wing — colloquially known as "CAG" — to report to his cabin forthwith.

While he waits for them to arrive, he recalls the events of the past few hectic days. They had been anchored at the US Navy's large base at Rota, Spain, and had virtually completed the process of "out-chopping" following a successful six-month tour of operations with the 6th Fleet in the Mediterranean. Briefing of personnel assigned to their relief carrier, the USS *Independence*, had been all but finished and they were within hours of sailing for Norfolk, Virginia when a "flash" signal directed them to delay departure and await new orders.

Those orders had not been long in coming. *Roosevelt* was instructed to head out into the Atlantic as if she was indeed going home. At the same time, a pair of destroyers which had been awaiting the arrival of their respective reliefs were also directed to put to sea, but departure times were staggered so as hopefully to mask their true intentions. Only when they were well out to sea did they rendezvous,

Left: Grumman F-14 Tomcats and a solitary Lockheed S-3 Viking share deck space aboard the parent carrier as a destroyer heads out to sea soon after dawn. Within a matter of hours, the carrier will also be on the move, heading west to a rendezvous point somewhere in the Atlantic Ocean.

Above: Only when it is well out to sea do deck crew set about re-spotting aircraft in anticipation of a resumption of flight operations. As it transpires, apart from the occasional fighter combat air patrol, there will be little in the way of aerial activity in the next 24 hours.

Below: Even though flying operations are kept to a minimum, the deck handling crew get little respite, moving aircraft from the hangar to the flight deck and sending those which are not fully mission capable below. Here, a Tomcat is about to be lifted up on one of the massive elevators.

casualties occurred when two aircraft dumped half-a-dozen cluster bomb units in a busy street market with quite devastating results.

Within hours of that air raid, Liberian diplomats attached to the UN had hurriedly gone to Washington where, at a secret meeting with officials of the US State Department, they had requested military assistance. It was as a direct result of that request that aircraft assigned to the USS *Theodore Roosevelt* now looked like being committed to action.

On the way south, the ''Rosy's'' staff had not been idle, conceiving a number of plans for contingency operations intended to discourage Guinea from pursuing her aggressive line and submitting them to National Command Authorities (NCA) in Washington. Some were based on direct action against purely military objectives, with airfields figuring high on the list of proposed targets. Others were aimed more at cutting off Guinea's ability to continue fighting. Options available here include the mining of harbours and attacks on shipping so as to institute a blockade.

''Sunflower'' was, in fact, a variation of the latter and was predicated upon attacking a small convoy. However, mindful of the international outcry that was bound to follow, the National Command Authorities had decreed that great care be exercised in attacking merchant shipping, with the inevitable result that many likely targets would be ruled ''off-limits'' by virtue of registry.

2313 hours

Turning to the signal annex which details the suspected make-up of the approaching convoy, the Captain peruses the short list. Two of the seven vessels were actually registered in Conakry so they, quite clearly, were fair game. As to the other five, he is hard put to restrain himself from laughing out loud. By some strange irony, all are Liberian-registered, a footnote stipulating that the Liberian authorities have given clearance for the attack.

2315 hours

''OK, gentlemen,'' says the Captain. ''It looks as if we might be in action before too long after all. I just got a message from CinCLant instructing me to prepare for ''Sunflower''. There's not a lot we can do right now but we might as well set the wheels in motion. What's the present ship and crew status, XO?''

''We completed underway replenishment on time at 2200 hours, sir, and we've been on minimal manning in non-essential departments ever since, to give ship's company a break. We're continuing to manoeuvre in the designated cruising area but we've only barely got steerage way on right now. As far as the tactical situation is concerned, I've just come from CIC (Combat Information Centre) and there's no evidence of untoward activity. In fact, it's all quiet on the eastern front, you might say.''

''Fine, thanks. How're things with you, Air Boss?''

''In pretty good shape. Serviceability looks good — last I heard we had about 65 per cent of Wing assets in FMC (fully mission capable) status and the stand-down has allowed AIMD

thereafter turning on to a south-westerly course and slipping past Madeira under cover of darkness before moving deeper into the Atlantic and skirting well to the west of the Canary Isles. About 24 hours later, yet another rendezvous — this time with two destroyers and a pair of nuclear-powered attack submarines — was effected, the entire Task Group then continuing to move southwards until it reached its designated operating station, roughly 300 miles (483km) offshore.

At the heart of all this activity was the deteriorating relationship between the People's Revolutionary Republic of Guinea and the Republic of Liberia. At first, overt acts of hostility had been confined to periodic clashes along the mountainous border region between the two states. These, while often bloody in the extreme, had taken place far from the Liberian seat of government in Monrovia and hadn't given rise to too much concern. Nevertheless, regular protests were

made via the medium of the United Nations but these were almost invariably ignored and were often followed by renewed outbreaks of violence. Finally, Liberia managed to prevail upon the UN to pass a resolution condemning Guinea's actions and calling for an immediate cessation of hostile acts.

More or less coinciding with the arrival of a considerable amount of Soviet-supplied military hardware and several hundred advisers, the UN resolution was particularly ill-timed and seemed to achieve nothing more than to prompt Guinea to step up the pace of its war-like activities. Two days later, her fighter-bombers had attacked a number of ''military'' targets in Monrovia, the capital's two airports being put out of action and the principal oil supply depot particularly hard-hit. Other targets bombed in succeeding raids over the next week or so included key government buildings as well as port facilities and it was in the latter area that the most serious

(Aircraft Intermediate Maintenance Department) to tweak most of the down-birds. Flight deck's in good shape and the problem on No.3 Catapult is being dealt with right now."

"Good. Anything to add, CAG?"

"Well, we managed to work through most of the scenarios on the way down here and I think we've ironed out all the bugs. We're continuing to hold two F-14s on five-minute alert round the clock but apart from one false alarm this afternoon it's been very quiet."

"Yeah, I heard them go. What was it?"

"Oh, one of our EP-3s ferreting about. You'd think those guys'd let us know when they're doing their stuff. I mean, that's the third time this week — same airplane too."

"Want me to hit ComSix (Commander, Sixth Fleet) with a message?"

"Eh. Oh, hell no, it keeps us on our toes, I s'pose. I just sometimes wonder whether they're watching us or the bad guys though . . ."

"Right, let's get on to actions." The captain stiffens his back and looks around at his officers. "Way I see it, there's no point in hitting the panic button and going to general quarters until we've got a lot more information. Let's just keep it nice and easy and notify only those who need to know right now.

"XO, you'd better start by bringing CIC to top line and then you might as well pull the department heads together since we're gonna' need them before too long. Oh, and you'd better bring comms up to full strength as well — I have a sneaky feeling that they're in for a busy night.

"Keep an eye on the catapult situation, Air Boss, and you'd better clarify just what the current FMC status is right now.

"As for you, CAG, you might as well get the squadron commanders together and put them in the picture."

 2330 hours

Personnel assigned to the *Roosevelt*'s communications centre most definitely earn their pay during the small hours when incoming and outgoing communications links fairly sizzle. Indeed, the ease with which it is now possible to relay information over vast distances via a multitude of channels seems to have been accompanied by an increase in traffic which at times looks likely to swamp the carrier's ability to cope. The problems experienced arise not so much from an inability to decode all the inbound traffic but rather from the need to ensure that it reaches the right people. With virtually every signal marked as "Urgent", it has become necessary to call additional messengers to ensure that delivery takes place with minimal delay.

McGraw thought that routine signals traffic might well be suspended but this is not the case. As a result, in addition to dealing with a mass of "Sunflower"-related message traffic — including rules of engagement, intelligence

Right: A brace of Intruders, an EA-6B Prowler, an S-3A Viking and an E-2C Hawkeye seemingly huddle together in the shelter of the island superstructure while they await their next tasks. Elsewhere, below deck, planners put the final touches to operation "Sunflower".

Above: *Utilising one of the small but powerful aircraft tugs, deck crew transfer a serviceable Tomcat to a parking spot near the rear of the carrier. Once there, munitions specialists will set about arming it with a load of AIM-7 Sparrow, AIM-9 Sidewinder and AIM-54 Phoenix missiles.*

Below: *Even though they will play no part in the forthcoming strike mission, at least two examples of the Lockheed S-3A Viking will be airborne in order to minimise the risk of a surprise sub-surface attack on the Navy Task Group as it launches and recovers its aircraft.*

assessments pertaining to enemy air and sea strength and projections of likely enemy actions and reactions — he also has to handle more mundane matters such as an enquiry originating from 6th Fleet concerning the whereabouts of a movie which has apparently gone missing. Needless to say, it is put firmly at the bottom of the pile.

The hectic atmosphere of the communications centre is matched by a rising level of activity elsewhere aboard the carrier, as more and more members of ship and air wing company are alerted to play their part in the forthcoming day's events. Hastily convened meetings, of which that between the Air Boss and his squadron commanders is just one, are for the most part concerned with more practical questions, such as aircraft availability — with hard information on the size and location of the convoy which is to be the target still not available, there is little point in wasting time on tactical considerations and battle plans.

Those details can be filled in later. For the moment, it is sufficient to know just what CVW assets are available and the picture that emerges is satisfactory. Some 74 per cent of the total complement are serviceable and ready for combat duty. In hard terms, this translates to 63 out of 85 aircraft, with 18 of the 23 F-14A Tomcats assigned to VF-13 and VF-62 being declared FMC. The latter squadron had lost one during transit when the arrester hook sheared on recovery. Fortunately, both crew members had ejected safely and

been recovered by the SH-3H plane guard within moments of entering the water.

Turning to the two dozen F/A-18A Hornets that are embarked, the picture is marginally less bright, VFA-104 having eight available while VFA-171 can put up nine. Other attack elements comprise the 10 A-6E Invaders of VA-135 and seven of these are ready, as well as three of the four KA-6D tankers that also form part of this squadron's complement. On the ASW front, seven of VS-34's 10 S-3A Vikings are operationally ready while five of HS-13's six SH-3H Sea Kings are fit for work.

Finally, there are the AEW and ECM resources. VAW-128 has three of four E-2C Hawkeyes in "up" status, and an identical return is declared by VAQ-142 which operates the EA-6B Prowler.

 0130 hours

Although only a relatively small number of the *Roosevelt*'s 6,000+ personnel have so far been apprised of the proposed action, the "bush telegraph" has been working overtime and few are now unaware of the fact that something is "up". However, political and geographical ignorance of the area in which they are at present operating has exerted a rather dampening influence on speculation by members of the crew and it is only the more perceptive and well-informed who reach the right conclusions.

By now, a variety of sources, ranging from a Central Intelligence Agency operative in Dakar, Senegal, to a KH-11 spy satellite orbiting high above, have provided a wealth of additional information with regard to the approaching convoy. When last observed, it had been near Dakar and it was obviously "coast crawling", proceeding towards its destination at a fairly sedate 10-12 knots just a few miles offshore. As suspected, it numbered no more than seven ships. Three moderately sized tankers were being accompanied by four cargo vessels conveying a hastily purchased collection of military hardware ranging from light jeeps through artillery to bombs and rockets, other heavy ordnance, and a substantial amount of small arms ammunition.

While the cargo may not give rise to much surprise, the fact that the convoy is unescorted does, although Guinea's modest Navy is for the most part confined to coastal patrol vessels that are better suited for "hit and run" raids, something which has been undertaken on a handful of occasions. Even though the US forces are unlikely to encounter anything in the way of naval opposition, it is agreed that extreme caution should be exercised, especially since Soviet naval forces are usually to be found serenely cruising the waters of the nearby Gulf of Guinea.

Shortly before three o'clock, the message directing the execution of "Sunflower" is received, the Captain first notifying his senior officers before making a general broadcast to ship's company via the internal tannoy system. Within minutes, the *Roosevelt* has come fully to life and nowhere is the activity more intense than in the various weapons storage compartments. Armament specialists are hard at work mating Mk.82 and Mk.83 bombs with fin and nose sections, completed bombs being transferred via elevator to the flight deck where munitions specialists wait to begin the muscle-wrenching work of loading them on to the weapons racks which hang suspended from the Hornets.

At the same time, the rather more sophisticated Harpoon anti-shipping missiles are removed from their storage crates and subjected to quick but thorough tests aimed at verifying that the complex electronic circuitry and guidance systems are fully operable. Only when that work is complete do these weapons also find their way to the flight deck, where other crew members set about positioning them in place on the five Intruders that will open the attack.

Even as the Harpoons begin to emerge from

Above left: *The ungainly Grumman E-2C Hawkeye, with its distinctive rotodome, is the most unusual type to operate from an aircraft carrier. It is also one of the most important, with the primary missions of augmenting the carrier's own radar, controlling fighter aircraft and managing strike formations.*

Left: *A jamming pod associated with the AN/ALQ-99 Tactical Jamming System can be seen beneath the wing of this Grumman EA-6B Prowler, one of four assigned to the embarked Carrier Air Wing. When the time comes, some of these will be responsible for emitting jamming signals aimed at disrupting enemy radars.*

their subterranean stowage, so too are other preparations well in hand, fuel lines snaking across the deck as aircraft tanks are topped up. A strident klaxon blast precedes a steady rumble as the deck edge elevator directly ahead of the island rises swiftly from hangar level. On it stands a solitary Prowler. Beneath its belly and wings are suspended three jamming pods which have already been programmed to deal with known and suspected radar "threats".

Nearby, other torch-bearing weapons technicians examine clusters of Sparrow and Sidewinder missiles at their storage point behind the island. Selected missiles are quickly manhandled on to trolleys for the short journey to their designated carrier aircraft while, below deck, planning staff are no less busy as they put the final touches to the proposed attack.

0530 hours

"OK, gentlemen, sorry to get you up so early," says CAG, motioning his squadron commanders and executive officers to be seated. "It looks as though some of us are going to get the chance to put all that training to good use at last. I know that all of you are aware of the broad objective and I think it's time to get down to specifics, since we now have NCA approval. The planning staff are presently putting together mission profile folders for all the squadron commanders. They'll contain the usual data — radio frequencies, routings, weather projections, target information and so on and I'm told they'll be ready by the time I wrap up this briefing.

"Essentially, we intend to execute a coordinated "Alpha"-strike against a convoy made up of seven medium-sized merchant ships. Point of engagement is just south of Biagos Archipelago and the actual strike package will comprise just 11 aircraft — five A-6s and six F-18s. The A-6s will open the attack, each launching two Harpoons in barrage fashion from a range of about 40 miles (64km). At missile. impact plus one minute, one F-18 will perform visual reconnaissance, by fire if necessary, relaying findings by secure voice channel to strike co-ordinator on the E-2.

"The second wave will go in at missile impact plus three minutes and will comprise six F-18s working in pairs and armed with a mix of Mk.82 and Mk.83 bombs. These will be used against any vessel deemed not to have sustained terminal damage. We'd prefer a single-pass attack but on no account are you to make more than three runs. If you have any ordnance left after that, dump it in the designated jettison area.

"Eight more F-18s with a mix of Sparrows and Sidewinders will provide CAP cover in the target area if the second wave is needed — four high CAP and four low. We're not really expecting any interference but stay alert and don't be diverted by events going on down below whatever happens.

"Moving further out, we're going to put up a couple of fighter screens, four F-14s to the north and four to the south which is where we would anticipate any threat to originate from. Since rules of engagement call for visual recognition before any missiles are launched, Phoenix is out, so ordnance will consist of Sparrow and Sidewinder, plus, of course, the

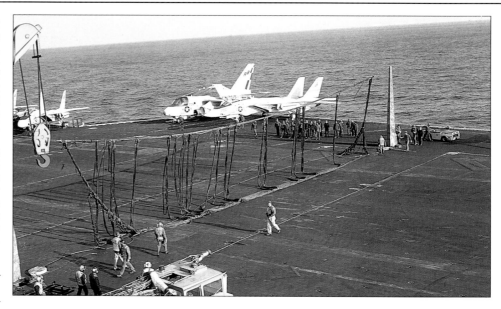

Above: As part of the preparation process, deck crew rig the emergency barrier in a routine drill exercise. Constant practice means that they have got this down to a fine art by now and it takes just a few minutes to erect. As it turns out, it will not be needed this time.

Below: Partially obscured by steam emanating from an adjacent catapult track, an E-2C Hawkeye winds up to full power in anticipation of launch. The first aircraft to depart, this Hawkeye will proceed to an orbit station from where it will monitor the ensuing strike.

Vulcan gun. The attack will go ahead during a period of low commercial air activity but we've given you the local airways frequencies so if you do run into any commercial traffic I'd suggest you try and talk them out of proceeding further. If that doesn't work, try a burst of gunfire and if that doesn't work, you'd better let them go but for Pete's sake keep the TARCAP informed. What we don't need is a repetition of the Iranian Airbus shootdown — remember.

"As far as threats are concerned, to the best of our knowledge there are no radar-directed guns or missiles but you'll almost certainly run into moderate small arms fire and you might also encounter man-portable IR-homers. You'll have flares available though — so use them and stay safe.

Below: With the massive jet blast deflector raised to divert exhaust gasses upwards, a Grumman F-14A Tomcat sits with engines idling as it awaits its turn to be thrust skywards from one of the two waist catapults. Alongside, deck crew relax.

Left: Silhouetted against a shining sea, the leading Hawkeye banks to the right just moments after launch, its gear already beginning the retraction process. Moving at a fairly sedate speed, it will take some time to reach its designated orbit point far ahead of the parent carrier.

"Enemy fighter forces consist of a couple of dozen MiG-21s but it seems that only about 10 are serviceable at any given time. There's no indication of increased air activity so it would appear that they are unaware of our intentions even though they probably know we're in the area. Our assessment of pilot ability is low, but they have been working with Soviet advisers recently and the quality may have risen slightly. Basically, though, we're aiming to be in and out before they can react, but we're also working on the assumption that they will try to intervene and the southerly fighter screen will be positioned along the most likely axis of approach.

"On the subject of ECM, we don't foresee any real need for this but we will have an EA-6 orbiting to the south, monitoring the situation. If it looks as though Guinea is putting fighters up — and, let's face it, that is a possibility — then he'll be well placed to jam their control radars.

"If they get gung-ho and try to follow you back to the ship, don't worry. We'll have a minimum of four and a maximum of six F-14s

Above: Guided by hand signals, a Tomcat pilot steers his aircraft into position on the catapult shuttle while deck personnel await the opportunity to hook it up for launching. Behind, the jet blast deflector is rising from the stowed position on the carrier's massive flight deck.

on BARCAP duty just waiting for them, and they'll be working in concert with another E-2 as well.

"Post-strike reconnaissance — at plus 20 minutes — will be undertaken by one of the TARPS birds with an F-14 escort. Finally, should anyone run into trouble, I wouldn't recommend looking for an emergency landing field 'cos there aren't any that can be considered as friendly for about 250 miles. The best course of action would be to head back towards the ship, but just in case anyone can't make it we're gonna' have a destroyer positioned on forward picket duty about 80-100 miles off shore. Their LAMPS bird will be airborne with a homing beacon emitting from zero hour to plus 30 minutes. If anyone hits trouble and doesn't think they're going to be able to get home, just tell them to head for the beacon and punch out. It's not a perfect arrangement but chances are we'd get to any downed pilot first.

"As far as fuel is concerned, it's tight but you should have enough. However, if anybody does need a drink on the way home, we'll have three KA-6s and a couple of buddy-configured F-18s up. Just don't all shout for fuel at once...

"Finally, with regard to surface and sub-surface threats, again I'd have to say we're not expecting trouble. The destroyer screen has been monitoring the situation since we arrived in the area but the most exciting thing they've seen has been a school of dolphins and we hope it's gonna' stay that way. Nevertheless, the S-3As and SH-3Hs will be maintaining a standing ASW screen throughout the day.

"And that's about it, I think, apart from to add that if you do the job the way you've trained, then we won't have to go back to tidy up any loose ends."

 0545 hours

Even as CAG is winding up the preliminary briefing, work on tidying up other loose ends is pressing ahead. Above, on deck, No. 3 catapult has been restored to operating condition, the shuttle of this and the other three catapults travelling up and down the deck a few times so as to confirm that everything is working satisfactorily.

Ahead of the island, arming of the strike component is virtually complete and a number of munitions specialists have moved aft to help prepare the CAP-dedicated Tomcats and Hornets which stand surrounded by heat-seeking and radar-guided missiles. Four fully-armed Tomcats are in the process of being manoeuvred into position on the four catapults, while personnel in pri-fly watch as a tractor begins slowly to pull a Sea King from its parking spot below the island towards the forward part of the angled deck. Once there, a gang of personnel secure it firmly to the deck with tie-down chains before they set about preparing it for flight, a process which entails freeing the rotor blades from their stowed position alongside the aft fuselage and unfolding the tail rotor fairing. Other crew members manhandle start carts into position, connecting umbilicals to aircraft, while the arrester gear crew examine the four cross-deck pendants that will be used to recover the aircraft, employing a massive pair of calipers to check that wear and tear is within safe limits.

Below deck, the seemingly more sedate degree of activity is perhaps misleading. In various squadron ready rooms dotted about the carrier, pilots and naval flight officers listen intently and scribble down occasional notes as squadron commanders brief those who are due to take part in "Operation Sunflower". Observers sitting in on the briefings are only too well aware that something unusual is going on by virtue of the absence of the usual good-natured badinage. In each of the respective ready rooms, several aircrew drink coffee; a few smoke; most wear flight suits bereft of the more usual adornments in the way of squadron patches; all look particularly serious, although that is hardly surprising since none has any previous combat experience.

With briefing over, one or two make for the nearest head in order to relieve themselves (there are few things worse than a full bladder and high g forces) before drawing flight kit — g-suits, bone domes and so on — from life support. Hastily donning the impedimenta associated with modern combat aircraft, they begin to filter out into the adjacent passages and head for the flight deck where their aircraft await.

Even as the aircrew are being briefed, preparations on deck move inexorably on, almost the final act coming when deck crew congregate at the bow. Once there, they begin a slow and steady march down the entire length of the flight deck, scanning the surface for foreign objects likely to cause damage during the ensuing launch. A routine facet of carrier-borne operations, the FOD walk-down produces a number of items ranging from various bits of fusing wire through a couple of small bolts to a discarded torch battery and a large spanner.

0730 hours

On the opposite side of the flight deck to the superstructure, a red-jacketed and helmeted ordnanceman desultorily examines his skinned knuckles, tangible evidence of a sweaty morning's work manhandling bombs on to the ejection racks which hang beneath each Hornet's wings. A veteran of two WestPac cruises at the tail end of the Vietnam War, he knows enough to savour the apparent calm which now envelops the carrier. For his colleague, whose first full tour of overseas duty this is, the day's events are infinitely more exciting and it is he who first observes the aircrew as they begin to emerge from the hatch at the base of the island, thereafter fanning out towards their respective aircraft. Although some time still has to elapse before the strike force begin launching, their appearance galvanises many other members of the deck crew into action.

On the bow catapults, a brace of F-14A Tomcats stand silently ready for launch, crew securely strapped in place with nose tow bars already engaged in the shuttle and with the hold-back restraint securely hooked up. Armed with a mix of Sparrow and Sidewinder missiles, they will be the first to go, heading out on BARCAP (Barrier Combat Air Patrol) duty. Moments later, a second cell will launch from the waist catapults, these too being earmarked for BARCAP.

Only then will attention switch to the Alpha-strike package, the 40-plus aircraft being scheduled to depart at carefully timed intervals. The E-2C co-ordinator will lead the way, several minutes in advance of the main strike formation so as to allow sufficient time for it to reach its orbit point between the carrier and the mainland and within the cover provided by the BARCAP Tomcats. From its lofty vantage point, 30,000ft (9,144m) above the sea, it will use its AN/APS-138 radar to pinpoint the convoy's precise location, subsequently providing course and turn instructions to the strike aircraft via secure data link equipment, while continuing to maintain airspace surveillance for enemy fighters, overseeing the developing tactical situation and co-ordinating rescue efforts should they become necessary.

0733 hours

"Stand-by to launch CAP" crackles out over the tannoy system, the brief message snapping the catapult crews into a state of heightened alertness. Elsewhere, aircrew are more intent on pre-flighting their aircraft, the "walk-round" being conducted rather more meticulously than is perhaps usually the case, with particularly close attention being devoted to weapons loads. One or two pilots, who possess greater faith in their crew chiefs than their colleagues, take time out to exchange a few half-nervous pleasantries with the deck crew. Another jumps down into the deck-edge catwalk and proceeds to disgorge the contents of his stomach into the flat calm waters of the Atlantic Ocean, many feet below.

"Sea-sick again, Boots?", shouts a fellow pilot, "I told you to go easy on the maple syrup..."

0735 hours

"Launch plane guard." For the past few minutes, the crew of the Sea King plane guard helicopter have been awaiting the order to move out on to station and within seconds of the tannoy's peremptory message the main rotor begins to revolve as the pilot quickly runs through the engine start procedures. Barely two minutes later, with a final quick scan of his instruments, the pilot eases back on

the collective lever, lifting the SH-3H clear of the deck before moving sideways over the port catwalk where several deck crew duck down to escape the worst of the downwash from the main rotor blades. Once above the sea, the helicopter swings sharply to the left, its nose dipping slightly as it sets course for its designated station slightly astern of the carrier and about 1,000 yards (914m) away.

0740 hours

Another terse message booms out from the tannoy. "Pilots, man your planes...." The tail end of this instruction is partially drowned by the sound of turbines spooling up as the four CAP aircraft simultaneously start engines, fumes and jet efflux being directed upwards by the massive jet blast deflectors which have, almost magically, appeared from the otherwise flat surface. Behind, the carrier's gently curving frothy wake provides visual confirmation that the huge ship is turning into wind, preparatory for launch.

On the bow, two green-shirted personnel scuttle left and right from the narrow safety corridor between the converging catapult tracks to check that both Tomcats are safely hooked up, notifying the yellow-shirted catapult officers that all is satisfactory by means of hand signals as they dart back to the centre of the deck.

Another hand signal from the catapult officer instructs the pilot to release the brakes and apply full power. The noise level increases to near the pain threshold as the twin afterburners ignite. For a moment, the Tomcat seems to want to shake itself free. Control surfaces flex to and fro as the pilot runs one last check before saluting to notify the catapult officer that he is ready for flight. A quick look round other deck personnel reveals nothing unexpected, and the catapult officer drops to a crouching posture, remaining motionless for a second or so before lowering his left arm and

Below: Deck crewmen huddle down to obtain some relief from the blast effect as, with afterburners glowing, a Tomcat hurtles down one of the two bow catapult tracks. In less than three seconds, the F-14 accelerates from a stand-still to a speed in excess of 150 knots.

touching the deck.

In the adjacent catwalk, a deck edge crewman sees this and sets an irrevocable course of events under way by hitting the catapult firing button. For the F-14 crew there is no going back. Amidst a welter of steam emanating from the catapult track and with a jolt that can be felt throughout the entire ship, they are momentarily subjected to six times the force of gravity, their aircraft accelerating from nought to 150 knots in just two-and-a-half seconds and less than 300ft (90m).

As the shuttle slams into the water brake which brings it to a halt in a matter of feet, inertia takes over and the Tomcat is literally flung clear of the deck, its nose undercarriage oleo leg extending so as to rotate the F-14 into the correct attitude for flight. Moments after leaving the carrier, the pilot initiates a gentle right-hand turn and begins to climb as he heads out to his CAP station.

Back on board the *Roosevelt*, the same routine is repeated three times in barely a minute, the four Tomcats that launch interposing themselves between ship and shore so as to prevent any potential attacker from having a clear run at the parent carrier.

 0742 hours

On the island superstructure, the catwalks which overlook the 4.5 acre flight deck — colloquially known as "Vulture's Row" — are unusually crowded — with aircrew with no part to play in the day's events enjoying the sights, sounds and smells of the launch.

Below them, in the lee of the island, stand a brace of E-2C Hawkeyes, the five-man crew of one having already clambered aboard and proceeded to their work stations. In the cockpit, pilot and co-pilot quickly run through pre-engine start checks while in the main cabin the combat information centre (CIC) officer, air control officer and flight technician verify that the various items of electronic equipment are in good shape.

Even as they busy themselves with the multitude of checks, the pilot signals to nearby deck crew that he is ready to fire up. A burst of compressed air provided by a "start cart" spins up one of the two Allison T56 turboprops, the massive four-bladed Hamilton Standard propeller revolving slowly at first but quickly blurring into a solid disc as power is increased, bleed air being diverted to start the second powerplant.

A quick final check to confirm that the engines are running satisfactorily is followed by yet another signal to one of the yellow-jerseyed aircraft directors before, with a gentle burst of extra power, the ungainly Hawkeye rolls forward a few feet. Once clear of nearby obstructions, it swings sharply to the right, the pilot receiving signals from a succession of directors as he carefully negotiates his way towards the bow. Skilful use of brakes and throttles enables him to steer a steady path between a host of parked aircraft and other deck equipment.

As the Hawkeye gingerly moves towards the No.1 catapult, so do the back-seat crew members complete their remaining checks. Their final action before launch is to swivel their seats through 90 degrees in order to face forward for take-off. Outside, deck directors

Above: Carrying AIM-9 Sidewinder air-to-air missiles on the wing-tip rails and AIM-7 Sparrows beneath the belly, an F/A-18A Hornet gingerly moves into position as it takes its turn to be catapulted aloft. In the foreground, an aircraft marshaller looks for the next to go.

Below: Resplendent in the coloured vests which signify their functions, deck personnel watch intently as the last Hornet leaves the bow catapult, amidst the usual cloud of vapour and flame. Now, all they can do is wait for the strike package to return from combat.

marshall the aircraft with inch-perfect precision, its twin nose-wheels passing astride the shuttle before yet another signal directs the pilot to stop and apply the brakes. At the same moment, he is also instructed to spread the wings. Hydraulic actuators propel these outward and then forward until they lock securely into place.

Behind, the jet blast deflector panels lift from the deck. Beneath the nose section, catapult crew members busy themselves positioning the nose tow link on the front of the shuttle and inserting the "T-bar". The latter forms a key element of the restraint system in that it acts as a link between the aircraft and the hold-back bar, being designed to snap under the stress incurred when the catapult is fired.

Elsewhere, another crew member holds up a weight board. The pilot checks and verifies that it accurately states his aircraft's weight, corresponding figures being dialled into the catapult system so as to ensure that the correct amount of steam pressure is used to accelerate the E-2 to a minimum single-engined safe flying speed at the specified take-off weight. In practice, of course, a reasonable safety margin — normally of the order of 15 knots — is built in to the calculations.

 0745 hours

Seconds later, in a reprise of the earlier Tomcat CAP launch, the Hawkeye hurtles down the deck under the impetus of the C13-1 steam catapult and sets course for its designated operating area. It initiates a fairly rapid climb so as to arrive on station at the specified altitude and at the correct time.

Back on the *Roosevelt*, a thinly veiled air of expectation is evident as the time to launch the strike package approaches. Pilots and naval flight officers are securely strapped into their respective aircraft, deck-edge cables having been used to align inertial navigation systems by taking positional data from SINS (Ship's Inertial Navigation System). "Vulture's Row" is now packed with onlookers. A ragged cheer had gone up as the Hawkeye departed, and those whose eyrie overlooks the bow deck area are now diverting their attention to the cluster of Intruders and the solitary Prowler that are spotted directly ahead of the island.

These are due to go first, launching from the two bow catapults. Facing them are half-a-dozen bomb-laden Hornets while on opposite sides of the landing area at the rear of the carrier more Hornets mingle with Tomcats. The missile armament fitted to both types confirms that they are earmarked for CAP duties.

 0750 hours

The tannoy barks again, as the Air Boss delivers the two-word message "start engines". Those below are galvanised into a state of frenetic activity, the start carts or "huffers" being much in demand. Above the scuttling deck crews, secure in their cockpits, pilots monitor their instruments as their engines come to life, checking the myriad small details which confirm that their aircraft is in good shape and up to the job that will soon be asked of it. Nav systems, flight control surfaces, refuelling probes, weapons computers, engine related instruments, radios and fuel flow gauges are all tested or examined. On this occasion the technicians have earned their pay, only two aircraft, an F-18 and an F-14, reporting minor "glitches", both of which are quickly put right.

Elsewhere, the launch plan looks like being thrown out of kilter by a faulty start cart, a problem with the steering gear preventing it from moving clear of the lead Intruder to another aircraft. Deck personnel — long used to dealing with such emergencies — hastily rethink their carefully orchestrated plan and "borrow" one from the F-18 line while a ground support equipment "trouble-shooter" goes to work on the defective huffer with a spanner and a screwdriver. Within 90 seconds, he has solved the problem. The offending piece of equipment moves out of the A-6's way barely 15 seconds before the Intruder is due to roll forward to the adjacent catapult for take-off.

The next eight minutes are impossible to relate clearly for the pace of flight deck activity is just too intense. The scene below is more reminiscent of a tightly-choreographed ballet, with aircraft seldom still for more than a few seconds as they jockey into position while awaiting their turn to make the short journey down one of the *Roosevelt*'s four catapults.

Meanwhile, deck personnel duck and dart out of the way of the constantly moving aircraft with apparent nonchalance, displaying evasive expertise that is perhaps only matched by Spanish matadors. Hand signals are the preferred — indeed, the only — method of communication, for normal speech is now impossible and even bellowed messages cannot be heard beyond a few feet. Periodic blasts of sound as aircraft wind up to full power before being flung from the flight deck amidst a storm of heat vapour raise the noise level to almost intolerable levels. Observers on the signal bridge overlooking the bow catapults are forced to inhale warm oxygen-depleted air made foul by burnt jet fuel. The smell of kerosene at times is almost overpoweringly strong, catching at the throat and, in conjunction with the wind generated by the carrier cruising at 20 knots, causing the observer's eyes to water almost continuously.

 0758 hours

Finally, the deafening racket ends almost as suddenly as it began, the last Tomcat blasting down the deck and clawing its way skywards as if impelled by the twin shafts of flame emanating from the exhaust nozzles of the TF30 turbofan engines.

 0830 hours

Far ahead of the carrier, the Hawkeye has reached its designated orbit area, the pilot throttling back and selecting ten degrees of flap so as to achieve the desired angle of attack which offers optimum radar performance. In the cabin, the three radar operators continue to monitor their display screens — apart from the carrier's own aircraft, there is little aerial traffic to be seen but the seven vessels which comprise the convoy are clearly visible.

Even as they watch, data link systems are already hard at work, information flowing from the E-2C to the combat information centre aboard the *Roosevelt*, from the F-14 CAP teams to the E-2C and vice versa, and from the E-2C to the inbound group of Intruders. The latter makes a small course correction follow-

Below: The cabin of the E-2C Hawkeye is a very busy place, being occupied by an aircraft control officer, a combat information centre officer and a flight technician. Each has a cathode ray tube display on which is presented data relating to the evolving tactical situation.

ing the receipt of more up to date information on the location of the targets which are still out of sight well ahead of them.

 0843 hours

Skimming across the calm sea at an altitude of no more than 50 feet (15m), the five Intruders begin to fan out into a loose line-abreast formation, allowing lateral separation between aircraft to increase to about 1,000 yards (900m). In five different cockpits, five bombardier/navigators (B/N) study visual display screens which provide a radar image of what lies ahead — as yet, there is little to be seen, their low altitude conspiring with the fact that radar is a line-of-sight sensor to prevent them from being able to "see" their targets. Another cockpit instrument, giving details of distance to run, relentlessly unwinds, electronically ticking off the miles as they approach the pull-up point, while the two Harpoons that each aircraft carries are "slaved" to the integrated package of avionics equipment which is crammed into virtually every nook and cranny aboard the Intruder. For this attack, the Bearing Only Launch (BOL) mode will be employed. Each weapon is programmed to fly down a specific bearing towards a target, the Harpoon's own Texas Instruments PR-53/DSQ-28 attack radar being activated early in the missile's flight so as to achieve a rapid lock-on, since there is little likelihood that the convoy will be able to take effective evasive measures or employ defensive ECM. Pre-departure planning has ensured that at least one missile will be targeted on each vessel. The three remaining weapons are earmarked for launch against the three "fattest" radar returns from the convoy since these will most probably be the tankers.

 0847 hours

As they cross the pre-determined pull-up point, the five Intruders rise as one, climbing quickly to 1,000 feet (300m). The respective B/Ns remain firmly "head-down", studying their radar screens which now betray the presence of the distant convoy and ascertaining the correct bearings to their respective targets. This information is relayed electronically to the missiles that hang suspended beneath five pairs of wings.

Moments later, with a slight jolt that is felt by each crew, ten Harpoons leave the weapon rails. Each is boosted to a speed of Mach 0.75 by an Aerojet solid propellant rocket motor which burns for just two-and-a-half seconds. Burn-out is followed by ignition of the Teledyne CAE J402 turbojet which provides power for the cruise phase of flight, but by then the launch vehicles have turned away and nobody actually sees the failure of one Harpoon, the now powerless weapon following a ballistic trajectory which terminates

Right: Even as the strike force nears its target, so too are the destroyers and S-3A Vikings of the defensive screen actively going about their task of preventing an undetected approach by surface or sub-surface vessels. SH-3H Sea King helicopters also assist in this duty.

Grumman E-2C Hawkeye

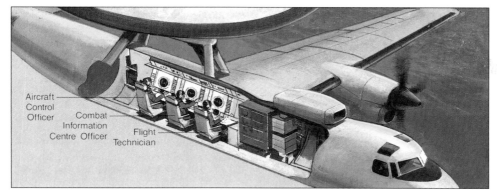

when it strikes the sea and breaks apart amidst a flurry of spray.

0851 hours

Shivering in the chilly air, a crewman from the galley of the leading Republic of Guinea ship is emptying a bucketful of slops over the aft starboard rail when he becomes aware of movement on the periphery of his vision. The first missile has left a thin trail of smoke as it homes unerringly in. At first, the crewman watches almost mesmerised and by the time his thought processes recognise it for what it is, he is in the water, flung there by the blast which follows just milli-seconds after the Harpoon penetrates the ship's outer skin to detonate in the cramped confines of the engine room, creating a cauldron of shrapnel and superheated steam.

On the bridge, the Captain instinctively ascribes the sudden and devastating blast to a boiler explosion. He is quickly disabused of this notion by the succession of booming detonations that ensue as other Harpoons hit home. Rushing from the bridge, he looks aft, his eyes being drawn first to the nearest tanker which has almost disappeared from view, engulfed in coils of thick black smoke shot through with sudden bursts of vivid red flame. Even as he watches, a sudden crack and a blossoming column of smoke and flame from another ship signal the arrival of the last Harpoon. It quickly becomes obvious that this phase of the attack has achieved most of its prime objectives.

Nine missiles have guided accurately, scoring hits on six of the seven ships. The tanker nearest the lead vessel has suffered worst, taking no less than three hits which have caused massive damage and an uncontrollable conflagration. The few remaining crew members are now more concerned with survival than with attempting to fight the fire. Barely 400 yards away, the second tanker fares somewhat better, being struck by just one missile which fails to detonate. This impacts in the vicinity of the crew's living accommodation, but the ship is otherwise undamaged. The Captain wastes no time in extricating himself from the main body of ships, pursuing a course which will take him considerably nearer to the coast in

the hope that "clutter" will reduce the risk of being hit in a subsequent missile attack.

At the rear of the convoy, the final tanker, which has been struck twice in less than three seconds, is also well ablaze, fuel pouring from a massive rupture near the bow seemingly causing the sea to burn. As far as the merchant ships are concerned, in addition to the lead vessel, two others have taken hits. One — laden with explosives and small arms ammunition — is literally torn apart by a truly massive explosion. The sole undamaged vessel immediately moves closer in a fruitless search for any survivors.

0853 hours

It is still there when the solo F-18 makes its reconnaissance run. The pilot's voice rises with excitement as he passes information to the Hawkeye which is still orbiting serenely some way off, its radar team having caused a flutter of tension among the Tomcats on southern CAP duty when they reported that a couple of small fighter-type aircraft had taken-off from a base in Guinea. Two of the F-14s were duly directed to move further to the south-east to forestall any attack and they are even now probing the ether with their Hughes AWG-9 weapons control radars as they head towards the suspect contacts.

Above: Flying a little way behind the main attacking force, an EA-6B Prowler stands ready to emit high-powered jamming signals should there be any indications that enemy fighters are attempting to intervene with the strike. On this occasion, the crew is content just to listen.

0856 hours

Further north, the strike-dedicated Hornets are closing rapidly at low-level. Navigation is now the least of their concerns since they can clearly see smoke rising from the blazing convoy on the horizon. Aware of the fact that two ships are still more or less fully seaworthy, they elect to split into pairs for co-ordinated attacks, this phase being opened by two aircraft armed with four Mk.83 1,000lb (454kg) bombs. One goes after the tanker while the other engages the undamaged merchant ship.

0857 hours

Running in fast at a slight tangent to the axis of the convoy, the lead pair employ a low-level lay-down method of weapons release. This is perhaps the simplest form of attack in that it allows a reasonable amount of time for each pilot to position his "pipper" over the target and hold it there while he activates the air-ground weapons release switch on the control column. From then on, the computers take over, performing a multitude of ballistics, wind, drift, altitude and speed-related calculations before automatically commanding weapons release. Bombs leave the rails in sequences which are carefully programmed to ensure the best chance of them effectively finding their mark.

On this occasion, in the absence of ground fire, it is perhaps too easy. Both pilots hold a fairly steady course and altitude as they rapidly close on their respective targets. Bomb patterns are extremely accurate, the tanker sustaining direct hits by two Mk.83s in addition to further damage from a third which explodes in the water barely five feet (1.5m) from the ship's starboard side, punching a sizeable hole in the steel structure.

The merchant ship is slightly more fortunate. One bomb clips the superstructure and removes a radio mast before detonating in a

mortar shells, the ensuing secondary explosion breaking its back. Within a minute, it has sunk beneath the surface, the only evidence of its passing being a large patch of oil and a few crates of deck cargo, to which cling three unhappy survivors.

lifeboat on the port side, most of the ensuing blast and shrapnel being directed harmlessly outboard. However, two near misses do cause a modest amount of damage beneath the waterline. Several plates are "sprung", and the ship's frightened engineers very quickly set about trying to staunch the flow of water.

0859 hours

Their determined efforts are destined to be rendered worthless by one of the next pair of Hornets. These utilise a dive-bombing attack to deliver their clutch of Mk.82 500-pounders. The attack begins with a 4g pull-up, both aircraft rolling inverted as they quickly climb to 2,000 feet (600m) so as to "eyeball" their respective targets as they pass "over the top", again exerting 4g on the airframe during this manoeuvre. Now in a fairly gentle diving attitude, they roll right side up, and the pilots position their "pippers" precisely on target and hit the weapons release switch. Moments later, relieved of their burdens, the F-18s tremble slightly as if anxious to be gone. Both pilots experience yet another dose of moderate g force as they pull out of their dives at low level, engaging afterburner and jinking quite violently as they speed away to safer airspace.

Behind, the thus far only slightly damaged merchant ship sustains a mortal blow. A bomb buries itself deep in the forward hold before detonating among a tightly packed load of

0900 hours

Above, the final pair of Hornets begin their delivery dives, choosing to administer the *coup de grâce* to the two least damaged tankers. In reality, of course, neither vessel is in any fit state to make a meaningful contribution to Guinea's war effort but, with opportunities to deliver ordnance against a "real" target coming only rarely, neither pilot is anxious to consign his load of bombs to "deep six". Moments later they are gone, turning on to a westerly heading and climbing to altitude

A: Five Grumman A-6E Intruders launch Harpoon anti-shipping missiles in barrage fashion from long range, before turning away and returning to the parent carrier. **B:** F/A-18A Hornets in second wave bomb convoy with mix of Mk. 82 500lb and Mk. 83 1,000lb bombs. **C:** E-2C Hawkeye orbits while performing strike control function and surveillance of hostile air space. **D:** Sparrow and Sidewinder-armed F/A-18 Hornets perform combat air patrol for bomber force. **E:** Missile and gun-armed F-14A Tomcats perform outer combat air patrol.

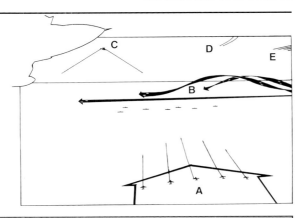

for the return leg to the *Roosevelt*. The high and low CAP Hornets — who have had to content themselves with merely observing the devastation below — follow less than a minute later after one last sweep over the area, during which two pilots utilise hand-held cameras to record the scene.

0902 hours

To the north, the four Tomcats tasked with screening the action begin to withdraw, while to the south, two more F-14s close with the as yet unseen radar contacts under guidance from the Hawkeye which is endeavouring to position them to the rear of the oncoming target tracks. Thus far, attempts to circle round have been forestalled for each time the F-14s change direction the opposing contacts swing on to a new heading. It eventually becomes obvious that an "eyeball-to-eyeball" confrontation is inevitable.

0903 hours

At this moment the EA-6B Prowler tilts the odds in favour of the US fighters, invisible signals emanating from the jamming pods inhibiting ground-to-air communications links between the control centre in Guinea and the two MiGs as well as the latter's own radar. Now rendered more or less blind, the two MiGs ought to turn for home, but for some inexplicable reason they continue coming, crossing the coast and heading out to sea.

0904 hours

Seconds later, the pilot of the lead Tomcat identifies them as a pair of MiG-21s on his television camera sighting device. Thumbing his microphone switch, he calls "Tally ho. Two MiGs at one o'clock", before reefing around into a hard right turn which invites the oncoming fighters to try for an infra-red "Atoll" missile shot at the F-14's now-exposed tailpipes.

Several thousand feet below, the wingman watches intently and, sure enough, he catches a glimpse of flame and smoke as the lead MiG-21 launches a missile. Immediately, he hits his own microphone switch and advises his leader of the shot.

Above, the lead F-14 pulls round into a hard left climbing turn, simultaneously ejecting several infra-red flares in order to decoy the

F/A-18 Air-to-Air Search and Track Modes

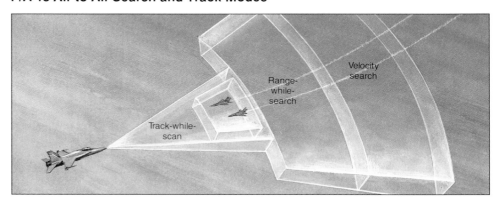

oncoming Atoll. Engaging afterburner, he continues to turn through 180 degrees before initiating a gentle dive towards the two MiGs which quickly abandon their fairly tight formation when confronted by the oncoming Tomcat. One breaks left and the other right as the F-14 passes between them. In the distance, a gout of smoke hangs like a punctuation mark in the sky. The Atoll has been fooled by one of the flares.

0906 hours

Having split the enemy fighters, the pilot of the leading Tomcat initiates a right-hand turn in the hope that he will be able to head off the lead MiG, a gambit which might have met with success had the MiG limited its turn to just 90 degrees. Instead, it manoeuvres through almost 180 degrees and makes directly for the coast at top speed. Undeterred, the lead Tomcat begins climbing in pursuit but it never seems likely to achieve a firing solution, the MiG pilot flying directly towards the sun as he heads for the shoreline, well aware that this offers his best — indeed, probably, his only — chance of survival.

Rules of engagement mean that the Navy pilots are hamstrung by the command to stay "feet wet" and are thus unable to continue pursuit once the enemy aircraft reaches the sanctuary offered by the coast. For the Tomcat pilot, this is particularly galling since he cannot determine whether his Sidewinder has locked-on to the MiG's exhaust or, as is possible, the sun. As a consequence, he elects to hold his fire in the hope that the other pilot will change course before crossing the coastline but it is not to be, and he reluctantly abandons the chase, cursing as he watches the MiG disappear from view.

Above: *In addition to its impressive air-to-ground capabilities, the Hornet's AN/APG-65 radar possesses a number of different air-to-air modes, all of which combine to make it a potentially deadly adversary in the aerial combat arena should it be called upon to engage enemy aircraft.*

0908 hours

His wingman fares rather better, the ploy of descending to quite low level possibly misleading the pair of MiGs into thinking that they face only one opponent. Whatever the reason, the second MiG seems concerned with staying well away from the lead Tomcat, turning on to a northerly course which takes him more or less parallel to the coast. He eventually passes directly above the wingman, for whom it is a relatively easy matter to manoeuvre into the classic six o'clock position. The growling tone in his headphones confirms that his Sidewinder has locked on satisfactorily. At a range of no more than one mile, he fires. The missile wobbles momentarily as it comes off the rail but then homes unerringly on the apparently unconcerned MiG, detonating alongside the rear fuselage of the fighter which sheds its port elevator and part of the rudder before flipping over into an uncontrollable spin.

Seconds later, the canopy separates as the pilot ejects, free-falling for a few moments before barometric pressure sensing devices activate his parachute as he drops through 15,000 feet (4,570m). The jerk of deployment causes the harness to bite uncomfortably into his groin but the pain is soon forgotten as he studies the scene below, his flight path having brought him close to where the devastated convoy now lies.

0917 hours

He is still bobbing around in his dinghy when, from the south, he hears the sound of approaching jets and he hunches down instinctively, half fearful that the noise heralds yet another wave of attacking aircraft. Some 3,000

Left: *Although far less pleasing from the aesthetic viewpoint, there can be little doubt that the Navy's switch to "low-viz" markings make its aircraft much harder to see. The aircraft above carries VF-84's markings of the 1970s while that below is in their present scheme.*

Tomcat Camouflage Comparison

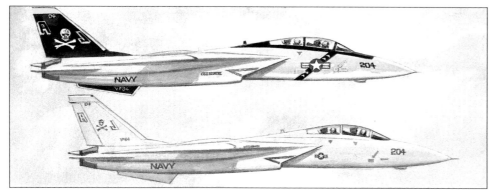

feet (900m) above, two Tomcats make a single pass along the line of the convoy, one using TARPS to perform post-strike reconnaissance while the other rides "shotgun" in the event of Guinea's fighters interfering.

0933 hours

From astern of the *Roosevelt*, two Tomcats appear, passing just to starboard and "hawking the deck" (checking it is clear) from an altitude of about 800 feet (240m) before breaking to port some way ahead of the ship.

The first Tomcat descends slightly so as to pass downwind at about 600 feet (180m) and roughly 1.5 miles (2.4km) abeam. Undercarriage, flaps and arrester hook are lowered while speed is allowed to bleed off, the final turn being timed to permit the aircraft to establish itself on the correct approach path at a distance of roughly three-quarters of a mile (1.2km) behind the carrier. At this time, the pilot visually acquires the fresnel lens optical landing system, or "meatball" as it is universally known. With the aid of this device, the F-14 flies a three-and-a-half degree glideslope which, if the meatball is correctly positioned between the horizontal line of green reference lights, will result in the perfect "trap", arrestment being accomplished by the third of the four transverse cables.

Needless to say, different landing weights — an A-7 typically comes aboard at about 26,500lb (12,020kg), while the Tomcat's typical landing weight is almost twice that, at 52,000lb (23,587kg) — require different degrees of tension. Hydraulic dampeners enable the correct degree of tension to be dialled into the system by a deck-edge operator so as to bring the aircraft to a halt within the landing area without it exceeding its structural limits.

0936 hours

On this occasion, the lead aircraft does indeed engage the No. 3 wire, at first appearing to gain on the carrier only slowly before suddenly seeming to accelerate as, wings waggling slightly as if in imitation of a duck about to alight on water, it slams onto the flight deck. Sparks fly from the skittering hook, white smoke blossoms from the tyres as another layer of rubber is deposited and black exhaust smoke issues from the engines as they go to full power before the crew's heads suddenly bob forward as the aircraft is brought to an

Above: *With the arrester gear cable paying out behind it, a Grumman EA-6B Prowler is brought safely to a halt aboard the carrier. In a few seconds, it will roll back a few feet, allowing the cable to fall free, before moving to a parking spot on the bow portion of the flight deck.*

Below: *With wings fully spread and the arrester hook dangling, a Tomcat hangs seemingly motionless above the flight deck as it returns to the carrier. Within moments, it will have been subjected to the brutal stresses and strains that are inherent in every successful "trap".*

Below: *Still carrying its missile armament, this recently recovered Tomcat turns to follow the directions of the deck crew as it heads towards a parking spot at the end of a combat patrol mission. For this crew, the sortie was uneventful but some of their colleagues have justifiable cause for celebration, having downed a MiG-21 with a well-aimed AIM-9L Sidewinder heat-seeking air-to-air missile.*

abrupt halt. Retarding the throttles, the pilot waits for a few moments as his aircraft rolls backwards to release the wire which disappears aft to be reset. Then, following the guidance of a deck aircraft director, he turns sharply right, taxiing forward to a parking slot adjacent to the island before shutting down the engines.

Seconds later, his wingman taxis into position alongside, the landing area now being clear for the Intruders that are breaking into the landing pattern. In the distance the first cell of Hornets can be seen approaching.

0940 hours

Most of the 50 or so aircraft that are airborne recover safely, the well-ordered procedure being interrupted momentarily by one F-14 which performs a victory roll. For the time being, though, not all of *Roosevelt*'s complement will come aboard, it being deemed necessary for BARCAP Tomcats and AEW Hawkeyes to continue to patrol between ship and shore until the parent carrier is well beyond range of any possible retaliatory action.

Index

PRINTED IN BELGIUM BY

proost
INTERNATIONAL BOOK PRODUCTION